Advanced Reef Keeping

Advanced Reef Keeping I

A Comprehensive Guide
to Setting up Your Reef Tank.

Book One

Theory
Equipment
Instrumentation
Installation

Albert J. Thiel

Printed in the United States by
Remar Printing Co, Bridgeport, Connecticut
Larry Palaia

Set in Stone Informal from Adobe® Systems
using Pagemaker from Aldus Corporation®
and a Mac Portable® Computer.

First Printing   January 1989
Second Printing   June 1991

91-77701925T

Aardvark Press
Box 1176
Mesilla Park, NM 88047-1176

Telephone (505) 526 4000
Fax   (505) 524 7313

Editing :   Albert J. Thiel
               Remar
Technical Assistance :   Leo Wojcik

Advanced Reef Keeping :
          Title
          1. Equipment
          2. Instrumentation
          3. Theory
          Bibliography
          Index
                    I.   Thiel Albert J. (1943)

ISBN- 0-945777-01-9

To
Sharon Thiel

Gordon Shearer

and

Sayssi

Advanced Reef Keeping I

A Comprehensive Guide

to Setting up Your Reef Tank

Albert J. Thiel

Foreword

Never has the hobby gone through such an amount of change as what has happened to Marine Fish and Invertebrate Reef Keeping in the last 2 years.

It all started with a series of articles by George Smit, and some articles I wrote around the same time which appeared in various magazines as well.

George was so "controversial" in his approach to keeping invertebrates, that no one interested in their well being missed any of his articles, printed month after month in FAMA (Fresh and Marine Aquarium Magazine).

Don Dewey, FAMA's publisher, certainly deserves many kudos for his forsightedness and determination in getting George's message across.

Suddenly, Hobbyists all around the country where confronted with a totally new approach, so drastically different from what they had been doing, and so unknown to them, that many were not only impressed with the amount of proof George included in his articles, but felt compelled to try out these new methods themselves.

And lo and behold the new techniques worked. Tanks started to look totally different and became Reef Aquariums, pieces of Living Furniture[1], as some call them, filled with corals, fish, and an assortment of invertebrates and macro-algae. The concept of the Reef Aquarium was re-born[2] !

Around the same time, Dupla Gmbh introduced their product line to the United States, through the Dupla Usa Inc. company, and not only applied George Smit's filtration techniques in a Dupla proprietary manner[3], but added a host of new products and tests, that made water quality management that more of a "serious" undertaking.

The combination of George's approach, and Dupla's products, supplemented by innovative approaches by other Hobbyists, that followed soon, changed the way many serious Hobbyists were keeping their tanks forever.

Whereas in the past, fish-only tanks relied mostly on biological filters, and combinations of biological, mechanical and chemical filters[4], Reef Tanks started to use special filters for each of these functions, as well as a host of new techniques to monitor and change the water chemistry[6].

This included pH meters and controllers, redox potential meters and controllers[5], carbon dioxide diffusion, and many others.

New lighting was being advocated, in particular the Actinic O3 lights introduced by John Burleson, and the HQI metal halides introduced by Albert Thiel as part of the Dupla System. Both went their own ways and appealed to different types of Hobbyists. Two years later this still seems to be the case. The controversy about what type of light to use has not abated.

In the interim however, newer, high Kelvin degree fluorescent tubes have also found their way into the hobby, and give excellent results as well.

The advent of all this equipment, all this instrumentation, and the newer filtration techniques, have unfortunately raised the complexity of setting up such tanks to a degree that is beyond the "simple" instruction sheets that come with such equipment.

Not only is the Hobbyist now confronted with PVC or flexible hose piping, using all sorts of water control valves, installing solenoids, electrically actuated ball valves, meters, controllers, float switches, and many such other implements that were never part of the "traditional" aquarium, but in addition to all this, he or she is expected to be able to make all these choices without much expert literature, or reference material, being available.

This has brought about the need for much more detailed information on what such equipment does for the water chemistry on one hand, and how it should be installed, as often many options exist.

It is also not clear to many Hobbyists whether or not they should use all of these instruments and all of the equipment, or whether many of them can be added at a later time, when more automation is being introduced.

Certainly, a lot of this equipment makes one's life easier and introduces more stability to the conditions in the Reef Tank. But are they really a requirement to be able to keep a successful reef? Or can we keep a successful tank with only part of all the recommended equipment?

These are the kind of questions that we need answers to. And these are the kind of subjects that are covered in Advanced Reef Keeping I.

In Advanced Reef Keeping II we will look in detail at the fish and invertebrates you can safely keep, and how you should care for them.

We hope you will enjoy both books, and welcome your suggestions and comments.

1. First used by Northern Tropicals of Grand Rapids Michigan, Jack Sievers, Owner.
2. It had been tried before, but because of the lack of adequate filtration, and the many disease problems, hobbyists gave up, and went back to fish only, and invert only tanks.
3. A more complete system that includes light, heat, water quality mangement and treatment.
4. E.g. Eheim, Lifeguard, PEP.
5. Sanders Gmbh and equipment from scientific instrument companies
6. All of these are discussed throughout this book.

Part One

Setting the Stage

1. Introduction

A few months ago, in an effort to assist Hobbyists in better understanding the mechanics of Reef Aquarium keeping, we published the Marine Fish and Invert Reef Aquarium book.

That book received a much better than expected reception; indeed it is now in its fifth printing and still selling extremely well. The 8th printing should be forthcoming soon.

That eighth edition will, more than likely, be sligthly up-dated and some photographs will be changed, as there are now several companies that make the instruments that we were discussing, and we no longer need to only show you Dupla products, which at the time the book was first written were the only ones available.

Some readers even pointed that out to us. Since, however, only one company made the instruments that we wanted to discuss, its name obviously came up quite frequently.

Although there may be some overlap between the two books, to get the complete technical and theoretical sides of Marine Reef Keeping, you should really have both. This is because the "Marine Fish and Invert Reef Aquarium" goes into more detail, especially where it comes to water chemistry and the instrumentation used.

It also explains, in layman's terminology, the majority of the chemical concepts that need to be dealt with, goes into great detail on the subject of filtration - especially the many kinds of trickle filters- and takes a more theoritical look at Reef Keeping, so you may understand the reasons for the instrumentation and what their measurements actually mean.

You could, in a way, consider this new book as a comprehensive set of easy to follow instructions on how to set up an advanced reef system.

Although in both books a great number of instruments and equipment are used, it should be made clear from the beginning that you do not need "all" of them to set up a successful tank. In an effort to be as complete as possible, however, we have inlcuded them all.

It became evident from the reactions we received to our first book, and from the questions we were asked, that Hobbyists needed a companion book, one that would explain the whole process of setting up a Reef tank much more in detail.

This is especially so because of the appearance on the market of advanced instrumentation for measuring pH and redox potential, using carbon dioxide, and other reactor-type equipment, and of course the newer methods of filtration.

The latter refers mainly to trickle filters, also called by some, wet-dry filters although we find that not to be a very successful name, as obviously no part of the filter is dry, but also the the mesh filters, and in particular to the BioMesh™ filter.

With this new book we are trying to fill the void. Using this book, you should be able to set up a Reef Tank, starting from scratch. Or, if you already have a tank set up, you may use the suggestions given to improve upon your existing system.

Either way, following the recommendations will result in a system that runs much better and smoother overall, and gives you less maintenance, and less trouble.

"Advanced Reef Keeping" is so named because it incorporates all of the modern technology now available and explains the whys and hows of those instruments and techniques in as much detail as possible. The book's sub-title should make that clear.

It is divided into several sections. The two main ones are :

• A description, and a short discussion, of everything you need to set up a Reef Aquarium, e.g. tank, instruments, equipment, skimmers etc...and
• A step-by-step look at how all the pieces fit together.

Additionally, there are sections on other materials that are useful to know, or techniques that you should be aware of as they may come in handy at some point or another, e.g. if sickness occurs, or if water chemistry deteriorates for some reason or another.

We hope that you will enjoy it, and welcome both your critiques and suggestions for improvement and inclusion in future editions.

Although this book was as complete as we could make it at the time it was written, we felt that we could enhance its helpfulness even further by producing a series of videotapes that can be used as complements to this book, and also to the "Marine Fish and Invert Reef Aquarium" (Thiel 1988, Aarvark Press).

There are 7 videotapes, taking you from step 1, to a tank that is cycled and ready to be enjoyed. Each tape takes you through some of the steps, and the set of 7 gives you the complete picture.

At the time of this writing, 4 videos were being shipped, for a price of $ 159.99 per set. Three more are in the works, and are expected to be released in March of 1989. They can be obtained from Thiel•Aqua•Tech.

We feel that because of the effort that went in to producing these tapes professionally, this really is excellent value for the money.

You will see a Reef Tank being started, from the time we drill the necessary holes in the tank, through installing the trickle filter, the water returns, solenoids where necessary, bulkheads, float switches, overflow box, the skimmer, the control instruments, place live rock and fish in the tank, and get the system up and running, then let it cycle, and finally end up with an aquarium that is complete and ready for all who see it to enjoy.

We assure you that making these tapes was quite an undertaking, both financially and in labor, but I personally enjoyed every moment of it.

In essence, you can use the book and if you want more visual aid, the videos, to set up a new Reef tank or to modify the one you already have.

We also remind you that you may keep yourselves continually updated on what is happening in the world of Reef Keeping by subscribing to "Marine Reef", the technical newsletter published by Aardvark Press. This newsletter which sells for $ 43.00 p.a. for 17 issues, is produced every 3 weeks for your enjoyment and edification.

At the end of the book we have included a relatively comprehensive questionnaire. Please do your fellow Hobbyists a favor by filling it in. We will compute all the answers and put out a summary and interpretation of the results, and we will send you a copy, free of charge of course.

This will give you an idea of what Reef Hobbyists at large are doing to and for their tanks and allow you to become a better Reef Keeper.

As our contribution, besides the compilation of the results, we offer you a choice of either 6 months of Marine Reef Newsletters free, or a one year's subscription (17 issues)for the very special price of $ 20.00.

Albert J. Thiel
Trumbull, Connecticut
Completed in December 1988

Advanced Reef Keeping.
A Comprehensive Guide to Setting up Your Reef Aquarium.
© 1988 1989 Albert J. Thiel

Dedicated to Leo Wojcik for all the inspiration that came of the many many discussions he and I had over the months it took to complete this book. With many thanks for his numerous and valuable suggestions. Leo I have great respect for your knowledge.

2. How to Use "Advanced Reef Keeping"

As already indicated in the Introduction, this book can be used in several ways :

- you may follow the guidelines to start a Reef tank from scratch,
- you may use the recommendations to make changes to your existing system,
- or you may just wish to learn more about what you could do to your Reef tank, at some later date perhaps, to improve upon the water quality and living conditions.

Whatever you do, be assured that we have tried to incorporate just about everything that can possibly be added to a tank to improve its efficiency and quality.

This does'nt mean that you should install all of the options that we have included. Though it is perhaps wise to include many of them.

If an item is really optional, we have so indicated, explaining its benefits, and also why it is not really a requirement, but as we say " a nice or neat addition" that perhaps makes life somewhat easier or that builds in an additional safety factor to help keep the water chemistry more under control in a more controlable fashion.

Moreover, some options are mutually exclusive, e.g. overflow boxes and syphons. But since different Hobbyists do different things, and since there are many ways to equip your tank, we have included them, to be as complete as possible.

Although you may skip sections and look immediately for what you are most interested in, it is best to read through the book chapter by chapter, to better understand how all the parts fit together, and how they need to be installed.

Even though we feel that the time of writing we were as complete as possible, progress is "fortunately" always made and newer equipment appears all the time. That is, of course, a boon, as it has brought us most of the instrumentation discussed in this book.

Some months ago, maybe 18 to 24 or so, there was really only one company that sold advanced instrumentation, and only one that sold reliable skimmers and ozonizers.

Now there are several, both foreign and domestic, and if this trend continues, we should start seeing some of the prices go down. By the time this book comes out, several German manufacturers should have their products on the American market as well.

Instrumentation from companies worth looking at include :

• MTC of New Jersey for filters, skimmers, reactors....

• Sanders Gmbh for a very wide assortment of skimmers, ozonizers and a redox potential regulator.

• Dupla Aquaristik Gmbh for advanced equipment in general, including pH, redox potential, lux intensity, carbon dioxide systems, and others.

• Tunze for power skimmers and advanced equipment, including a trickle filter with spray bar.

• Thiel•Aqua•Tech, my own company, for Redox Potential Regulators and strong ozonizers, air dryers and nitrate and phosphate removing products, protein skimmers, turbulence makers (Ocean Motion), Twin probe conversions units, fertilizers, macro-algae nutrients, trace elements, Reef salt and more. all made in the USA.

• Eheim, for canister filters and large protein skimmers.

• Coralife and Energy Savers of Torrance California, for foods, additives, skimmers, and many forms of advanced lighting.

• and of course a number of scientific instrument supply houses, including Cole-Parmer, Markson's, Omega Engineering, and others still.

It should not come as a surprise, that those are the names of the companies that you will find mentioned over and over again in this book, as those are indeed the instruments that we will be using in setting up our tank.

Some equipment can be built, home-made that is, by the enterprising hobbyist. Most instruments cannot however, mainly because components are not widely available.

And even if you are electronically proficient, you would not want to assemble many of them because of the dangers involved. For instance, ozonizers run at several thousand volts, and even though the amperage is very small, you could get seriously hurt if you experienced such an electric shock.

It is sometimes difficult to explain in words exactly and clearly, what needs to be done to install a particular instrument or piece of equipment. We have tried to use simple language and describe procedures and terminology in every day words.

Sometimes, however, you may need to read a section several times, to visualize what we are talking about. This is especially so if you are not in the habit of working with plastics, glass, equipment and instruments.

Don't let this bother you. If you read the sections over again, you will no doubt know exactly how to do what you set out to. No specific knowledge is required, just general handiness perhaps.

This is not a picture book, which explains the lack of color photography of invertebrates and fish. The charts and diagrams and some gray scale pictures should, we feel, suffice to achieve what the intent of this book is, namely to make you a better marine fish tank hobbyist, specializing in tanks containing corals and invertebrates, and be able to do all that work yourself.

The fact is that there are already quite a few excellent picture books on the market, anyway. There is no void there.

Keep in mind too when reading this book, that it is not intended to be the final word on the matter, and that it is not a scientific text. We have tried to simplify all explanations as much as possible, to the detriment sometines of chemical accuracy.

Technology evolves and new products appear all the time. Sometimes equipment that exists, but is not used in the Hobby, finds its way into stores and wholesalers, and is suddenly recommended for use. Case in point : oxygen measuring devices and meters.

Consider it fortunate that this happens, as that is exactly how Reef Keeping becomes a more serious and professional hobby in the long run.

Always remember, too, that "quality pays both in the short, and in the long run".

Good luck in your Reef Keeping endeavors, and please, let us have some feedback on how you feel this book can be improved so that future readers may find it even more useful.

3. Review of Basic Equipment

3.1. Selecting an Aquarium

3.1.1. Glass or Acrylic

No one ever seems to agree on whether it is better to use glass or acrylic. Both have advantages and both have disadvantages. The two main plus features of each are that glass is long lasting and does not easily scratch, on one hand; and acrylic is light and easy to drill, on the other.

Some of the disadvantages of each include that glass is heavy and not easily drilled, and that acrylic scratches and becomes yellow over time, especially under certain types of light.

Just think for a minute however about what we normally will be putting in our Reef tank. Live Corals, stony or dead coral formations, and many other such materials can easily scratch the acrylic, or what most hobbyists commonly call "plexiglass", although that is a brand name.

Is it still such a good idea to use acrylic? Personally, I do not think so.

Acrylic is excellent for the filters and for the reserve water vats that you may be keeping, but for the aquarium itself, it is too delicate in my opinion.

Of course, as time goes on, forms of acrylic may appear that change these negative aspects. My own opinion is only my own, and you may disagree, especially if you are on the West Coast where the use of acrylic is much more popular and widespread.

Besides the scratches from sharp corals, which cannot be removed (except on the outside), algae growth will also invariably result in additional scratches. These then turn into patches that lose their transparency somewhat and look very unsightly after a while.

Blushing may also occur. This is the tendency of the bonding agent used to become whitish and opaque, and this happens, of course, at the seams. However, not all solvents or bonding agents change color over time. The problem is that when buying the tank you have no way of knowing whether yours will or not.

Don't let this not discourage you if you already have an acrylic aquarium, You will just have to be extra careful not to scratch it in any way, and remove any algae that may coat the inside panes as soon as they appear. This will prevent them from taking hold too firmly, or, in the case of diatoms, start encrusting. Use your hands to get them off, or an extremely soft piece of cloth.

Diatoms and encrusting algae are more difficult to remove, as their shells scratch the acrylic while you remove them, so be super careful. Be extremely careful too, when moving rocks and corals around.

3.1.2. Size

It is not the size of the tank that determines whether you will be successful or not. Too small a tank however is not recommended, (refer to the Marine Fish and Invert Reef Aquarium for more details). Start with at least 50 to 55 gallons.

The best looking tanks are the ones that are wide : meaning the front to back measurement. Fifty gallon breeder tanks make excellent reef aquariums because they are usually 24 inches wide, they are however not easy to find. Wide tanks allow you to build up a section in the middle of the tank that slopes the way a real Reef does, which makes it much easier for you to position the invertebrates, corals and other animal life that you will acquire.

To be able to keep a large variety of animal life you will need a somewhat larger tank. In this book we will be looking at how to set up and maintain such an aquarium. We have opted for a 150 gallon, because it can hold a large biomass, and because it is still well within the space considerations that most hobbyists can deal with.

Larger aquariums might sound nice to have, but fitting an 8 foot by 2 foot by 2 foot (240 gallons) tank in a living room is not within everyone's possibilities. This is not to speak of the 300 gallon plus aquariums. If however that happens to be the size you will be setting up, just substitute your size number wherever we mentionned 150 gallons.

The principles are of course exactly the same. And if you do have such a large tank, you will be able to enjoy it even more thoroughly after you have applied some of the techniques we describe.

3.1.3. Glass Thickness

For those of you who are inclined to build their own tanks, it may be useful to know that the thickness of the glass is determined more by the height of the tank than by its width or length.

Runs of 4 or more feet need to be braced at the top with a strip of glass, about 3 inches in width, that runs from the front to the back.

Blue-prints on how to build aquariums are available and even advertised inte hobby magazines. You would however be wise to either have a professional build it for you, or buy a stock aquarium.

We have seen a lot of the work done by World Class Aquarium in Brooklyn, New York, but there are many such companies all around the country. Yellow Pages are probably your best source for names.

3.1.4. Tempered & Non-tempered glass

Tempered glass is stronger than non-tempered glass and makes a better tank of course. The problem is that tempered glass cannot be drilled.

The holes needed for the filter inlets and outlets have to be drilled before the tempering process takes place.

This is usually not practical and you will, in all likelihood, have a tank that is made of non-tempered glass.

3.1.5. Height

To many of you this may not seem an important subject to deal with, and most Hobbyists never think about depth implications when buying an aquarium.

In my own mind however it is , because the deeper - top to bottom - the tank is, the harder it will be to service.

Even some 150 gallon tank that are 27 inches deep are hard to clean at the bottom without standing on a step stool, and getting into the water with your whole arm...

Tall tanks may be visually more appealing, but they are much harder to care for. Keep this in mind when selecting your own tank.

3.1.6. Shape

Although not as important as height, some tanks with odd shapes can be hard to service in all spots, e.g. the sides and the back.

We have seen triangular tanks that fit nicely in a corner, but one can never really get to the back to clean the overflow box, or back glass pane.

Although we are not saying that you have to stick with the traditional rectangular or square shape, remember these remarks when buying an aquarium. This is especially the case if you order a custom built model. All parts must be easily accessible. This will indeed influence how often, and how willing, you will be to service your aquarium.

In my experience, the easier it is to access the filters to clean them, the more often you will be inclined to do so, and doing so regularly is very important indeed.

3.1.7. Location of the Tank

Because of the weight of the whole aquarium, you must make sure that the spot where you will, or have located yours, can support the great weight of the tank. On average, figure that you must multiply the number of gallons that the tank can hold by 10, and then add the weight of the tank, and also the weight of the stand.

Coral and other types of rock weigh about 1.5 times the amount of water they displace.

Tanks are best placed against a wall, at a 90 degree angle with the beams in the floor underneath. That way they are well suported. This is especially important in older houses and does not apply to modern appartments perhaps. But check anyway.

3.2. Drilled or un-drilled ?

Personally, we feel that a drilled tank is much easier to deal with, but you can certainly get by with a non-drilled tank that is outfitted with an overflow syphon arrangement, e.g. the ones sold by Route 4 Marine Technology, or Summit Aquatics, Nautilus Aquatics and T•A•T.

Make sure that the syphon you order can handle the flow that you will be pushing through the tank. It is important that the syphon be sized properly to allow for good water flow; otherwise, you will not be able to obtain the water quality that you will be looking for. The outflow pipe should be at least one inch in internal diameter (I.D.).

If you have the choice, drill or have the tank drilled. If you have an existing system and want to make modifications based on the recommendations in this book, but you do not want to take the tank apart -which is understandable-, you will, of course, have to make do with a syphon system.

This syphon should be self-starting (self-priming). This means that when your pump stops the syphon stops as well ; and when the pump re-starts, the syphon does the same.

Only two such syphons have withstood the testing I did. One is the one already mentioned, and the other one is made and sold by Dupla Aquaristik. This does not mean that there are'nt any others, of course, or new ones may have appeared since this book was written.

There are quite a few on the market, and you may want to check the ads in the hobby magazines that you regularly read.

Remember that the two criteria to look for are :

• self starting & re-starting, and
• able to handle high flow rates.

A syphon that can hold pre-filter material is better than one that cannot. Indeed, the water from the aquarium needs to be pre-filtered before it enters the trickle filter, regardless of the packing material that you use. Make sure that such material is easy to remove and clean.

It is our experience that the easier that is to do, the more often the filter will get cleaned, and the better off you and your tank will be.

If you are using an overflow area in the corner of the tank, that same area will be the pre-filter chamber. You may fill it with natural sponges for instance, or other materials that remove gross and medium particulate matter. The latter include the EfiGross by Eheim, BioMech, Bioporon, floss, and many other materials that can trap dirt and particulate matter.

I have used natural sponges for many years - the kind you buy in auto parts places are excellent - and have not really had to replace them.

Just wash them religiously every week and place them back in the overflow. This will prevent them from plugging the overflow, and from reducing dissolved oxygen levels as a result of organic decay (more on this later in this book).

Installing such a mechanical filter ensures that the water that reaches your trickle filter is free of gross impurites, e.g. pieces of algae, or food, that may otherwise pollute the sump.

Or such matter may get stuck in the trickle filter, start decomposing, use oxygen in the process, and add ammonia and other impurities to the tank.

This is to be avoided as much as possible, as it is probably the quickest way to lower your water quality and stress the tank's inhabitants unduly, and for reasons that can easily be avoided.

3.3. Overflow, Automatic Syphon, Stand-pipe

Water is required to flow, on a continuous basis, from the aquarium to the trickle filter. There are several ways to achieve this.

You are probably familiar with all of them. If you are not, the various methods are explained here briefly, and in much more detail in The Marine Fish and Invert Reef Aquarium book :

- Corner overflow box,
- Siphon, automatic or not,
- Surface skimmer and siphon combination.

Platinum Series Trickle Filter with all accessories

• Stand -pipe.

All of these methods will work. In order of efficiency, however, the order is as follows:

• Corner overflow
• Wide Stand-pipe (1 1/2" minimum)
• Surface skimming automatic syphon
• Automatic siphon (double assembly type)

Corner Overflow Box :

Built within the aquarium, e.g. in one of the back corners. Can be rectangular, triangular, circular, square, or any shape you want. Does not have to run all the way to the bottom, either.

If that is the case, you will need a hole in the back or side of the tank, to guide the outflowing water to the trickle filter. Such a set-up works better however if it does go all the way to the bottom, since, because of more gravity you will get a much better flow rate.

Most tanks have square or rectangular overflows. The reason seems to be that only 2 pieces of glass or acrylic are needed to build them. Of course, a triangular box requires only one piece.

Alternatively you could use a cylindrical piece of acrylic pipe and set it in place with a bulkhead fitting (for explanations on fittings, see the Marine Fish and Invert Reef Aquarium).

Check the picture of the Nollmann Aquarium and take a good look at how the corner overflow fits and sits in the tank.

Of course you could conceivably make a full square box, of the height you require, and tighten that into the aquarium with a fitting. That way you do not have to glue anything. You just need the holes drilled, or you need to buy a pre-drilled tank.

Such an overflow looks like a tall rectangular or square container, with a bottom. Through that bottom a hole is drilled the same size as the hole in the tank. To put it in place, slide a bulkhead fitting through it, and tighten from underneath the aquarium.

The height of that box assembly will determine the water level in the tank. Usually it should be approximately 1 3/4 inch shorter than the tank's height. This will maintain the water level in the aquarium at about 1 1/4 to 1 1/2 inches from the top.

If that is too low to your liking, make the box one quarter inch taller, and the level will be from 1 to 1 1/4 inches from the top.

There is still another way of getting water down to the trickle filter, which consists of hanging a little 2 box assembly on the tank. One actually hangs in the water, and the other one, on the side of the tank.

The first one skims the surface tank water, which runs into the box through slits. The box looks like a comb at the top, and from there the water is siphoned with traditional siphon tubes to the second box,

Modern Aquarium with Corner overflow box, and holes in the bottom

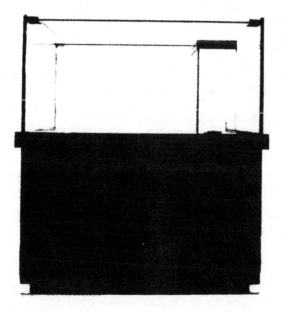

where the siphon breaking and restarting is controlled.

There are several manufacturers of such systems : MTC and Summit Aquatics are two of them. Thiel Aqua Tech is another one.

The 2 boxes can be either close to each other, e.g. one on each side of the aquarium glass, or distant from each other. In fact if the second box is at a certain distance, and one or two feet lower than the first one, the syphon will develop a stronger suction capability, resulting in a higher water flow.

The outflow pipe should in all cases be at least 1 inch I.D., and preferably 1 1/4 inch. This will allow for enough water to go down through the trickle filter, especially when using strong pumps.

We prefer 1 inch on medium tanks, and one and a quarter inch on larger tanks. This means 55 to 110, and 110+ respectively.

When starting with a new tank, the choice is rather obvious; go for the overflow corner box. If you are converting an existing tank to a reef system, the 2 part box assembly made by M.T.C. and the Summit Aquatics and T•A•T models will all give satisfactory results.

Stand pipe :

This type of overflow operates on the same principle as the corner overflow, except that it has certain disadvantages :

- it cannot be used as a pre-filter
- flow adjustment can be tricky resulting in slurping noises
- to do the job, the pipe needs to be quite large and becomes unsightly

It's advantage however is that it is easy to install and totally safe in its operation.

Obviously it can only be installed if holes have been drilled in the bottom of the aquarium.

Since stand pipes need to be of a large internal diameter, they usually require a rather large hole in the bottom of the tank. The hole to accommodate a 1 1/2 inch bulkhead will be around 2 1/4 inches. Make sure that whoever is going to drill your tank has drilling equipment that can handle that type of a job.

Plastic fittings used in swimming pool set ups are usually not as thick.

3.4. One or several water returns ?

Water can be returned to the aquarium from either the top using hose
or pipe to guide it there, or by means of holes drilled in the bottom of
the tank.

Either way is fine of course, but if you are drilling a hole for the overflow
box anyway, you may as well drill one or more holes for returning the
water to the tank.

The question is how many returns should there be. In smaller tanks one
hole, or one return by means of pipe or hose, will certainly do. In larger
tanks, two or more holes are desirable. In tanks up to a 150 gallon tank
we recommend two water returns.

Where are they positioned ? One on each side of the tank, about 2 to
3 inches away from the side panes of the aquarium. Angle them
towards the side panes, using a 45 degree angled fitting in which a
short piece of pipe is stuck. The latter is done to obtain a uniform
outflow.

Directing the water towards the side panes breaks up the flow, and
pushes it back towards the center of the aquarium, ensuring in the
process that there are no dead spots. The more centered the return is
(between front and back glass pane) the better the water distribution
will be.

See Section 3.5 for additional recommendations on returning water
behind coral rock formations to improve the flow through the aquarium even more.

To achieve even water distribution you will need to install a ball valve
in each return line, as this will enable you to adjust the flow that comes
out of each of the returns. It is always a good idea to use true union, or
single union, ball valves for easy disassembly and cleaning.

You will need a check valve in each line as well, to prevent water from
flowing from the aquarium backwards - this is called back syphoning-
when the pump is at a stand still, or when a power failure occurs.

If you "alternate" the currents (see 3.1.6), you will not need the check
valves as the solenoids that you will be using act as check valves when
there is no current going to them. Normally closed solenoids close
when the current to them is shut off.

3.5. Spray pipe behind the Corals and Rocks

Hobbyists who keep corals, invertebrates, and who build reef-like structures in their tanks, need good water circulation behind these structures. This removes undesirable materials and prevents dead spots where water gets replaced slowly or not at all.

One way to achieve that is by piping a long piece of PVC -that has been perforated with a regular drill bit at 1 inch intervals- into the bottom rear of the tank.

Position the holes in such a way that water is pushed out in vertical, 45 degree and horizontal ways. To clarify, the first hole is pushing the water downwards, the second one, one inch further, is pushing it backwards towards the rear pane of the tank, the third one backwards but at a 45 ° angle, and so on. All holes are 1 inch apart.

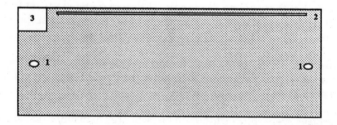

This will create strong water movement in the back of the reef looking structure, and ensure good water movement. It is most important, when piping in this fashion, to install a ball valve **and a check valve** in line with that pipe, to be able to control the actual amount of water that will be diverted behind the rocks.

Setting this up requires an extra hole in the bottom of the tank, smaller than the other holes. Make sure that the water intake of that pipe is positioned before the branch-off to your two main water returns (the ones that alternate), otherwise that water return will only let water into the tank half of the time, because of the alternating effect of the solenoid valves, or other device that you use to create this change of direction in the water flow.

To get this system to work efficiently you may need to run it with a dedicated pump. Remember, you are looking for good flow.You will not need a strong pump; about 200-400 gallons per hour, depending on the size of your tank.

An easy way to solve this is to use the pump that runs your cooling unit, and return that water behind the coral rock formations in the tank.

Also see the Section on "Cooling", for an explanation on why we think you will need such a unit.

3.6. Location of the Water Return Holes

There are various ways, of course, to return the water to your tank.

Some Hobbyists will run a line from the trickle filter to the tank itself, using either flexible hose, or hard pvc, or other pipe. This may be an arrangement where the water gets back into the tank by means of one return, or sometimes by means of several, (usually two - one on each side of the tank), and some even use spray bars to make the water break the surface, to increse oxygenation. That is one way of doing things, the traditional way. In Reef Systems, we try to return water to the tank in more efficient ways!

Returning the water from the top :

• run pipe or flexible tubing behind the tank, up to, and over the top.

• do this on both sides of the tank. This means that there will be a water return on each side.

• angle the returning water in such a way that it "shoots" downwards and towards the sides of the tank. This creates currents that not only stir the bottom up, and move detritus to the filters, but it reduces the likelihood of deadspots.

• run a third line, smaller perhaps than the first two, up and over the top, and then all the way down again, so its output is behind the coral formations that you will be placing in the tank.

Make sure to angle its output sideways. This will prevent the formation of so-called "dead spots", where water moves slowly, behind these coral formations. The latter would result in oxygen depletion, stagnation, and lowering of the overall water quality, and this is, of course, undesirable.

Returning the water from the bottom of the tank :

The principle just described can be achieved by returning water from the bottom of the aquarium rather than from the top, and in a more efficient way of doing so.

This requires the drilling of three holes through the glass (or acrylic). One on each side, and a third one, towards the back of the tank, as close to a side as possible, in essence in a rear corner.

The illustration shows clearly where the holes are located. The size of the holes will depend on the size of the tank, which, in turn, determines how much water you will be circulating.

The larger the tank, the more water you will want to circulate and the larger the holes will have to be. Consequently you will also need a larger pump.

Both hard piping and the use of flexible tubing, held in place with clamps, are possible. Bulkhead fittings (tank fittings) will be required to ensure that no leaks occur where the holes have been drilled. More on this in Part Four of this book (See also The Marine Fish and Invert Aquarium book).

3.7. Alternating or continuous current

When you install more than one return, the water being returned can be alternated between the two returns. For instance, the system could be set up in such a way that the water is coming back for 15 minutes through one opening, and then for 15 minutes through the other one.

For that matter, you can set the switch-over time from one return to the other at any level you wish.

How often you can make the water alternate depends on how you have your system set up. If you use one pump with 2 solenoid valves and a timer, the frequency of switching is determined by the fine tuning you can achieve with the timer that you are using.

Grasslin Corporation (New Jersey) manufactures a number of timers with switching capabilities as low as every minute and a quarter. Several scientific instrument supply companies sell digital timing devices as well (Such timers will run you anywhere from S 30.00 to $ 70.00 for the more sophisticated multi-channel models).

More frequent switching can be attained by using two pumps and a relay that is preset to switch current input to the pumps for any interval that you select. This could be every second, or few seconds, which, of course, is not very practical. On the average a switching time of around 2 minutes seems to work well.

There is no reason to recommend any particular switching time, or prefer one over the other. The only consideration to take into account is that it should be relatively short, say every 10 minutes or so. Or every 30 minutes. This is very much a matter of personal preference.

When including this in your system set-up, you are in essence duplicating the motion over the reef that is the result of wave movement.

Leo Wojcik, a Hobbyist from New Jersey, alternates the currents about every 30 seconds, using a a sligthly more sophisticated set up, which we will describe later, and which is based on the use of 4 power heads, two on each side of the tank, which alternate on the mentioned 30 second interval.

Leo seems very satisfied with this timing, and when you look at the inverts, you can see them sway from one side to the other. The opening view of tape one, of the series of videos on Reef Tanks that we produced, shows this device in action.

Units to alternate the flow are sold by Thiel•Aqua•Tech (Ocean Motion), and also by MTC and Route 4 Marine Technology (Wave Maker). More on these units and how they are installedlater in the book.

Ocean Motion wave making device

3.8. Surface skimming

If an overflow box or a siphon arrangement is used, the top of the aquarium, meaning the surface of the water, is skimmed of accumulated dirt and oils.

This is very beneficial, as it improves the air—water interface, especially for gaseous exchanges, for instance oxygen, and this results in better oxygenation of the water.

A surface skimmer incorporated in your siphon—overflow is the best of both worlds. Corner overflow boxes automatically skim water from the surface of the aquarium, as they pull water down from the top.

Since the matter that is skimmed needs to be removed from the water altogether, fine filtering material should be present in the overflow corner box, or in the siphon. Floss, natural sponge, bonded blue—white filter pads and the like will do.

The key is to clean them as frequently as required, certainly at least once a week. Any detritus that is caught will decompose, remove oxygen from the water, and lower the dissolved oxygen level in the process.

And that is something that is to be avoided at all cost. Moreover, anything that decomposes adds pollutants to the water, and eventually increases the amount of nitrates, phosphates, and other undesirable - even non organic- compounds present.

3.9.   Pulsed water return ?

You may elect not to push water back in to the tank at a steady rate. Or push it in at a steady rate for some time, and then switch to a pulsating mode for a while.

Whenever the water is pulsed, uneven currents are created and the aquarium water is moved about in a more natural way. This is not something that we feel is absolutely required, but since it recreates the uneven water movements that occur on natural reefs, it is certainly a worthwhile option to consider.

It is not difficult to achieve this, and all you will need is a controller that allows you to vary the pump output in that fashion. At the time of this writing no such pulsators were available in the USA, although my own company is trying to obtain rights to distribute a German unit in the near future.

What we do sell though, is a unit that allows you to alternate the output of two pumps.You may also wish to check with some of the plumbing supply places or scientific instrument companies to determine availability of similar devices.

3.10.   Using Flowmeters

Should you want to carefully monitor how much water is actually being moved in and out of the tank, a flowmeter is the device you need. Several companies market units that can be safely used in salt water environments, e.g. Cole Parmer, Omega and others. No Aquarium product company has one available to our knowledge.

All parts, including the float, must be salt water safe and salt water resistant. Glass, 316 stainless steel, or an inert plastic material are therefore a requirement. Salt water resistant is not enough, the parts must be totally inert.

Flowmeter

The problem with the latter floats is that they are light, and cannot be used in small meters that have to control a high flow since they do not offer enough resistance to the force of the water flowing through the pipes.

The inside of a good flowmeter is tapered. You should not buy flowmeters that are spring-loaded. The spring offers too great a resistance and, as a result, you will get less flow out of your pump. Additionally, the spring is usually made out of metal.

Of course, flowmeters can also be used to determine the amount of air that is produced by your airpump, the amount of air you are blowing into your ozonizer, or the amount of Carbon dioxide, or air-ozone mix, etc. that flows into your system.

Whether there is any merit to knowing those numbers is really up to you to decide.

It is however helpful to know those numbers if you use a carbon dioxide reactor or an oxygen reactor (for more details on both, see Part 2), or if you are injecting enriched air or oxygen into the water, under pressure or not, via a similar reactor.

With such reactors you may have to adjust the flow rate, and it is therefore helpful to be able to monitor more accurately, how much of a gas you are presently injecting into your system.

3.11. Power Heads

Power heads can be used to create additional current inside the aquarium, e.g. behind the coral rocks where dead spots could occur. Or they can be used to simulate wave motion by alternating their operation.

This is not really a good description of what they do, creating turbu lence inside the aquarium, would be better, but there is not one word that describes that action accurately. At T•A•T we call it Ocean Motion.

They can also be used to move more water around, inside the tank, and be run continuously. The Aquaclear 400, by Hagen, moves a good deal of water and is not really large. In tanks of 180 to 300 gallons, you may wish to use one, or several, of the 800 models.

Since they are sold in several power versions, it is easy to size them properly And remember to adjust the flow direction for maximum efficiency.

Ideally that is from one side of the tank to the other. In this way the water goes all across the tank, hits the other side pane, and then fans out and comes back, creating a nice flow that will make your invertebrates sway every time the current is changed from one power head (or set of power heads) to the other.

Although they are very helpful in achieving this, their drawback is that they need to be cleaned regularly. Failing to do so will result in the intakes clogging up, the motor overheating , and eventually motor or impeller failure.

Of course, no water movement will occur as a result. Cleaning them regularly is also important to prevent the impeller and its shaft from breaking or getting stuck and becoming noisy at start up.

If you are prepared to include their cleaning in your regular maintenance schedule, by all means use them, as they greatly improve internal water circulation, and do so easily.

Alternating the current to the power heads requires the use of a relay which switches current output between the various power heads that you are using, thus pumping water in one direction for a while, and then reversing and pumping from the other direction. Both MTC and Thiel•Aqua•Tech make such a device.The latter one is solid state, and totally noiseless.

When using intricate rock formation set ups in your tank, using one or more power head is always recommended to ensure that good circulation is obtained within that coral rock formation.

Just place the power heads in the correct locations, behind the coral rock, e.g. about 10 or more inches under water. Make them accessible, as you will need to clean their intakes from time to time. Adjust their output if neccessary, and plug them in.

If, on top of that, you have decided to use an alternating device, your sytem will be more efficient, but this is not a requirement. It is an optional improvement.

3.12. Submersible Pumps

As we have indicated earlier, creating additional current in the tank to improve water circulation and prevent dead spots where dissolved oxygen levels are low or depleted, can be achieved by using one or more of the many submersible pumps on the market.

March, Little Giant, Teel, and several other companies make such pumps..

The key is to position them in such a way that they move water away from behind the coral formations, and bring it back into the main water flow inside the tank.

You will also need to make sure that you can easily retrieve them, as they will obviously need to be cleaned from time to time.

Whatever pump you use, make real sure that it is totally salt water resistant. If any metal parts are visible, you may want to cover them with one of the silicone paints (they are usually called dips) available in paint and hardware stores.

You can achieve the same result by "sinking" one or more Power Heads behind these same corals. Again, be sure that you will be able to remove them to clean them from time to time. More on the installation procedures later in this book.

3.13. One or Several Corner Overflows

Some Hobbyists are concerned that, to handle large flows of water, one overflow corner filter box may not be enough.

In our own experience, a properly sized overlfow can easily handle 1000+ gallons per hour, and should suffice in most cases.

The outflow pipe should be one inch, or one inch and a quarter. Often indeed, the problem of "good" flow is not the number of overflows, but the dimension of the drain pipe at the bottom of the overflow box.

Of course, there is nothing wrong with having more than one such overflow, and in tanks of more than 250 gallons we would recommend that you have at least two.

Not so much because one corner overflow cannot handle the amount of water you want to move around, but because drawing water from

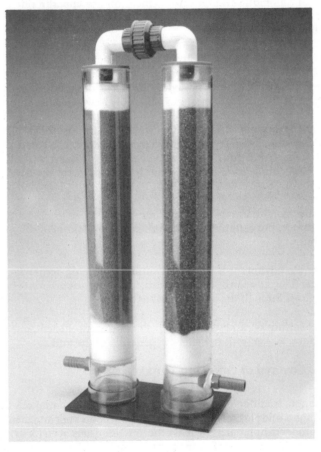

Double deionizer

two areas in the tank will give you a more thorough turnover rate (new water coming in - old water going out).

All such overflows should be sized so that they can accomodate pre-filter material. And they should be easy to access, to enable you to clean the pre-filter material regularly (once a week is our recommendation).

If you have only one overflow corner filter and you would like to add a second one without taking your tank down to do so, you may simply add an automatic syphon arrangement on the opposite side of the tank. You will in essence now have an overflow in the left and in the right corners of your tank.

This is not a difficult modification at all -you will just need to run additional hose to the top of your trickle filter, and may need to place a Tee-fitting in line to accommodate the second down flow going to the biological filter because most such filters oly have one inlet at the top.

Alternatively you will need another water inlet into the trickle filter for that additional water coming down from the tank. You can drill this hole yourself and add another bulkhead fitting. The system will now accommodate 2 down runs of water from the tank to the biological filter.

Having more than one surface skimming overflow is obviously an advantage, but certainly not a requirement in tanks of less than 180 gallons.

The main advantage is that better surface skimming occurs and that greater flow rates can be achieved, thus increasing the amount of water that flows through the biological filter column.

Better surface skimming means a better and more efficient, air/water interface, which leads to better oxygenation of the tank.

3.14. Covered or Open top Tanks ?

Although, traditionally, we have all been used to covering our tanks with lights and plastic frames with or without lights built into them, the more modern approach is to leave the top completely open (or as much as possible since acrylic tanks are partially closed on the top to reinforce them structurally).

The reasoning behind this newer method is :

• an open top allows a much better view of the top of the reef.

• the air-water surface interchange occurs more naturally and also more efficiently with an open top.

Many recognized authors recommend this method and endorse it fully. This includes P. Wilkens, J. Lemkemeyer, H. Kipper, and many others. It is also the way most advanced Hobbyists in Europe keep their tanks.

Many of you will ask "What about fish jumping out?"

The incidence of fish jumping out of Reef systems is so small, that we may as well discount it altogether as a source of problems. Jumping occurs mostly as the result of aggressive behavior of some fish in the tank, chasing the others, ultimately driving others to try to escape by jumping out of the water. This sometimes happens to be out of the tank as well.

Such aggression will not exist if you carefully select your tank's inhabitants. You will find many recommendations on which fish to keep in Reef tanks in recent books, as well as in Advanced Reef Keeping II, which as we have already indicated will be out later this year..

The benefits of increased oxygenation, thanks to a better water-air interface exchange, far outweigh the possible loss of a fish. Do not forget that most Aquarists lose fish for many other reasons, and never make any particular issue out of it.

3.15. Undergravel Filter Plates

We do not recommend the use of "undergravel" filtration in Reef Tanks. The reason for this will become clear to you, as you progress through this book.

This does not mean that such filters do not work in Reef Tanks. They obviously do, but as we will see, they are not necessary as we will be using far more advanced methods of filtration.

Does that mean that if you are still using an undergravel filter you should dismantle your tank and start all over again? Of course not. You may add a trickle filter to such a system, but must also continue to run your undergravel, lest the water underneath the plates will foul.

You may, however, elect to run your undergravel at a slower rate or let it run the way it always did. Make sure that you clean the gravel or substrate regularly to remove detritus that may break down and consume oxygen in the process.

The above remarks apply to both regular flow, and reverse flow undergravel filters.

3.16. Conversion Units - Siphons

As you browse through the Hobby magazines you will see ads for so-called conversion units. Most of them are simply siphons with or without a pre-filter assembly.

There are some, too, that incorporate some form of biological/mechanical filtration, e.g. the Matrix-Matrex and other such systems.

As we have pointed out before, we do not like to use any filter that combines the biological and mechanical filtration functions in one unit.

Let us re-iterate the reason : mechanical filters need to be cleaned. Anything that traps dirt promotes decay and enhances the oxygen reduction process. This is contrary to good systems approach techniques.

Moreover, each time such a filter needs to be cleaned, part of the biological filter will be killed off. Not exactly what we want, do we ?

Although conversion units can be used meaningfully, trickle filters will give you much better results.

If you decide on a conversion unit, use it as a mechanical filter only, and clean it at least once a week. In this fashion you will have excellent fine filtration and reduce particulate matter in the water, plus the benefit of a siphon system.

3.17 Conversion units - True, complete filters

Lately, true modular filter conversion units have appeared on the market as well. You simply hang them over the back of the tank and run them with a strong power head type pump.

This is a promising development and should prove interesting to watch and test, once larger models are available.

4. How important is the stand ?

The stand has no bearing on the performance of the tank. The only reason for mentioning it in this book is that the size underneath the tank, the cabinet, has to be able to accommodate whatever trickle filter you will be buying and installing.

With larger tanks, you will need to be able to remove the top of the stand to lower the trickle filter inside. Indeed the larger models do not usually fit through the small doors of the cabinet.

This may entail being able to actually remove the top plate (if any), or removing the supports, to slide the trickle filter in.

When ordering a trickle filter, or when looking around for one, make sure that you know the exact inside dimensions of your cabinet. This will save you a lot of trouble when installing your system.

If you are just starting you must make sure that you get the stand and the filter to match. If they do not, you are up for a lot of installation problems.

Some cabinets have open backs, or partially open backs. They are better than the fully closed ones, inasmuch as you have more space to work with and easier access to all the parts of your system.

You may also be able to remove the supports in the back of the tank to slide your filter in, and then re-assemble the stand supports. These are excellent types of stands as they give you more flexibility.

If you build your own, keep in mind that salt water is very heavy. The stand needs to be very sturdy. It can be done, and many a Hobbyist has, but you should buy plans for such a stand from a company that has a tested model that has been around for some time and has proven itself. Dont't be the guinea pig.

Stands with more than one door are better, as they allow more access to all interior parts, especially the trickle filter's compartments, once it is installed.

Also, stands without a divider in the middle are easier to work with than those that do.

To those of you who have tanks this whole issue may seem trivial, but to the beginner it is not, as, having the right stand will make servicing and installing all the equipment and the filter all that much easier.

5. Selecting Pumps

Most Hobbyists do not pay enough attention to the type of pump they buy. This is very unfortunate, because the pump is the "lifeline" of the Reef Tank.

It needs to run day after day, month after month, year after year without failing. That requires a real good quality pump. Do not forget that you are entrusting the lives of your fish and invertebrates to that same pump (and thedollars invested in the system too, for that matter).

If the pump fails, even if your fish do not die, you may still lose your biological filter, or worse, have to start all over again. We therefore recommend that you do not skimp on the cost of the pump.

Additionally, pumps should be installed in such a way that they are easy to clean and they should not warm up the water. Most magnetic driven pumps are either water or fan cooled. You will be better off with fan cooled pumps as water cooled pumps transfer the heat generated from the motor to the water. This cools the motor down but heats up your water, and may add several degrees to the aquarium's temperature.

Fan cooled pumps use the outside air to cool the motor and, as a result, less heat is transfered to the water. Two excellent pumps you may want to look at are the Aquapump by Aquarium Sales and Services, and modified Iwaki pumps, as sold by Thiel•Aqua•Tech and Dupla USA.

The modification, which is not major, is required to ensure that the pump will resists salt water for extended periods of time with minimal maintenance; this makes it totally safe as opposed to just salt water resistant.

The most important feature to look for besides salt water safe and salt water resistant parts, is the pump's rated output.

Output is what determines the flow of water through the tank and consequently through the filter. Keep in mind that most pump ratings are given at a head of zero feet. This is the output when the pump pushes the water straight out, not up, into a pipe, and also not against additional head pressure and friction created by the fittings that are in-line with the water flow.

It is not uncommon for a pump to lose 25 to 30 percent of its rated output when the actual flow is measured, meaning the flow that reaches the tank.

To determine the pump model that you will need to buy, you need to know the flow rate that you should try to achieve in your tank; the number of gallons you should move through the filter.

In Aquarium literature, flow rates are usually refered to as how many times per hour you should turn your tank over. Multiply that number by the water content of your tank, and you have the flow rate.

Once you know that number, you can determine which pump model you should buy.

The problem is that this is a very debated area. Various Authors differ greatly in their flow rate recommendations. Does that mean that some of them are wrong ? No, not at all.

The recommendations individual authors make are based on their personal experiences over the years, and must have obviously worked for them, lest they would not recommend them.

It may also have to do with the fact that many of the books were written quite some time ago. The choice of pumps then was certainly not as large as it is nowadays and the recommendations usually refer to fish-only tanks.

How do you then make sense out of this? Well, surmizing from several suggestions and taking my personal experience into consideration as well, I recommend from 3 to 5 times the water content of the tank, per hour.

The lower number applies if your tank is not heavily populated, and the higher number if you are keeping a rather large number of inver-tebrates and marine fish at the same time.

The latter would be the case for most Reef Keeping Hobbyists, since once the system is up and running, a considerable bio-load is placed in the aquarium, and since that bio-load is usually increased as time goes on.

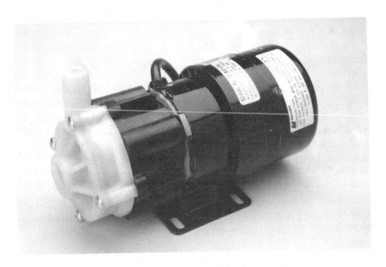

Thiel Aqua Tech Model Zb pump

Practically, this means that you need to look for the following types of flows :

Gallons	± GPH
55	265
70	350
110	550
125	625
150	750
180	900

Gallons = the water content of your tank, and GPH the flow rate you will need to achieve.

These numbers may seem high to some of you. They are in reality not because to get an even and strong water distribution in all parts of your tank, you need to move quite an amount of water on a continuous basis in and out of the tank.

To obtain these kind of flows, you will need to look for a pump that is rated at at least 25 percent more than what you need, especially if the rating of the pump that you are looking at is at zero feet of head.

Find out from the company you are buying from what the rating really means, and then chose a model number. The Iwaki pumps we use are rated at 4 feet of head.

Pumps to consider include :

• Iwaki pumps, now sold by several companies. Thiel•Aqua•Tech modifies them to make them totally salt water safe for the long term.

• the Aqua Pump, which is a greatly modified Grundfos pump. In fact, about the only thing left that is Grundfos is the motor. The volute and impeller have been changed to plastic materials. This pump will deliver !

The small version, a 3-speed pump, will put out an easy 900 to 1000 GPH (gallons per hour). We strongly recommend it. It is a great aquarium pump, quiet and powerful.

• Teel, an excellent pump made for marine use and often found in boat equipment stores. They even come in low voltage versions. They are not normally sold in pet stores.

• a number of others, including Marlow, Hydrothrustor, Little Giant and so on. Keep the remarks made at the beginning of this section in mind though, especially with regard to suitability for long term use in salt water.

• Un-modified Grundfos pumps can be used as well, but you should change the seals holding the volute in place to Viton, to assure long term protection against corrosion from salt water.

Noteworthy too is the fact that to get a strong flow the output opening of the pump should be 3/4 to 1 full inch. Otherwise the size of the out-flow restricts the amount of water that can be moved.

This is not always the case as some manufacturers use special impellers which deliver great quantities of water even with small size pipe. More on impellers later.

You may not reduce the size of those fittings, especially not the intake side, as that will lead to "cavitation". This happens when too little water enters the pump's volute, the impeller chamber, and that water gets swirled around so strongly, that it gets broken up.

As a result the dissolved gasses come out of solution and you will then get a stream of fine bubbles entering the tank. This is unsightly and dangerous, and reduces the output of the pump not to speak of the wear on the motor.

Pumps can be outfitted with different types of impellers, each having their own characteristics. That is the reason that some pumps have different outputs although they use the same motor.

One can categorize these impellers into three broad categories :

• medium head, medium output
• high head, medium to low flow
• high output , low head

Remember that "head" is not only the number of feet that the pump has to push the water up, but that it also includes the resistance offered by the pipe itself and by the fittings that are used in line (the loss is often referred to as pressure drop).

The total head is really the number of feet up, plus the frictional head. All this gets deducted from a number that differs and is based on the feet above sea level that you happen to be at.

This number can be either positive or negative, and all these calculations (which we are usually not even aware of) then determine the real head, and how well our pump will work.

Suffice it to say that for our purposes you do not need to get involved with all this, and that you really only need to count the height the water has to be pushed up, and that that usually will come pretty close to what the real head is, unless you are using intricate piping and many elbowed fittings.

The main point I am trying to make is do not buy a pump that has a maximum head that is close to the height the pump will have to push, as if you do that, the real flow you are getting will be low, and probably insufficient.

It does not really matter whether you use flexible hose or hard pipe to hook the pump(s) up. Hard pipe will last much longer, but that may not be a requirement in your case. Of course, to install pumps in that manner you will have to work with both PVC primer and cement.

Always use hose clamps with flexible hose connections. This is particularly important on the suction side of the pump, as, if air gets drawn in the pump will air-lock over time, heat up, and may be even burn out.

A pin hole on the suction side draws air in to the line; it does not leak. Leaks occur on the pressure side, on the side where the water is pushed back to the aquarium. Such leaks are usually pretty obvious.

If you have a leak, or suspect one on the suction side, tighten the clamps more. If you used PVC pipe, add some PVC cement, it will be drawn in and close the hole (more than likely anyway).

You do not even have to stop the motor to do so. On the pressure side however, you will need to stop the pump. If you used clamps, tighten them more. If you used hard pipe, put some more PVC cement and wait a few minutes. If the leak does not stop, you will, unfortunately, have to re-do the cementing.

This can be pretty laborious, may require emptying the filters, and stopping the tank from running for the time it takes to do the job.

Take great care, therefore, the first time you glue or cement. You will save yourself quite a bit of trouble later.

Always use primer and PVC cement on hard pipe installations. Do not risk having to re-do the work over. It is really problematic once the tank is running.

Coconut Shell Carbon

6.   Float Switches

The Marine Fish and Invert Reef Aquarium book went into quite some detail on float switches. You may wish to refer to those passages again.

Float switches are used to protect the pump, prevent it from running dry, and also to get uneven currents returning to the tank.

Let's take a look at what happens when the filter is running and the pump is pushing water back to the aquarium.

The water entering the tank comes from the sump of the trickle filter, where it collected in the first place as a direct result of the same pump adding water to the aquarium. That made the overflow box or the syphon overflow, which brings the water back down to the sump of your filter. This is of course a continuous process, as long as the pumps operate.

If the level of the water in the sump becomes too low, for whatever reason, e.g. evaporation, a moment will come where the pump begins to suck air and water at the same time. This will eventually become so much air that the pump will air-lock, start heating up, and stop.

The latter occurs because most pumps nowadays are thermally pro tected. This means that if the motor reaches a certain temperature, it will automatically stop.

If this happens once in a while, not too much damage is done. But if this happens frequently you will eventually ruin the motor and your pump will have to be replaced as it will fail to operate. This is usually due to the shaft bending slightly because of the repeated heating up and cooling down cycles. The end result is seizing of the shaft.

You can easily prevent all this from happening by installing a float switch in the sump.

Here is a short description of the main types of float switches :

6.1. Reed Switches :

These very common float switches regulate water levels by means of a magnetic on—off cycling device. There are usually two assemblies that slide over each other.

One is stationary, the other one moves up and down with the water level. Mounting is done by means of a bracket, or a threaded tank fitting.These parts are normally not supplied with the switch and you will have to buy them at a plumbing place, or at a hardware store.

As the magnetic contact is triggered by 2 encased magnets moving alongside each other, the electrical device (in our case pumps) will be switched on or off.

Reed switches can be very small and are made out of many kinds of materials. Luckily these include most of the ones that are totally salt water safe and resistant, e.g. plastics and their derivatives.

The problem with most reed switches however, is that the types that can handle stronger pumps, with high amperage ratings, get real big and are not that easy to install.

Keep in mind that you always have to match the "amperage" rating of the switch, with the amperage rating of the pump. If you don't, your reed switch will stick. This means that it will no longer work . That is the same as saying that you do not have a float switch.

They will stick in either the open, or closed, position, and that means that either your pump will run "all the time", or "not at all". Both, of course, defeat the purpose to begin with.

Reed switches with amperage ratings lower than your pump's can be used, but only if a relay is placed between the pump and the reed switch. Although this can be done, it is not practical unless you have elecrical knowledge sufficient to deal with such an installation. Most Hobbyist's don't of course; they would have to rely on an electrician, making the use of such switches rather prohibitive.

6.2. Mercury Switches :

These switches are so called because mercury moves around freely inside a glass (usually) tube that is installed in a watertight float, often made out of plastic or stainless steel.

Depending on the position of the float (see drawing), the mercury will move to a location where it will, or will not, make contact and let electricity through.

The latter triggers the on and off cycle of the device that the switch is controlling, which in our case is a pump.

Float switch assembly

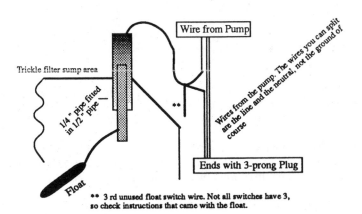

Trickle filter sump area

1/4 " pipe fitted in 1/2 " pipe

**

Wire from Pump

Wires from the pump. The wires you can split are the line and the neutral, not the ground of course

Ends with 3-prong Plug

Float

** 3 rd unused float switch wire. Not all switches have 3, so check instructions that came with the float.

These are very reliable switches and they come in many amperage ratings, to match just about any pump you may be using.

Their size, even for larger pumps, can be kept small. This is important as not too much space is available in the sump of most trickle filters to begin with.

They are usually more expensive than Reed switches, but we feel that their increased dependability warrants the extra money.

How to install these switches has been discussed in detail in The Marine Fish and Invert Reef Aquarium book, and is reviewed in Part 4 of this book as well.

6.3. Solid State Switches :

Such switches have no moving parts and are the top of the line in water level control.

They are unfortunately about 2 to 3 times as expensive as mercury switches, which are already double or more as reed switches.

If, however, you want the best and you want to control levels very accurately, then this is the type of switch to get.

They require you to use rods, usually made out of 316 SS, and lower them in the water to the height where you want them to either activate, or de-activate the device that you are trying to control. Additionally a grounding rod will have to be installed.

They are extremely dependable and very accurate because they have no moving parts. You can buy such solid state switches from Thiel• Aqua•Tech and from certain plumbing supply places.

316 Stainless steel is safe for usage in saltwater and will not deteriorate for many many years. Cleaning the rods from time to time is the only maintenance required when using these types of switches.

6.4. Air Pressure driven switches :

These reliable and relatively inexpensive switches are made out of plastic materials. They are totally safe for use in salt water aquariums.

They operate on the principle that, as water rises, it increases the pressure of trapped air (that is part of the assembly) and as a result, can trigger a pressure switch to make or not break an electrical contact.

This results in your pump, (or other device to which switches are hooked up), to either operate, or not.

They are small, easy to install, and require no electrical connections or wire stripping and cutting.

The unit comes in two parts, one is installed in the sump of your trickle filter or vat, and the other one is a receptacle into which you plug the device that you wish to control. That's all there is to it.

Some also incorporate pressure transducers which control an outlet box in which you can plug your pump.

6.5. What can you control ?

Unit that monitors 1, 2 and 3 or more different levels exist:

• the "normal" level in your sump,

• a slightly lower level that triggers the reserve vat pump to come on and top-off your water level,

• a third level, which is the "low" which stops your main pump if it is about to run dry.

The most interesting feature about the T•A•T switch assembly is that, even if it starts adding water to the sump to compensate for evaporation, it will only do so for a pre-determined amount of time.

This is to prevent the refilling process from continuing in the event that you had a "leak" somewhere. Indeed it that happened, and such a protection was not built in, more water would spill.

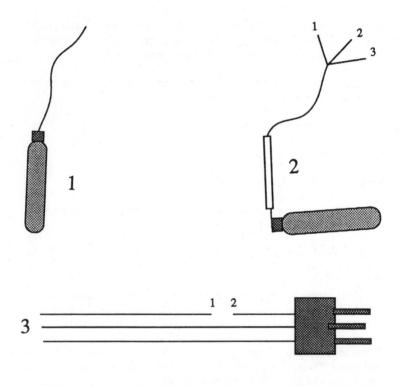

*The float switch :*1. *a float switch, mercury type, by Dupla* 2. *the same float switch showing the 3 wires, and also a piece of rigid pipe or tubing that has been sled over the wire, to within 1.5 inches of the float*   3. *the electrical cord from your pump, showing one wire cut. Exact installation instructions can be found in part two of this book.*

7. Airstones, or other aeration devices

Reef tanks operated with trickle filters do not require aeration other than in the biological filter area itself.

As air is blown inside the so-called "dry" section of the filter - the area where the biological activity takes place - oxygen is being provided at the same time, since air contains over 20 percent oxygen.

Nitrifying bacteria, Nitrosomonas and Nitrobacter, require a great deal of oxygen. By providing this oxygen by means of said air injection, we ensure that a sufficient amount is present at all times.

This is the result of one of the very important advantages of trickle filters. If set up correctly and with the right packing materials, they will promote much higher levels of dissolved oxygen.

Typically, when using trickle filters, it is not uncommon to see the dissolved oxygen levels reach saturation or super-saturation levels easily . This has always been very hard to achieve in more traditional filtration systems such as undergravel filters, cannister filters, etc...

Other than that there is no real need to provide additional aeration.

Bubbling air stones has, in addition, 2 drawbacks :

• They cause salt spray and unsightly salt encrustations,

• They chase dissolved gasses, i.e. CO_2, out of the water, which is what we want to avoid because the symbiotic algae harbored by corals and some invertebrates require carbon dioxide while photosynthesizing.

If the trickle fitler alone cannot increase the dissolved oxygen levels, to the range, or amount that you are aiming for, **a dissolved oxygen reactor** should be used.

Such a device "will" increase that level, and does it without complicated equipment or laborious intallation procedures. Such units can be bought for anywhere around $ 250.00.

These units are discussed in detail in both Part two and Part three of this book, including how to install them.

Of course, airstones are used in columnar foam fractionnators, and effectively assist in the removal of organic material before it can breakdown and pollute the tank's water.

Limewood airstones are to be prefered because they have proven, over time, to produce real small bubbles. The latter are more efficient in the skimming process.

Ceramic airstones are now also available and can be cleaned and re-used. We have not had the opportunity of trying them for long enough to report on their suitability. We will however do so in **Marine Reef**, our newsletter.

8. Fittings and Valves

Although we discussed fittings and valves in great detail in The Marine Fish and Invert Reef Aquarium, I felt that it should be covered here as well, albeit not in such great detail.

The best places to be obtain the valves and other fittings you need are, in order of preference :

• your local plumbing supply place
• a large hardware store
• your local pet store who is into Reef Tanks
• through the mail, from, for instance, U.S. Plastics in Lima, Ohio
• from advertisers in Hobby magazines, e.g. FAMA or Aquarium Fish Magazine, TFH and so on.

Prices of valves and fittings can vary greatly, so my advice certainly is to shop around.

You will need fittings such as T-connectors, male adaptors, female adaptors, couplings, 90 degree elbows, 45 degree elbows, and perhaps some barbs and some endcaps. For an explanation on all of these, please refer to The Marine Fish and Invert Reef Aquarium.

Most of those are rather easy to obtain and should not constitute too much of a problem for you to figure out.

We will be mentioning the ones we used ourselves while setting up our 150 gallon tank, as we go along.

If you are not familiar with what they look like, refer to the book just mentioned.

Valves are another matter altogether. And it is an important one, as their use, or non-use, determines greatly how easy it will be to service your aquarium down the line.

Using the right kind of valves also greatly improves the built in safety features to prevent overflows and back syphoning.

The type of valves you will be needing include :

- **Ball valves of the true union type, or of the single union type**
    These are valves that allow you to control the rate of flow and can also be used to disconnect the pump and take it out of the piping for cleaning or servicing. The flow can be adjusted by means of a valve that easily adjust and makes relatively minor changes possible. More details in Part 2.

- **Check valves of the true union type**
    These are used to prevent water from flowing back, from the tank to the filter through the holes in the bottom. These valves are a must in any decent Reef system.They are also called one-way valves and, because they are true union, one side can be easily disconnected when for instance the pump needs to be serviced. More details in Part 2. They come in ball and Y form.

- **Solenoid valves, also called Magnetic Valves**
    These are relatively expensive valves used to control the direction of the water flow when more than one return is used. They are activated or de-activated by electrical impulse, from e.g. a timer or an instrument such as a pH regulator (when controlling Carbon dioxide output). More on these valves in Part 2. Solenoid valves may cost over $ 150.00. In certain cases they are a requirement, as we shall see later

- **Chemical Needle valves, also called Chemcocks**
    They perform the same function as ball valves, but are used where very fine adjustments of small amounts of water flow are necessary.

- **Bulkhead fittings, tank fittings**

    You will more than likely need several of these fittings to install your water return lines. This fitting usually consists of 2 parts made of PVC and one O-ring. One part slips through the hole in the tank, and the other part is screwed onto the first one. The O-ring is fitted between the two parts, on the outside of the tank, underneath the bottom. We also suggest that you run a bead of silicone sealer between the fitting and the aquarium glass. This will ensure a real water tight seal. Plumbing supply places, some hardware stores, or a plastic pipe and fitting wholesale or catalogue mailing house are good sources. Shop around as the price of these fittings can greatly vary.

- **Angle Valves - 90° Valves**

    These valves allow for very fine adjustments, much like needle valves, but they give you a larger flow capacity. They come in handy when you are trying to fine tune the outflow of a foam fractionnator, or the water going to some of the reactors that are now used on Reef Tanks.

- **Electrically Actuated Ball valves**

    These ball valves can be opened and closed automatically based on whether or not they are energized. If you have a small sump and want to prevent it from overflowing should you lose power, use such a valve on the output side of your skimmer. When the current fails, the valve closes and your skimmer cannot empty itself in that sump. This is only one use. There are many others.

9.   The Aquarium Water

9.1. Introduction

You need to pay extra careful attention to the type of water that you will use to :

- fill the tank when you start it,
- top-off the aquarium when necessary,
- make water changes,
- dilute additives

Until maybe as recently as a year ago, it seemed normal to use tapwater and not worry about its quality. No thought process actually took place. It was just done. That's, after all, what all the books and articles told you to do. So did Pet Store personnel.

Things are finally starting to change, and many a hobbyist now tests the water he or she uses before actually preparing it with salt for addition to the tank.

That is exactly how it should be ! Indeed you may be surprised at what you find in tap and well water, for instance :

• nitrates
• phosphates
• nitrite
• and many other pollutants too, most needing to be removed by chemical methods, e.g. activated carbon, or better molecular absorption filters.

Since water is the element in which your fish and invertebrates spend their life, 24 hours a day, you better make sure that it is of superior quality. This may require that you treat it before you actually use it.

A good way of doing this is to drop a few Poly Filters in the reserve vat in which you store your "water change" reserve water, and circulate the water in that vat (a large plastic garbage can will do) by means of an air pump airstone arrangement.

If you presently do not have such a vat, you should set one up. As we just said, a good quality plastic garbage can will usually do, or you may want to buy, as we did, a 35 gallon Polypropylene vat.

9.2. What type of Water should You use ?

The choice is not very large, but there are several types that you use :

> • distilled
> • de-ionized -demineralized
> • spring
> • tap
> • well
> • R.O. water (reverse osmosis)
> • real Seawater
> • mineral

Distilled, de-ionized and spring waters should not give you any concerns, as they are pure enough to be used right away. Because of their expense you should buy a de-ionizing unit. You will recuperate its ± $ 150.00 cost very quickly.

It is often reported that some commercial "distilled" waters contain quite some impurities and sometimes even copper.

This is due to the distilling methods used and the fact that you are buying single distilled water. Pharmacy brands, and triple distilled water do not contain impurities, but they are more expensive. Tap and well water need to be tested for nitrates, phosphates and especially copper. Heavy metals such as copper will create havoc in a Reef Tank.

If you have copper piping in your house (which most of us do) let the water run for about 3 minutes before using it, and do not use the hot water line. Hot water dissolves heavy metals better than cold water, and can easily create additional problems.

Running the water lines for a while will get the water that may contain dissolved copper from the pipes to go down the drain, and not in your aquarium.

Of course the use of spring or distilled or de-ionized water involves a greater expense. Perhaps as much as 75 cents per gallon. But if the water in your area is really bad, those 75 or 80 dollars spent for good quality water are certainly worth the investment, and represent only a small portion of the total cost of setting up a reef tank anyway.

Then again, as already indicated, a de-ionozing unit will run you around one hundred and fifty dollars, and will make a considerable amount of water before being exhausted.

A typical dual cylinder mixed resin bed set up will bring the price of the water down to pennies per gallon. You will have paid for its cost after a few hundred gallons of water.

You may be lucky, and your tap or well water may be of excellent quality (do not forget chlorine and chloramine), in which case you can use that source to fill the tank, top it off, and make water changes.

Bacteriostatic filters are usually cartridge type filters that contain a very high grade activated carbon and silver, to prevent the formation of bacteria. Silver is a excellent anti-bacterial agent, but unfortunately not in the aquarium.

If your tap water is not of good quality and you do not want to buy better quality water, you can always resort to purification methods, e.g. reverse osmosis filtration and the already mentioned de-ionization. Both cost about the same, but deminelarization gives a water of better quality.

Reverse osmosis, new to the hobby, but not new at all in water treatment, is explained in a later chapter in more detail, and is also covered in The Marine Fish and Invert Reef Aquarium book.

R.O. filters come in various sizes. Since you will not really be needing water constantly, and immediately, there is no need to buy a large model. A 5 gallon per day unit will usually be ample.

Let's assume you have a 125 gallon tank and you will be doing 2 percent water changes every 3rd day. This requires in reality only 2.5 gallons of water. If you also need about 2.5 gallons extra to top the aquarium off, your total requirement is 5 gallons every 3 days.

The small unit that we just mentioned can in fact give you 15 gallons in that period, which is already more than what you need.

All you need to do is hook the reverse osmosis filter up to a water supply and collect the water it produces in some vat. You can then use that water for whatever purpose you require it, adding salt when appropriate, and using it as it is, when topping your tank off.

Such units sold for around $ 120.00 at the time we wrote this book and there are now at least 3 different models being advertised.

Reverse osmosis filters rely on membranes to perform the cleaning function. The better the membrane, the better the quality of the effluent water and the more expensive the unit will be. Do not assume that there is only one type. There are many and their quality determines how purified the outcoming water is.

Other types of water purification units are easily found, e.g. in DIY stores, some hardware stores, and in some of the larger department stores.

They usually consist of units that are plumbed in line with the mains water and often work with replaceable cartridges that are sold seperately, and are meant to improve taste, odor, color, and remove e.g. iron flakes from the water.

They usually contain activated carbon and some fine filtering device that removes fine particulate matter. As such, they are excellent to use, but the cartridges are costly and you may wish to carefully consider other ways.

You may even consider plumbing them directly into the water return to the tank, with the necessary shut-off valves, to enable you to change the cartridges easily. If you install such a filter, look for a cartridge with a 25 micron rating.

Smaller ones (meaning less micron) are available too, but they clog up rather quickly, need frequent replacement, as they cannot be cleaned. Their cost is usually around 7.00 to 10.00, making this an rather expensive way to go.

You could of course purify the water from the well, or mains, by using a diatomaceous earth filter that can also take powdered carbon. If you opt for this solution, fill a vat (e.g. a plastic garbage can) with water, and attach the diatom filter to it.

The Vortex XL™ model, and the System 1™ will both do the job. Do not use either without the carbon as you require the chemical filtration effect to purify the water before you use it.

Using a diatomaceous earth filter directly on the tank can be done too of course. If you install one, make sure that it runs on its own separate pump, and that you clean, or "re-charge" it regularly.

Diatom filter usually only work for about 24 to 36 hours, depending on how much particulate matter is in your tank and how strong the pump is that runs them.

Using any of the above water purification methods makes filling the tank, changing the water, and topping the aquarium off a little more cumbersome, but it is well worth it in the end. Plus, once you get in the routine of doing this, you will not even notice that additional time it will take you.

You may wish to keep a supply of carbonate hardness adjusting compound handy, so that you can increase the KH before adding the water to the tank. We suggest you use liquids rather than tablets, because we have found that they are easier to dispense and do not make your skimmer foam excessively.

For details on KH and how to adjust it, why it may need to be adjusted at all, and to what levels, see The Marine Fish and Invert Reef Aquarium book, and Part Three of this book.

9.3. Water changes

In hobby literature you will find many differing recommendations on water changing . These range from never changing any water whatso-ever, to certain recommended percentages every couple of days, to changing very large amounts of water changes every few weeks.

Who is right ? Rather than deciding who is right and who is wrong, let us try to find out what we are really trying to achieve, and then form an opinion of our own.

Whatever the quality of the water that we start with, over time this water becomes of lesser quality, as impurities of many kinds enter the tank and the aquarium water.

This is unavoidable and no reason for concern. That's what filtration and water changes are all about. It is also the reason why good maintenance practices are mandatory if you wish to be a successful Reef Keeping Hobbyist.

There are several kinds of pollutants :

• **particulate matter** : this can be removed by mechanical filtration, e.g. floss, bonded pads of dacron, cartridge fine filters, diatom filters, and so on. Just remember to clean them regularly.

We will repeat this piece of advice many times. It is important, and you need to make a habit of cleaning your filters religiously. We suggest at least once a week.

• **pollution of organic nature** that results in the build up of ammonia and ammonium ion in the tank. This is taken care of by installing biological filtration units : trickle filters in our case.

We will be looking at these filters in great detail in a later chapter. Protein skimmers also remove some of the organics, especially if the skimmer is correctly sized. See The Marine Fish and Invert Reef Aquarium for more details on skimmers.

• **dissolved compounds** not removable by either mechanical or biological filtration : dyes, urea, acids of protein breakdown, etc. These compounds are removed by using chemical filters : activated carbon, and perhaps other resins. Carbon of good quality is very efficient, but needs to be installed properly.

This is not complicated to do, all that is required is that as much water as possible flows **through** the carbon, and not just over it as is often the case when such carbon is placed in bags.

A more modern way of chemical filtration involves the use of Poly Filter pads, from Poly Bio™ Marine, a method which we feel is to be preferred over the use of carbon. These pads adsorb undesirable compounds, including organics, heavy metals, phenols and so on, and do not release any of these compounds back into the water, even when the pad is spent.

Besides the "pad" shape, they can also be obtained in disc shape placed in cannister filters which can be installed in line with the water circulation right underneath the tank.

• **compounds that cannot be removed by activated carbon or Poly filters either** : mostly airborne pollutants, nitrate, phosphate, and other such chemical compounds. Airborne pollutants include nicotine, aerosol sprays, perfume essence, pesticides, and so on.

Although you would not knowingly introduce them into your tank, they get in there anyway from the air above the tank, from the air you may be using to run an air pump, and from the mains or well water. Since nothing removes several of these compounds, they build up and continue to do so over time.

Although there are now products on the market that remove nitrate and phosphate, e.g. X-Nitrate™, most of the other compounds mentioned will not be removed.

Reducing their concentration by replacing some of the tank's water seems the only way to lower them and prevent damage to the Reef's lifeforms. Replacing some of the water = making water changes.

Denitrification equipment that operates under anaerobic conditions, is presently finding its way into the hobby too. No conclusive results however are available that demonstrate that this method is really safe. They work, there is no question about that. They can really bring your nitrate levels down to practically zero.

Unfortunately they are still hard to adjust. We have tested several units. The one that we had the most success with is manufactured by MTC, and sold by Route 4 Marine Technology. The Sera unit, which can be hung on the back of the aquarium, came in a very close second. Of course, testing such units is difficult and somewhat subjective.

Thiel•Aqua•Tech is now working on a fully automated unit that will take most of the regulating problems out of these devices. It should be available sometime around mid 1989. In the interim that company offers a 24 inch advanced unit and a specially developed nutrient mix to reduce the incidence of hydrogen sulfide production.

It appears that, after having reviewed all the forms of pollution that your water can contain, it is clear that not changing any water at all does not make sense. I personally feel that anyone who recommends such practices, fails to understand the pollution process of aquariums accurately, or does not grasp the potential harm that some of the pollutants can have on Reef tank life.

Having said that, how much water should we then change ?

Our recommendations which we already outlined in detail in The Marine Fish and Invert Reef Aquarium book, are based on the following principles :

• removing polluted water, and adding non-polluted water, dilutes the overall concentration of the noxious compounds,

• repeating such a practice regularly must, over time, stabilize or keep such concentrations at acceptable levels, providing the amount of water changed is sufficient,

• this means that more of the pollutants need to be removed, than accumulate between two water changes,

• changing water frequently, in small quantities, prevents big fluctuations in the concentration of any pollutant.

Infrequent water changes let the pollutants build up to a larger amount, and then remove more of it, because the amount of water changed is greater as well. This puts more stress on the tank's lifeforms because of the greater fluctuations in water quality and water chemistry,

• changing a little water at a time reduces the changes in water parameters less than a large water change, and thus gives the fish and invertebrates a more stable environment to live in. And we know that stability is better than frequent variations and fluctuations.

This applies particularly to temperature, salinity, pH, and especially redox potential. A 25 percent water change, every 3 weeks, as advocated by some, reduces the redox potential by a considerable amount.

For example, if your R.P. is 325 mv, and the R.P. of the freshly mixed new salt water is 230 mv (this is by the way just about what it will be 10 to 15 minutes after you mix in the salt), the redox potential of your tank will go own by at least 65 to 95 millivolt. Sometimes even more, depending on the kind of salt that you use.

Having said all this, and feeling that we have made our case for frequent water changes, what is our recommendation ?

Very simply :   **4 percent a week, or 2 percent every 3 days.**

The latter being the better of the two. Our own tanks run on automatic water changers, and we change ± 0.75 percent every day. We have used the 2 percent every 3 days for a long time, before automatic water changers were installed and vats filled with salt water allowed us to run the water changing procedure on a daily basis.

How to set up such a water changing system is explained in more detail in Part 2 of this book, as well as in Part 4.

It may sound complicated but it is not at all. All you will need is a reserve vat, a float switch, and a timer.

To fully automate water changers you will also need a drain to which the excess water can flow. If you cannot guide the excess water to a drain hole or pipe, a way to circumvent that problem exists too.

You can pump the water that is removed to a vat, and then empty that vat once a week, or on some regular schedule which depends really on the size of that vat.

10. Hospital - AcclimatizationTank

While still on the subject of tanks and water, we want to devote a few paragraphs to what is commonly refered to as the "hospital" tank.

Athough this is not a requirement for success with Reef Tanks, having such a tank set up at all times will prove to be very helpful.

It is basically a small conventionally set up aquarium, may be 20 gallons in size. Running it with an Eheim cannister, filled with the appropriate Eheim packing materials, will do the job. This tank does not need light, but does need a good heater.

Do not set it up with an undergravel, as this will tend to complicate its maintenance unneccesarily.

Whenever new fish are acquired they should be placed in that tank for a few days, to make sure that they do not develop any diseases.

If need be, treat the fish with the necessary medications. Make sure that you remember to change water during the course of the treatment and after the medicating period is over.

It is in fact a good idea to keep diseased fish in the hospital tank for a few days after they have healed. You will additionally need to run the water through an activated carbon filter if you wish to remove most of the medication, once the treatment is completed.

Both Cora and Dupla make a superior carbon. So does my own company; we carry medical grade activated carbon.

It may even be that you have to change all the water. This will depend on the type of medication, and what level of concentration you have used.

Keep the tank at the same pH, salinity and temperature as the main Reef Tank.

Make sure that you regularly service the cannister filter, or whatever other filter you may be using to ensure that the hospital, come acclimatization tank, is always ammonia and nitrite free.

This also means that if you do not have any animal life in the tank, you will lose your biological filter, since no pollution is created. It is therefore recommended to keep at least one or two small invertebrates in that tank. When you then need the aquarium, you remove the inverts, and place whatever fish you need to, in the tank.

Newly acquired invertebrates can usually be placed directly in the reef tank after dripping tank water in a bucket, or styrofoam container, in which you have placed them, for about 30 minutes.

You may need to clean the live rock you buy beforehand. An excellent article on how to do this appeared in the August edition of Fresh and Marine Aquarium Magazine and the whole procedure is discussed in Advanced Reef Keeping II.

Keeping such a tank will save you a lot of headeaches if problems occur at some point or another. And believe us, they will !

11. Preparing the Water

11.1. Introduction

Having reviewed water and its sources, at least as far as keeping Aquariums is concerned, we now need to prepare it before we can use it, and add it to our Tank.

This consists mainly, although not solely, of adding an artificial salt formulation to bring the water to the right salinity or, as it is usually called in the Hobby, specific gravity, or "s.g.".

That presumes of course that you are not using real sea water, in which case this chapter does not apply to your situation.

There are many problems though with using real seawater , not the least of which are :

• availability,
• cost,
• and mainly, how to treat it before using it.

For those of you who are interested in exploring this avenue further, we suggest you read, or re-read, Seawater Aquariums, A Captive Environment, by Stephen Spotte, published by John Wiley/Wiley-Interscience.

You will find, as I did, that although you certainly gain in quality, you will be looking at a far greater expense.

In this chapter we will only deal with the addition of aquarium salt. Other water additives such as vitamins, fertilizers, and trace elements are covered in Part 1, Chapter 12.

11.2. Aquarium Salt

There are many types of artificial salts on the market. Most national brands are, in our experience, of excellent quality.

Some dissolve better and faster than others, but that should not really be a consideration. **You should not use freshly prepared salt water immediately anyway.**

Some contain more impurities than others, and that is a consideration as the impurities affect the overall quality of the water, both in the short and in the long run.

It is not the purpose of this book to make recommendations as to which salt you should use. You must any way rely on which ones are available in your area, as not all salts are available in all markets, even national brands.

It may be that the local wholesaler/distributor does not carry more than one or two, and as a result your store may only have those two for sale.

A good quality salt must contain :

• a good mix of the trace elements that are commonly found in sea water, and the national brands that we know of, all do. Whether you use Instant Ocean, Tropic Marin, Cora, Hawaiian Marinemix, or some other brand, is really not important in the the long run.

They all have their merits, and they all have their drawbacks : they are all artificial, not the real thing! But we have no choice and we have to be happy that such artificial sea salts are in fact available, or we would not have a Hobby.

• a good salt must be able to bring the carbonate hardness of your water up to at least 8 to 9 German degrees of hardness.

If you are of the school of thought that it should be higher, and I am, then you can always adjust it upwards by using one of the many buffer solutions or tablets that are available in pet stores.

• a good salt must be consistent in its quality. That is one of the reasons why you must buy a reputable brand that has proven itself, and that does not change in appearance or make up, every time you buy it.

• a good salt must be available on a continuous basis. New products, although they may be excellent, sometimes are hard to find on a regular basis. That forces you to change brands often.

Then again, some advanced hobbyists advocate alternating at least two good brands, in an effort to get an overall wider range of trace elements and nutrients.

One salt may contain elements that the other one does not, and vice-versa. There may be a lot of value to that in fact, and as long as you make the conscious decision to follow this method consistently, you should not have any problems with running your system that way.

Most salts are sold in plastic bags, in dry form. Others come in crystals, or in a moist semi-dissolved mix, in buckets.

H. Kipper Author of "The Marine Optimum Aquarium", 1987, Aqua-documenta Verlag (not available in English), was in favor of that particular form of salt; he felt that trace elements were less likely to precipitate when mixed with water.

I am personally not of that opinion, as the processes used by most manufacturers ensure that the trace elements remain in solution anyway, as long as you stay within the parameters of pH and temperature that are normally recommended for Marine Aquariums.

We use a proprietary Thiel•Aqua•Tech salt "Tech•Salt", made in small batches to ensure freshness, and sold only in 25, 50 and 100 gallon quantities.

If you want to keep your Tank looking "healthy" all the time, with very low levels of both nitrate and phosphate, you may want to use a salt that is low in both, or has quantities that are so low, that standard aquarium tests do not detect them.

This is easy to check. Just add some of the salt that you use now to some distilled water, and test. Then decide whether the levels are acceptable to you. Keep in mind that they will never be zero, but should be very close to it. For example a phosphate reading of 0.1 or 0.05 ppm should be acceptable to all.

If you run a sophisticated filtration system, as we advocate, that same system will be able to remove any such small excesses anyway.

Tech•Salt is a very high quality salt; try it some time. And if you have good results with it, as we are sure you will, tell others about it. It took me about 2 years of trial and error to perfect it. The end result should give you the same satisfaction as it gives me.

11.3. Salinity and Specific Gravity

This has been covered in detail in The Marine Fish and Invert Reef Aquarium book. Let us just recapitulate :

• salinity measures the amount of salts dissolved in the water, usually in parts per thousand. We recommend 33.5 to 35 ppt. Our own tanks are now kept at 34 ppt, although for the longest time we maintained them at 35 ppt.

To measure the salinity we use a "refractometer" with a dual scale, the second one indicating the actual salinity. This unit is discussed in Part Two of this book.

• if you stay within the above ranges, you will be at the right levels. Once you have decided on an exact level, keep the tank at that level all the time.

The latter is perhaps more important than the exact level itself. Remember that stability in all water quality parameters is what we are looking for.

• to maintain that stability, automatic brine addition and/or automatic freshwater addition devices can be used.

They are discussed in Part Two, and their installation is explained in Part Four. But you can do all this manually just as well. Check the salinity on a regular basis, and make sure, above all, that the water you use to make water changes is of that same salinity.

That is yet another reason why you cannot use freshly prepared salt water: salt takes time to dissolve completely. Most of it does, but quite a bit does not.

Waiting for 24 to 36 hours and aerating it well, will ensure not only that the pH stabilizes itself, but also that all the salt you added has in fact dissolved, and that you can measure the true salinity of that mixture, since no more salt needs to dissolve.

That amount of time will also ensure that chlorine that may be in the tap water (if that is what you use) will have disappeared as well.

Most Hobbyists however do not measure salinity, rather they measure the specific gravity, which can be explained as the effect that all the salt you added has on the water. This is however a very temperature dependent measurement, and therefore not as accurate as salinity.

The positive side is that much less expensive equipment is necessary to measure it. A good hydrometer will do.

We recommend keeping the water at a s.g. of 1.022 at 75 degrees Fahrenheit, which corresponds to 34 ppt salinity. Conversion charts to different temperatures exist, and were published in at least two books that you are probably familiar with : Seawater Aquariums by Stephen Spotte, and the Marine Aquarium Handbook by Martin Moe.

Although you may find other recommendations, they may not necessarily be better, or worse, for that matter. There is no real "ideal" specific gravity.

Indeed, you are likely to keep such a variety of animal life in your tank, that come from such different areas on the reef, and from so many different reefs, that they are all really accustomed to different salinities and/or specific gravities. The salinities may be close to each other, but they are often different.

The key, in our opinion, is to stay as close to the general guidelines as possible, and then maintain "stability". That would indeed seem to be the most logical approach, and the one that is easiest to achieve.

12. Water Additives

12.1. Trace Elements

Many Hobbyists wonder whether they should use trace elements on a regular basis. They even wonder whether they should use them at all, and if so, which ones, and how they should dispense them.

There is no simple and single, answer :

• You probably do not need them if you follow our recommendations on water changes , and really change water regularly as we suggest all along.

Changing water regularly adds trace elements every time you do, and should make it clear that you do not need to supplement their concentration even further.

It turns out that most hobbyists do not change water regularly, or not to the extent that we recommend, and as a result, and if you are part of that group, you "will" need to add trace elements regularly.

• Many Reef Keeping Hobbyists use ozone. Ozone and foam fraction-nation remove many elements from the water that are undesirable. But the process removes some desirable elements as well, which obviates the need to add trace elements (we obtained convincing evidence of this fact by sending scum from a protein skimmers to a lab for an assay for a number of the components that are normally added to aquariums, for instance iron, manganese, vitamins, and some of the well known trace elements contained in sea water).

If you use trace elements, do so sparingly and certainly not more than the manufacturer recommends. Indeed, some of the trace elements can be noxious to invertebrates when used in too large quantities. This is another case where more is not better!

• if you do use them, try to spread their additon out as evenly as you can over the course of the day (best) or the week.

Ideally this is done by using a metering or dosing pump. As far as we know, Thiel•Aqua•Tech and Dupla USA are the only companies to offer such metering pumps for sale to the Hobbyist. At the time we wrote this their price was around $250.00-400.00, depending on the model.

If you do not use such a metering pump, do not add one large quantity once a week. Try to add a little every day, or every other day. In this fashion the water chemistry is changed much less, which is much better for the animal life.

Various preparations are sold in Pet Stores. Buy a quality brand, one that has been around. Hawaiian Marine and Coralife are two that come to mind.

Tropic Marin, the maker of an excellent salt, also sells a trace element mixture, but it has a tendency to make your skimmer work a little too hard if you are not careful with the quantity you are adding. Keep this in mind when using it. It is however an excellent product.

Route 4 Marine Technology now also offers such an additive. In fact the last time we checked, they were planning to introduce a whole range of products specifically designed for Reef Aquariums.

And of course we offer Tech•Reef•Elements in 4, 8 and 32 fluid oz sizes through T•A•T.

Freshness is definitely a consideration. Do not buy products that look as if they have been around for too long. They may have lost their potency. Quality is everything when it comes to water additives !

Follow the manufacturer's recommendation with regard to quantity carefully. Each preparation is different and we can therefore not give you a "so many drops per gallon" suggestion or recommendation.

In fact, this remark applies to just about everything you do to your Aquarium. One cannot recommend a dosage that applies to everybody's situation.

Every aquarium is different in what it contains. Different amounts of fish, different amounts of invertebrates, different amounts of algae, both micro and macro, and different forms, and-or sizes of filtration. This results in each tank "using" additives in a different fashion, and as a result requiring different amounts.

12.2. Vitamins

Vitamins benefit both fish and corals, providing they can be readily absorbed. Some vitamins are more important than others and need to be dispensed in somewhat larger quantities. B-12 and Biotin are two of them. Commercial preparations take these requirements into account, providing they are correctly manufactured.

Adding them directly to the water reduces their effectiveness but is still quite beneficial. The reason the effectiveness is reduced is because they are diluted, removed by filtration (e.g. foam fractionnators) and are not as easily absorbed by the fish and invertebrates.

Adding vitamins to the food is a more desirable method. Soak the food in a small amount of vitamins for 10-15 minutes; even flake food if that is what you are using, and then add the food to the water or feed the invertebrates with it, targeting each one specifically.

We have, over the years, refined a special formula that we now offer for sale. It is both water soluble and stabilized for the 8.0 to 8.4 pH range. We call it Tech•Vita•Trace Complex. It comes in 4 and 8 oz containers, and for stores also in quarts.

Another excellent formula is Dick Boyd's VitaChem for marine tanks.

Again, adding a little at a time, but every day, would be the best method to dispense vitamins. We use a metering pump to ensure as even a distribution of our Vita Trace mixture over a 24 hour period as we can achieve.

Our own 150 gallon aquarium requires about 38 drops per day to maintain the desired level, which we measure by determining the presence of the B-12 Vitamin Hydroxocobalamin (we use ozone as well as protein skimming & therefore have a higher vitamin requirement).

We mentioned freshness already when we spoke about trace elements. This is even more important when it comes to vitamins. Remember also that Vitamins "smell" like Vitamins, not like something else.

Dosage is again dependent on the manufacturer's instructions. Quantities are usually pretty low. Something in the range of a few drops per gallon per week for most of them.

No generalizations are possible here either. Our own formulation requires more drops, but that does not mean much because it is the amount of vitamins, not the amount of drops that is important.

Important note : any Hobbyist using ozone on his tank, should use much more vitamins than normally recommended, as ozone breaks the vitamins down (Wojcik, 1988).

You may wish to double, or even triple the recommended dosage. Doubling will usually do however (Thiel, 1988, Research on Vitamin B-12 in Salt water Tanks running on Ozone, 21 page monograph).

12.3. Marine Fertilizers

Fertilizers are only required if you keep and try to grow macro algae. If you do not keep such aquatic life, you do not need fertilizers.

A good fertilizer should contain iron, manganese and a few other elements, (that we do not wish to disclose as they are major components of our two T•A•T fertilizers, one for freshwater plants, and one for marine macro-algae) **but no nitrates and no phosphates**. The tank will have plenty of those all the time anyway...

Fertilizers come in tablet or liquid form; the liquid form is to be preferred because it is easier to keep in solution on a controlled basis, and fish will not be tempted to nibble at the tablets.

Check for iron by using an iron test (Fe) to determine whether the product that you are now using meets the requirement.

It is recommended that the iron levels be maintained at : 0.05 to 0.1 ppm at all times, meaning on a continuous basis.

Because salt water has a tendency to make iron and other elements fall out (precipitate), you should buy a product that uses chelated chemicals during the manufacturing stage. This will ensure that the iron, for instance, stays in solution for much longer. The better products use EDTA in the chelating process. Phosphate based chelators (bi- and triphosphates) should be avoided. They add phosphates to the water.

Coralife, Dupla and Route 4 Technology manufacture such products. Again, the easiest way to dispense fertilizer is on a continuous basis, by using a metering pump, e.g. the Tech•Doser.

You may wonder how many dosing pumps you will need to dispense all of these additives. Indeed, we have already mentioned at least three products. The answer is : one, just one.

You can prepare a mixture of all the additives, in the right proportions, and then have the metering pump dispense that mixture over a period of 24 hours. How to do this was explained in great detail in The Marine Fish and Invert Reef Aquarium book, pages 96-97-98.

Most fertilizers require that you test their effect on your tank to determine the quantity that needs to be used. That makes real sense as, indeed, a tank with a lot of macro-algae will require more fertilizer every day than a tank with only very few macro-algae.

As the fertilizer gets depleted more rapidly, it will obviously need to be replenished more frequently, or in larger quantity.

Tanks with lots of light are tanks in which photosynthesis takes place at a very high, or at least higher level. Such tanks will use more fertilizer and also more carbon dioxide in the process (Theoretically easy to understand; experimentally proven by Leo Wojcik in Dec. 1988)

12.4. Carbonate Hardness Generators

Any Hobbyist who wants to keep a Reef Tank with corals, needs to pay careful attention to the carbonate hardness of the water.

This is the total of the carbonates and bicarbonates (hydrogen carbonates) mostly of calcium and magnesium, that are dissolved in the water.

Besides having an influence on the pH stability, because of the chemical buffering effect, it provides the corals with the hardness and the calcium that they require, and are accustomed to in their natural environments.

Most expert German Hobbyists recommend levels of anywhere between 12 and 22 dKH (German degrees of hardness).

Several years of experimenting have convinced me that the best levels
are between 12 and 18 dKH, and we have kept corals alive successfully
for long periods at 15 dKH. We therefore strongly recommend that
latter number (Thiel, 1986,1987, Carbonate hardness and marine aquarium
lifeforms: 43 pages of research notes. Lab book n°16).

Newly mixed salt water will give a dKH of around 8 or 9. This is normal,
as aquarium salt mixes are buffered that way.

If we are to follow my recommendation, we will have to increase the
carbonate hardness quite a bit to reach the 15 dKH level.

**You should never do this in one adjustment session, lest you want
problems.**

You must adjust the carbonate hardness slowly, and only raise the it
a little at a time, and over a period of several days or weeks, depending
on how many dKH degrees the change is. Perhaps no more than
1degree per 12 hour period. This is in fact what we recommend for the
Tech• Reef•KH that we market.

Raising it too rapidly will have very adverse effects, especially on fish,
and also on the corals that are not of the calcareous type (reef building), because each time you raise the carbonate hardness you are
making significant changes in the carbon dioxide, buffer and pH
equilibrium (Lab book n°16 cfr above).

Those interested in the chemical explanation of this phenomenon are
referred to Stephen Spotte's Sea Water Aquariums, A Captive Environment, published by Wiley Inter-Science.

Various products exist that can be used safely. Again, and you may feel
that we are repeating ourselves company name-wise :

• Instant Ocean : tablets
• Thiel•Aqua•Tech : liquid
• Route 4 Marine Technology : liquid
• Dupla : KH tablets

Each product affects the carbonate hardness differently. You must therefore follow each manufacturer's instructions carefully.

The key is to make the rise come about slowly, but steadily. In this respect a liquid KH generator would be more desirable than a tablet form, as the former could be added by a drip method, or by a Tech•Doser metering pump.

Many German Hobbyists prepare their own carbonate hardness generating mixtures, and they are usually refered to as "Kalk Wasser", or Lime water.

We do not advocate that you try this, because you may find that suddenly your pH has risen a great deal too much.

An article describing this whole process was published in "Marine Reef" the technical newsletter by Aardvark Press. It is a cumbersome and laborious process that requires both a CO_2 supply and a good pH controller.

Most Hobbyists will probably not want to experiment with this system. It is much wiser to rely on the research done by others, and buy a commercial products that does the job.

12.5. Ozone : O_3

Ozone can be considered a water additive, but is better classified in the filtration section, as it should be used either with a foam fractionnator, or with an ozone reactor, or with both.

We will therefore deal with it extensively in Part Two and also in Part Four, when we explain how to set these pieces of equipment up.

Let us just say that to reach the levels of Redox Potential (see Part Two) that are usually advocated by seasoned hobbyists, protein skimming and ozonization will definitely be required.

Excellent ozonizers are now available from several manufacturers, and availability no longer seems to be a problem.

Ozone is still a very controversial additive or "water treatment method".

Perhaps the main reason being that is largerly misunderstood, and therefore mistrusted. People feel uneasy using it, do not understand its effects on both tank life and the environment (your house, appartment, etc..), and shy away from its use.

Ozone is a strong oxidizer, with a very high redox potential, over 2000 mv, meaning it can do a lot of damage if used improperly.

But it can really clean up the water, if used correctly, and has therefore a lot of positive effects as well.

Understanding the process is a must for every Reef Keeping Hobbyist, so that he-she can take advantage of the many positive effects that ozone can have on the tank, while at the same time avoiding the negatives.

In Part Two we will therefore be dealing very extensively with ozone and its use in the Reef Aquarium.

12.6. Oxygen : O_2

All life in the aquarium and in the filters revolves around the availability of oxygen. A lot of oxygen !

Just as we need it in the air we breathe, fish, invertebrates, bacteria, plants, macro-algae, etc... need it to survive, thrive, and grow.

Not only is a lot of it needed to promote all forms of life, but it has to be constantly replenished, since the animals and bacteria "use" it up.

This replenishment happens through contact with the air, on the top of the aquarium mainly, but also inside the trickle filter, where droplets, or small streams run down. The process is enhanced by blowing air inside the filter's column.

Of course, oxygen also gets taken out of the water by so-called oxidation processes : in simpler words this means decay. Anything in the water that breaks down, for instance excess food, will remove oxygen from the system in the process of decaying.

To keep the levels of dissolved oxygen at their maximum, ensure that filters are clean, that you do not overfeed, etc...

Oxygen enters the water from the surrounding air, inside the filter, but also as a result of oxygen transfer in the protein skimmer (Kipper, 1987).

There is however always a limiting factor :

Water can only hold a certain amount of oxygen, and that amount is different for any given temperature. The higher the temperature, the less oxygen the water can contain. The lower the temperature the more oxygen it contains (within limits).

That maximum amount is called the saturation level, and it is different for every temperature. Running tanks at 82 or more degrees Fahrenheit automatically reduces the amount of oxygen that can be dissolved in the water.

That is another good reason not to run your tank at such high temperatures. As dissolved oxygen levels are low, fish and other animals have to breathe harder to get the amount they require, and that obviously will stress them more and make them more prone to disease.

Since lowering the temperature, and automatically, without doing anything else raise the level of dissolved oxygen, we should certainly strive to maintain our tanks at the recommended 75 to 76 ° Fahrenheit.

Another easy way, already pointed out, to increase dissolved oxygen, or at least preventing it from being unnecessarily depleted, is to adhere to good husbandry techniques.

Clean anything in the tank that can function as a mechanical filter regularly - for a detailed list of techniques, see The Marine Fish and Invert Reef Aquarium book.

Besides that, blowing air in the biological filter column, using a protein skimmer, and perhaps an oxygen reactor, are other methods. They are not as easy to implement, and cost more money, but they are certainly available to you.

The better way to go, in our opinion, is installing an oxygen reactor that can be kept under overpressure.

Here is a short list of saturation levels of dissolved oxygen in seawater at 35 parts per thousand salt content :

Temp . C°	Mg/L O$_2$	Temp. °F
22	7.07	71.6
23	6.95	73.4
24	6.83	75.2
25	6.71	77.0
26	6.60	78.8
27	6.49	80.6
28	6.38	82.4
29	6.28	84.2
30	6.18	86.0

Reprinted with permission from Marine Reef. ©1988

As you can see, the level drops quickly as the temperature goes up. At around 75 - 76 degrees, saturation levels are around 6.80 mg per liter. That is the "normal" level. If you measure less than that you must try to determine the cause, and correct the problem.

Around the real Reef saturation is generally always exceeded because oxygen is produced more rapidly than it can escape (tests taken in many different locations, and on many different Reefs, confirm this empyrically over and over).

And here is the last, but very important source of dissolved oxygen : the algae, both micro and macro. This happens during the day, when the sun and the light is strong, and photosynthesis takes place.

A tank with macro-algae will therefore typically have a higher dissolved oxygen level during the daytime, than one that does not have any, or very few (providing you are using strong lighting).

This is covered in the section where we describe how **Leo Wojcik** grew dozens of types of algae using very high light intensities and regularly measured up to 11 mg/l of dissolved oxygen.

This book will deal with lighting extensively, and attempt to give you a better insight in the many factors that need to be taken into consideration, besides "wattage".

If you maintain your tank with dissolved oxygen levels in mind, you will probably find that they will rise, because you will avoid those situations that have a tendency to lower them.

Test your disssolved oxygen levels regularly. There are now various tests on the market. They are accurate to usually within 0.5 mg per liter, which for our purpose is enough. More accurate measurements can be obtained with better tests, or ideally with an oxygen meter that can be adjusted for salinity.

12. 7. Medicine - Disease Treatment

You should not, we repeat, not, under any circumstance use medicine directly in your Reef Tank.

If disease breaks out you must, unfortunately, catch the fish, and treat them outside of the aquarium.

We know this is of course easier said than done. But adding medicine of any kind to your aquarium will do more damage than you bargained for, and is therefore not an option available to Reef Keeping Hobbyists.

The solution is to spend more time trying to get the fish out. Use 2 nets to try to catch the more difficult species. Use acrylic jars with a little food in them to lure them inside, then, with a net, close off the opening of the jar and lift out the fish.

I am sure you have your favorite method, and that is fine, as long as you catch the fish, and then treat whatever the disease may be, in a hospital or seperate tank.

Many of the available medicines are antibiotica, and result in the loss of your biological filter when added to the water.

Other types of medicine contain compounds that invertebrates cannot tolerate at the dosage the medicine is prepared with, or the chemicals are just plainly noxious, even in low concentrations.

Quinine hydrochloride is rumored to be safe for invertebrates. We have had no such experiences.

12. 8. Liquid Foods

Liquid foods are great. They are easy to dispense, hold up well, and can be stored easily, usually not even in the refrigerator.

We use them too, but you must be careful with the dosage, as a lot of it never gets eaten and just pollutes the tank.

If you keep corals that cannot be fed larger pieces of frozen foods, try soaking them in the liquid food, in a small aquarium, without filtration, for about 20 to 30 minutes. Then place them back in your tank.

If you keep lots of corals, this approach may not be practical. It is also probably the reason why so few aquarists resort to it.

There are several brands on the market, and we have tried them all. Personally I have a preference for Coralife's line of foods, and the not yet for sale food by Route 4 Marine Technology, which I had the opportunity to try out as well, and which you should definitely try once it is on the market.

Whatever brand you use, use it sparingly, and follow the manufacturers' instructions carefully. You don't need additional pollution in your tank from excess food.

When using liquid foods, you should turn the pumps off, and let the syphoning to your trickle filter end. Once that has happened you can add the food. Do not forget to turn your pumps back on a few minutes later. Alternatively, use a device that will switch the pumps back on automatically after a period of time that you can set .

Thiel•Aqua•Tech sells a device that allows you to stop your pumps for up to 10 minutes. They will turn back on automatically after that.

The same device has a few other features : it can also make your pumps alternate. It is solid state and has no moving parts. You just plug your pumps, or powerheads in it, set the desired alternating time, and you're done.

Liquid foods are often supplemented with vitamins and other elements. You may wish to keep that in mind when deciding on how much extra vitamins you should add yourself.

Often the foods contain extracts of many forms of food, and are therefore very nutritional, and complete.

T•A•T's Coral Reef Nutrients, a liquid extract of the foods corals normally live off on the reef, is special in as much as it is prepared in small numbered batches that also indicate an expiration date after which you should not use the food. It is only available in 4 oz bottles.

12. 9. Carbon Dioxide

CO_2 although not a true water additive, is a form of "fertilization" and we have therefore included it in this section.

During photosynthesis, macro-algae, micro-algae and zooxanthellae, the symbiotic algae, require carbon dioxide. That is a known fact, and not much different from what happens with terrestrial, and aquatic plants, including freshwater ones.

It is a very important part of the growth process of algae, and in the case of symbiotic algae, it benefits the corals or anemones. The latter has been written up by many much more qualified experts than myself, and is documented in several books, articles, and research papers.

Carbon dioxide is present in the water as a result of fish respiration, and also enters the tank from the surrounding air. Some is always present; the problem may be however, that not enough of it is available to satisfy the needs of all those lifeforms that require it.

Unfortunately, once you have a fair amount of corals and algae, a carbon dioxide deficit is very often the case. This means that there is not enough CO_2 available for all the "users" of it in the tank.

This can be alleviated by adding carbon dioxide, either manually, or with an automated system. Dupla sells one, and so do Coralife, Poisson, and Route 4 Marine Technology.

Although there is no set rule for determining exactly how much there should be "ideally", German circles usually recommmend around 4 mg per liter, on a continuous basis during the time your lights are on. Depletion occurs continuously, and the more light is used, the more rapidly that takes place. Consequently, more needs to be provided.

Tests for carbon dioxide are available, but not many of them exist. Scientific supply places, laboratory suppliers and Dupla, are three sure sources.

Keep in mind that, as carbon dioxide enters the water, it will form carbonic acid. This will lower the buffer of your water, and also affect your pH.

You must therefore ensure that :

• Your carbonate hardness is high enough to be able to deal with this addition of CO_2 : recommended levels go from 12 dKH to 18 dKH, with 15 dKH - German degrees of Hardness - probably being a good average.

For those of you measuring in ppm (American degrees of hardness) multiply the dKH by 18.5 to get ppm, or divide ppm by 18.5 to get dKH degrees.

• You do not add excessive amounts of carbon dioxide, and follow the ins-tructions from the manufacturer scrupulously.

Controlling the quantity added, safely, by observing its effect on your pH, is probably the best and most recommended method.

Proceed as follows :
• measure your dKH (carbonate hardness),

- adjust it if necessary,
- measure your pH,
- start adding CO_2, first just a small amount (30 bubbles a minute),
- wait about 10 minutes and measure your pH again,
- if it has not changed, increase the amount of CO_2 that you are addding slightly,
- wait another 10 minutes, measure the pH again.
- Keep doing this until your pH has dropped by 0.1 degrees.
- Then leave the carbon dioxide dispensing equipment set as it is.
- After about one hour, you should re-test your pH to make sure that it has not changed, and dropped further.
- If it has, you must reduce the amount of carbon dioxide being added slightly, and go through the above steps again until you have it set for the right amount.

When using carbon dioxide, make it a point to check your carbonate hardness at least once a week. Adjust it whenever necessary with liquid buffer (best), or with tablets (second best).

Alternatively, use a Thiel•Aqua•Tech "Tech•Doser" pump, and dispense it automatically.

Adding CO_2 will provide additional carbon dioxide, and is totally safe for fish and invertebrates, as long as you follow the above instructions.

Those interested in more details may wish to read, or re-read, the section on carbon dioxide in The Marine Fish and Invert Reef Aquarium book.

Often you will read that CO_2 kills fish. We assure you that if you use it wisely, and follow the above simple instructions, it is totally safe.

Corals and algae will greatly benefit from the addition of CO_2. Adding it may just make the difference between being able to grow macro-algae, or not; even if you are already using fertilizers that contain iron and manganese.

12. 10. Permanganate : KMnO4

In an effort to improve the tank water's redox potential, or increase the water quality, Hobbyists sometimes resort to the use of Potassium permanganate.

Yes, $KMnO_4$ will oxidize organics, and yes it will raise the redox potential very quickly, and yes it will "polish" the water, and yes it kills bacteria. But it is too dangerous a chemical to use, unless you are a chemist and know what you are doing and are familiar with the dangers involved.

It is a purple crystal that, while dissolving, will turn the water of the tank purple too, especially if you use several crystals at a time.

As it oxidizes it turns to brown, and a slimy brownish film will form on the top of the water, stick to the glass (or acrylic) and to anything else it comes in contact with.

It is very difficult to remove and makes the tank look real unsightly for several hours, even after you clean it up. It is sticky, messy, and something you do not want in the tank.

At the same time, your redox potential may go up by several 100 millivolts very rapidly, and stress the fish so much that they may actually die of shock.

Its effects on the redox potential are very temporary. Of course, the quantity used will determine for how long your redox potential will stay high, and how high it will go. Just remember that sudden changes, especially such drastic ones as occasioned by permanganate, can wipe out your tank.

Invertebrates do not seems as sensitive, but they will close up if you increase the redox potential very rapidly to levels over 600 mv, and the sudden highly increased oxidation capability of the water may damage them permanently.

Unless you know what you are doing, stay away from this chemical, especially in its pure purple crystal form.

Diluted versions are available as well and are a lot safer. They can be used for temporary improvement of the water quality, but only if you absolutely must. Check carefully to determine whether these contain any other chemicals that may be noxious.

12. 11. Hydrogen Peroxide

H_2O_2 , or hydrogen peroxide can be used in diluted form, usually 3 percent, to momentarily, but rapidly, raise the amount of dissolved oxygen.

The effect is very short lived but if, for instance, your pump fails or if a power outage occurs, you could use hydrogen peroxide to keep a sufficient amount of dissolved oxygen in the water, until the power comes back on.

The usual recommended dose is 15 drops of a 3 percent solution per gallon, up to a maximum of 3 times per hour.

Adding hydrogen peroxide does not solve your problem at all if your dissolved oxygen level is habitually low. It only lets you raise that D.O. quickly if you notice a sudden deficiency and your fish are in distress.

If your D.O. is always low you must try to find why and then correct whatever is necessary to bring it back up to normal levels.

This includes, as indicated several times already, good and regular husbandry techniques, the use of a properly sized trickling filter, with the right packing material for biological growth, and possibly the installation of a dissolved oxygen reactor.

Although the use of hydrogen peroxide will, in the long run, increase your redox potential, in the short run it will bring it down very significantly and quickly.

If you find that you will have to use hydrogen peroxide to increase the dissolved oxygen levels for some time, for example during a long power failure, the drip method is the best method to use.

Take a bottle of 3 percent H_2O_2 and perforate the cap, making an opening just large enough to push airline tubing through. Strike a little silicone around the opening in the cap after you have inserted the tubing.

Let sit for 10 to 20 minutes. Hang the bottle upside down over the tank or filter. Clamp the air line tubing shut. Pierce the top of the bottle with a needle, so air can enter and no vacuum is created inside the bottle (it will not flow if such a vacuum exists).

Open the clamp slowly until a drop comes out about every 2 seconds.

During the power outage : remove all mechanical filter material from the filters to prevent the start up of anerobic decay. As soon as the power comes back on, remove the bottle of hydrogen peroxide, perform a 15 percent water change, replace pre-filters with new material, and start the system back up.

12.12. Resins

Although obviously not a true additive, resins perform a funtion similar to some. Indeed by removing elements from the water, they purify it, and make it more suitable for use in Reef Tanks. This is similar to what a number of additives do.

Of course, resins can also be classified in the filtration section since they filter many noxious elements out and absorb them by ionic exchange processes.

De-ionization and demineralization are new to the hobby. In fact we strongly believe that the only company offering a D.I. system is T•A•T.

De-ionizers use resins, which are artificial compounds. How they are made and what they contain is not important. It is their function that we are interested in as it assists us in bettering the water quality.

Resins come in two main types : gel resins and macroreticular types. The former are not porous, whereas the latter have a definite internal structure. They are referred to as continuous and discontinuous phase resins respectively. Macroreticular resins are not commonly used as they are extremely application specific, and also much more expensive.

Resins each have narrow and specialized applications. To truly deionize we must therefore use more than one type.

Resins are usually classified into the following types:

• Strong acidic cation exchange
• Weakly acidic cation exchange
• Strongly basic anion exchange
• Weakly basic anion exchange

One of the reasons that we ourselves use such resins, is that we can treat incoming and previously reverse osmozed water, and remove all remaining traces of silica, the main culprit in our opinion of micro-algae outbreaks (based on experiments with raw tap water containing silicic acid, and subsequent appearance of large colonies of so-called micro-algae and diatoms.THIEL, 1987).

Mixtures can be made up of combinations of the above resins. The desired effect determines which resins are used, and also whether the resins are kept seperated, or whether they are placed together in one and the same treatment column.

Many combinations can be made up and only experienced water treatment specialists will be able to adjust the mixtures to perform more optimally.

At Thiel•Aqua•Tech we have invested in both the cost of researching which mixture of resins would work best, and in the time required to do so. The end result is the Tech•Ultra de-ionization unit which is now commercially available, and can be obtained both in a standard size and in a system-size custom unit for larger set ups, e.g. pet stores.

If you are looking for excellent quality water at a much lower price than buying treated jars, Tech•Ultra should be your choice.

Keep in mind however that these units are not meant tobe hooked in line with the tank's filtration. They are used prior to adding salt to the water. All you will need in addition to the unit itself is a pump and a vat in which you keep the water to be treated.

Because of the high chloride content of aquarium water, sodium exchange resins do not work, and hydrogen cycle resins used on their own would not give the right result.

Resins that can work in this harsher environment are however presently being tested.

13. The Substrate

13. 1. Introduction

Whereas in traditional systems thick layers of substrate are the norm, in Reef Tanks you should only have minimal amount of substrate, mainly because of the different type of filtration that is used. In fact, you do not even need substrate (J.Sprung, A.Thiel 1988)

Since little or no water circulates through the substrate we want to eliminate the possibility of anaerobic activity, as such activity brings about a set of problems that may well wipe out your tank. To prevent anaerobics, use only very small amounts of substrate.

It is also our contention that you are better off using non-calcareous substrate, as opposed to a calcareous one.

The maximum thickness that we recommend is 1/8 to 1/4 inch, with perhaps some small areas with a little more, but only if needed for burrowers.

Anaerobics, even small amounts, in spots of the substrate, will produce hydrogen sulfide. This is a very toxic compound and will harm all lifeforms in the tank.

Anaerobic activity results from bacteria in areas where no oxygen is present. These bacteria break down the sulfates in the artificial seawater, which combine with hydrogen to form hydrogen sulfide.

Black spots are a clear indication that such anerobic activity is taking place, the black being a precipitated iron compound. Whenever you see such spots, you must suspect that anaerobic activity is taking place. You must syphon that area out of the tank with a hose or similar device.

Stirring up these black spots is not recommended, as if hydrogen sulfide is present, you will mix it with the water.

13.2. Dolomite - Crushed Coral

Most manuals on keeping Salt water aquariums will tell you to use either crushed coral, or dolomite. Both are heavily advertised, and claim to buffer the water, and aid in long term pH stability.

Both are calcareous materials and are made up of carbonates and bicarbonates of calcium and magnesium.

The reason for this recommendation is simple : they are supposed to increase the buffer, and therefore assist in stabilizing the pH.

This may be so for a few days, or perhaps for a few weeks at the most. After that, both dolomite and crushed coral cover themselves with slime and detritus; the exchange between your substrate and the water stops. The buffering process is no longer taking place.

To re-activate it, one would have to wash the substrate regularly in an acid bath to remove the impurities, and that is of course not practical at all. Just cleaning the bottom of your tank does not help either, as you are only removing loose particulate matter and not cleaning the surface of the granules themselves.

Additionally, the magnesium ion in the water and the magnesium ion in the substrate seek a chemical balance. This also results in both types of substrate being covered with a very thin layer of magnesium that inhibits any further exchange.

It has also been established, over time, that both these materials have a tendency to bring the pH down to 7.6 - 7.8.

References for this process include Guido Hueckstedt, Stephen Spotte, as well as hobby literature.

It would therefore appear that the only benefit of these materials is the natural look they give to the reef tank, not the chemical implications that are made about what they do for the buffer and the pH.

The **process** that is being referred to works; it only does so however in the presence of acids, for example in carbonate hardness reactors, while carbon dioxide is being injected.

So why do they get used so much? We do not know, but we recommend that, because of the additional negative side effects of precipitating trace elements (Preis 1988), Reef Keeping Hobbyists, should stay away from them, and opt for different kinds of substrate materials altogether.

Shells, Florida crushed, Oyster shell, and other such materials, do not really do us any good, except maybe aesthetically. And even that only for a while, since, as soon as algae grow on the substrate, one can hardly see it anymore anyway.

Tanks kept with such substrates do not retain their carbonate hardness any longer than tanks that use different compounds.

pH stability should come about, not as a result of the type of substrate that is used, but through control and adjustment of the carbonate hardness or, better still, through the use of a carbonate hardness reactor. This equipment is described in Part Two of the book, and its installation is explained in Part 4.

Crushed coral can be used to promote buffering of the water, providing this is done in an environment conducive to the slow release of carbonates and bicarbonates in the water (mostly bicarbonates), because of the lower pH and the presence of carbon dioxide. Cylindrical tubes are used to do this. The process is described in Part Two, as already indicated.

If you are presently using such a material, you should ensure that it is kept free of detritus and, as bits are syphoned out in the cleaning process, replace them with a different substance, or better still do not replace them at all.

Using dolomite and crushed coral will certainly not damage the tank environment but will, in our opinion, not contribute to the purported stability of the pH either. It can be used for that purpose, but only in certain ways. The carbonate hardness reactor is one of them.

13.3. Non-Calcareous Materials

This should be the prefered material in Reef Tanks. We know of no such product offered for sale, on a large scale, in the Pet industry however.

Since recommendations with regard to the effects of substrates on trace element and water chemistry paramaters are new even in Germany, and has only recently been given recognition and credibility, not many such products are available there either.

As the facts become better known in the USA , importers will start to bring in such products, and local manufacturers will start packaging such non-calcareous materials as well.

In some areas of the country a rock generally referred to as cave rock, can be found in granular form as well as in large blocs. Such rock is suitable for marine use.

Of course, ground zeolites make perfect substrates, even adding some calcium to the water for a short period of time and then becoming quiet inert.

Zeolites, and at least 22 different ones are known, give off calcium and take up sodium instead.This is a very short lived process and will not affect your salinity.

Zeolites are used extensively in the freshwater hobby, but for different purposes. In freshwater certain zeolites remove ammonia.

13.4. Other Substrates

These include sand, silica sand, Carribean white sand, quartz sand and other such products. Although they give the tank a real nice look, they are of no value to the reef tank.

The main reason for this strong stand against the use of sand, is that sands "packs" very easily and will lead to anearobic activity much more rapidly than some of the other materials that you may use, or have used.

Stay away from silica sand especially, as you want to avoid increasing the amount of silicate in the tank. Silicates promote both the appearance and proliferation of diatoms. Diatoms can make the tank look very unsightly, and are the cause for some of the so-called "red algae"

Silicic acid, a component of tap water, often anyway, also promotes their growth , and only good quality reverse osmosis units and de-ionizers with the correct resins,will rid the water of it. Of course, using distilled water has the same effect.

Removing silicates is a difficult process that no one seems to have resolved yet, at least not in a manner that is not dangerous for the tank life, unless it is done before salt is added to the water.

13.5. Conclusion

Use a non - calcareous substance, or no substrate at all.

In the latter case the tank may look a little odd for a few weeks, but the bottom will soon be covered with algae and other life forms that came in with the rock that you placed in the tank.

Soon you will not even realize, that there is no "real" substrate in your tank, because the whole bottom will be covered with alltypes of life.

Alternatively use zeolites. If you are using dolomite and/or crushed coral, make sure that you monitor the carbonate hardness of your tank regularly and add buffering solutions as required.

KSM Strontium Chloride supplement

14. Heating - Cooling

We have dealt very extensively with heating and with the types of heaters that you can use, in The Marine Fish and Invert Reef Aquarium. Please refer to that book for more details.

We wish to stress again that it is important to lower the temperature to much more realistic levels than the ones normally found in many Reef Tanks.

We personally advocate 75 to 76 degrees Fahrenheit at all times.

This not only takes some of the stress out of the environment in which your fish and invertebrates live, but it also enables you to achieve much higher levels of dissolved oxygen. That, in turn, lowers additional stress.

Besides keeping the tank at the right temperature, it is important to maintain that temperature as stable as you can.

Large and frequent temperature fluctuations stress the fish and other lifeforms, and often results in disease break-outs, especially parasites. One way to prevent that from happening, is to ensure that whenever you change water, the temperature of the new water that you are adding is the same as the tank's.

A good quality heater is a must, as heaters that either keep on for much longer than they should or heaters that stick, will only lead to problems down the road.

Perhaps one of the best ones on the market is the Ebo-Jaeger heater, especially since it is totally submersible.

Since we wrote The Marine Fish and Invert Reef Aquarium book, newer heaters have appeared on the market :

• quartz heaters with separate thermostats,

• electric pads, that can be placed underneath the aquarium, against the glass,

• 24 volt, rather than 42 volt heating by Dupla, although at the time we wrote this book it was not available in the United States.

Heating is of course important, especially if your tank is in a room where the temperature "fluctuates"rather widely, e.g. warm enough or real warm during the day, but much colder at night.

This will lead to great differences in the tank's temperature during day and night time and is one of the reasons for stress on the animals in your tank.

This will ultimately lead to disease, often as a result of less resistance to parasitic infestations. The fish can no longer fight these parasites, which manage to suddenly find a weak host , start multiplying, invade all or several of your fish, and suddenly you start losing fish to these infestations.

As indicated earlier in the book, if, for example, you need a total of 300 watts of heat, it is better and safer to use several smaller heaters, totalling 300 watt, rather than just one unit.

This spreads the risk of heat loss because of heater failure. Indeed, it is unlikely that all your heaters will fail at the same time. This only happens when the power fails, but if the latter happens, the only thing that will save you is having a generator.

The best generators are the ones that kick in automatically when the power goes out. Those are however expensive units (several thousand dollars for a unit that delivers 5000 watt).

Although your heater must be of excellent quality to be able to deal with such possible fluctuations, it is our experience that most hobbyists do not really need to heat their tanks, rather, they often need to bring the temperature down with a cooling unit.

Although coolers are relatively expensive, they are a good investment if your tank is always running at high temperatures and you lose fish to disease, cannot keep anemones for very long, and generally measure low levels of dissolved oxygen.

Aquarium Sales and Services makes excellent units, in a variety of sizes, for just about any size tank.

Although most cooling units nowadays are relatively quiet, one cannot really say that you will not hear them either.

If you have no alternative but resorting to a chiller to bring the temperature down, then it is really as wise investment. The savings made, over time, by not losing fish and invertebrates, will help defray its cost.

X-Phosphate bottle and compound

15. Lighting the Reef Tank

15.1. Introduction

Over the last two years, Hobbyists' opinions with regard to which light to use over a Reef Tank, have gone from just plain fluorescent tubes to using specialized ones - including actinic lighting - to installing various types of metal halide lighting.

The aim of all this is, of course, to provide both the right kind of lighting, spectrum wise, and enough intensity for corals, invertebrates and macro-algae.

Whereas oxygen is a most important component of the animals' environment and regarded as such by most Hobbyists, lighting does not always receive the kind of attention it deserves.

Is this because of the cost involved? Or is it because of the many misconceptions that still exist about what light does, and how it does it? Or is it that Hobbyists just do not understand what factors to look for when talking about light?

My guess is that it probably is a combination of all of the above.

Lighting is indeed not an easy subject to understand because of the many concepts that need to be dealt with. Let us look a little closer at some of the concepts that I feel are really important .

Hopefully, this will contribute to a better understanding of all the factors that are involved, and help you in selecting a light for your aquarium with a better grasp on the subject.

15.2. Lighting Intensity - Lumens

Intensity is expressed in Lumens, and refers to the output that a particular light source gives off.

When you buy a bulb, one of the numbers you will find on its spec sheet is this output. It could be 6500, or over 10 000, or even higher. It could also be much lower. The magnitude depends on which type of bulb you bought.

High intensity lights such as metal halides, typically give off 10,000 or more Lumens. Sometimes you will see two numbers, one for initial output and also one for average output over the life of the bulb. The first number is higher than the second one, and their names are self explanatory.

What this implies is that if Lumen output is high, the bulb will give you a lot of light, even if you measure that light intensity one, two or more feet away from the bulb.

Fluorescent tubes and incandescent bulbs are not lights with a high output; their Lumen rating may therefore only be 4000 to maybe 5000 Lumens for the stronger ones, and usually much less.

It should be clear that you will need quite a few more fluorescent tubes than metal halides, to obtain identical levels of intensity. Two to three fluorescent tubes for one 150 watt metal halide is not uncommon.

This can be a real problem because space above the aquarium is very limited, and you cannot cover the aquarium completely, because you need to have access to it from the top too from time to time.

We would therefore logically want to recommend that metal halides be your light of choice. But not just any metal halide. You must keep reading, until you have all the concepts under control.

You will, as a result, be able to form yourself a better opinion of what kind of lighting you will want to use over your own aquarium, and better understand what the lights that you are now using do, or don't do.

We mentionned "regular" fluorescent tubes a little earlier. The reason for that qualification is that there are other types :

• high output (HO)
• very high output (VHO)

Because both of these have higher Lumen output ratings, they could possibly be used over a Reef Tank.

The problem is that :

• VHO tubes lose their spectrum (see later in this chapter) too rapidly, and are therefore not useable; besides they are quite expensive,

• HO tubes are expensive too, and need special end caps and a special ballast to operate.

Although this does not exclude them, it does not make it as practical to use them as it first seems. However, HO tubes with a high Kelvin degree (see later in this chapter) rating are definitely your second best choice.

Besides "metal halide", which really is a generic name just as fluorescent tube is, the bulb needs to be qualified by some other characteristics.

What we mean is that to do the job, we need some very specific type of metal halide. We need Halogen quartz metal halides (Thiel, 1985).

Tungsten quartz metal halides are not a correct choice for our purpose. They give off a light that is much too yellow. It has intensity, yes, but the color of the light is wrong.

The same applies to mercury vapor and sodium vapor lights. They are not suited for Reef Tanks either because the color of their light is also not what we are looking for. It is too yellow.

Again, both meet the intensity criterion, but they do not meet the other criteria that we will place on the bulb that is best suited for a Reef Tank.

As we progress we will define our criteria one by one, and narrow the choice of bulb down to what we think is the bulb that you should be looking for.

The first criterion is defined : high intensity, preferably very high intensity. This high intensity can be achieved with metal halides and with certain fluorescent tubes.

15.3. Light measured in Lux

Even though a bulb may have a very high Lumen output, that does not mean that it can make that intensity travel a great distance. In our case that means to the bottom of the tank, or to the areas of the tank where we have placed corals and macro-algae.

If you wanted to know how much light intensity reached a given spot, a specific spot in the aquarium, you would measure that intensity with a special meter and express that strength in Lux.

In Europe it is usually measured in foot candles. Foot candle strength multiplied by 0.0929 = strength in Lux. For example, 100000 foot candles wich seems like a very strong light, equals only 9290 Lux, slightly more than the lux reading you would get from 150 watt metal halide at about 18 inches distance.

Since most of what we keep in our Tank is not necessarily close to the light source, but sometimes a good distance away from it, we can define the second criterion :

Whatever bulb used must be able to penetrate the water well, and bring enough light to the animals and algae in any given spot of the tank.

A bulb that has a high intensity, but cannot bring the kind of light that we want to one feet under the water for instance, is of course not an ideal bulb.

It may give off a lot of light, and you may feel that your tank is well lit, but unless the Lux you measure is of the magnitude that the animal who is at the spot where you are measuring, needs, the bulb you are using is not ideal.

Light measured at a specific spot is expressed in Lux, as you may have surmized. It is known that most macro-algae require Lux readings of up to 16,000 or more for at least several hours of the day. Many corals benefit from similar strong light on the reef, for a good part of the day as well.

Of course, one bulb may not be the answer. You may need to use 2 or more, depending on the size and depth of your tank. This may be the case, even though the bulb you have selected is very strong and has a very high Lumen output.

Halogen quartz metal halides certainly qualify, as they fit both the Lumen and the Lux requirements that we have set forth.

Incidentally, the "quartz" in the above name refers only to the fact that the glass of which the bulb is made, is quartz glass. Nothing else. And there are many types of quartz bulbs on the market.

Most of these, in fact, do not fit the criteria that we have already set. So do not buy just "any" quartz bulb. You will need to be much more specific than that to get the right kind of bulb.

Regular fluorescent tubes do not have the output that will give you high Lux readings. Some High output fluorescent tubes do. But to match the Lux readings that you get from HQI (halogen quartz iodine) bulbs, you will need to use more than one.

Typically two such high output fluorescent tubes are needed to match the strength off one low wattage HQI.

We already pointed out, and want to repeat it, such bulbs require special transformers and special endcaps as well. They will not fit in regular fluorescent tube fixtures.

Ballasts that can run 2 bulbs are available, both for 4 and for 6 foot HO fluorescent lights.

So if Lux is the measure of how much light in fact reaches a specific spot in the tank, then how do we decide on what that intensity should be ?

That is the trick. Every form of life you have in your tank has a different optimal requirement, depending on its location on the reef in the real world.

Trade offs are therefore necesssary, and positioning of the animals, based on their individual requirements is therefore suggested. This was extensively described in The Marine Fish and Invert Reef Aquarium book, in the lighting section. (Thiel 1988)

We suggested various light zones in the tank, and still stand by that position, as we feel that it best replicates the true Reef.

In essence, we plan for those lifeforms that need the most light, and then position the others in such a way, that if they need less light, they are somewhat protected from it.

Algae and corals both need very high intensities, many over 10000 Lux, and some even more. But they do not need this strong light the whole day.

Just think of what happens over the real Reef. The suns comes up in the morning and, as the sun rises further, more and more light reaches the animals on the Reef, until the sun starts going down again in the afternoon.

Optimal aquarium lighting should therefore duplicate that phenomenon by staggering the way in which your lights go on and off.

This can be achieved by using timers that allow multiple on and off cycles. Several such timers exist; when we last looked Micronta timers by Radio Shack were available in 3 on off cycle versions.

Let us assume that you have 3 HQI metal halides over your tank. One would go on at 9.00 a.m., a second one would go on at 10.00 a.m., and the third one would go on at 12 noon.

All three lights stay on until 3 p.m., at which time one goes out. A second light goes out at 9.00 p.m., and the third one goes out at 10.00 p.m.

These on and off times are just illustrative, and you should substitute your own numbers and times. This will work with as many lights as you may wish to use. All you will need is a timer that can handle the number of sets of lights that you are using over your tank.

Recommendations on how long to leave your lights on, range from 10 hours to 14 hours. We keep ours on for 12 hours, but we do not start until 11.00 a.m.

This allow us us to enjoy our tank at night with lights on until 11.00 p.m. This obviates the need to use timers, as not too many people are home at 11.00 am to turn on the lights.

Of course, so goes the reasoning, more hours of a weaker light will make up the difference. If your light was not strong enough, you would leave it on for say 16 hours a day. That is a completely false reasoning.

The only correct way is to provide strong enough light, for a normal 10 to 14 hours maximum, but provide it in such a way, that it gradually increases for a few hours, then stays stable for about 3, and the starts going down again.

Higher light intensities result in more Lumen, and result in higher Lux readings in any given spot in the tank. Approximating the true Reef situation is not something that we are likely to reach, as around noon time you can measure up to 150 000 Lumen.

Leo Wojcik however has done just that on an experimental basis, and we will discuss his set-up later in this section.

As you increase the amount of light, all life processes increase, and photosynthesis is a good part of that.

Running, for instance, 1200 watts of HQI light over a 150 gallon may seem like overdoing it, but it can easily be achieved, and does not negatively affect the life in the tank.

To the contrary, Leo Wojcik has been running such intensities for quite some time now, and reports superior results with both corals and macro-algae.

Whoever decided that metal halide lighting "burns" your corals, should have a word with Leo, and should have a look at his tank to convince himself that such is not the case. Not even with nearly 10 watt of light per gallon of water.

Leo's tank has never been in better shape. In fact his Elegance corals (Catalaphillia plicata) have never been as large, and his macro-algae have never grown so well.

The one requirement however is that you have water of extremely good quality, with very low nitrate and phosphate levels, nl practically zero mg per liter, or zero ppm of both.

If this is not the case, micro-algae will grow too. Not as a result of the light, but as a result of the nutrient availability. Light is only a catalyst.

Light by itself does not make micro-algae appear, but if nutrients for them are present, and you provide strong light, they too will photosynthsize more and grow more rapidly.

Whenever you resort to very strong lighting, you must also consider that at higher levels of photosynthesis, more fertilizer (e.g. iron and manganese) must be added, and that CO_2 will have to added to the tank as well.Keeping fertilizers in solution on a continuous basis can be achieved only with EDTA chelated products, and it would be better to dispense them in minuscule amounts on continuous basis, e.g. by using a chemical metering pump.

In fact, we were so impressed with Leo'slighting and the results that he is obtaining, that we have decided to set up similar lighting over one of our own tanks, to duplicate, and study the impact of much higher intensities on Reef life.

From what we have seen so far, all effects are very positive, and we will be reporting on the results in Advanced Reef Keeping II, which will be out in mid 1991.

15. 4. Spectrum - Kelvin degrees

Every bulb, whether incandescent, fluorescent or other, - whether trea- ted or untreated with compounds such as phosphorus - gives off light of a particular color.

Just think for a while and you will agree. Take, for instance, "sodium vapor" lights that are commonly found along highways: they give off an extremely yellow light.

What we see as the "color" is not just one color, but the result of a mixture of colors in which the predominant one prevails, and gives us an overall impression.

Some bulbs, such as the mercury vapor lights often used over fresh water aquariums, look rather yellowish-white but they have a lot of red in the overall light output as well.

This is usually only "visible" to us for a few moments, when we switch the light on, and the bulb "warms" up; but the red light is there all the time as an integral part of the total number of different colors of light that such a light source emits.

The mixture of all the colors that a bulb, or fluorescent tube, or any other light, gives off, is called the "spectrum".

This is the third criterion that we must take into account, when selecting a light source for our Reef Tank.

We have already defined three :

- Intensity in Lumens,
- Measureable light strength in a specific location in Lux,
- and now we have Spectrum.

Spectrum is expressed in a numerical value : Kelvin degrees. A high number means that the light is really white and "cool", a low number means that the light is off-white, usually with a predominance of reds and yellows. High Kelving degree rated bulbs also have alot of blue in their spectrum.

A mercury vapor bulb, with a yellowish color, would probably have a Kelvin degree rating of around 3700. One with a more reddish look to it, e.g. the phosphorus coated bulbs, would show a lower spectrum of around 3300 Kelvin degrees.

Each type of light, spectrum-wise, has its own reason for existing. Manufacturers developed them because obviously the spectrum means something to the user.

Mercury vapor bulbs of around 3300 Kelvin degrees are used as "plant lights".

Others, for instance, general use fluorescent tubes, are usually just plain "white" are inexpensive to make. They are at the bottom of the ladder in quality, may not have a specific use, and are installed for no other reason than to provide "light".

De-luxe white fluorescent tubes are a little better, and are often used in stores, to make merchandise look more appealing.

Warm white fluorescent light is softer on us, friendlier perhaps, and is often used in offices.

What we are getting at, it that the "color" or "spectrum" influences not only how we "see" things, but also how the make up of the various colors in a light, can affect our vision.

And that introduces the fourth criterion that we need to pay attention to: the color rendition index, or CRI.

Because CRI and spectrum in our case go hand in hand, we are treating them together in this section.

We know that Hobbyists pay attention to the type of light they use and they do so for a totally different reason.

Blue lights, as in Actinic blue light, are added to hoods to try to provide the corals and invertebrates with a light that approximates what happens in nature.

Blue has the best depth penetration of all the colors in the light spectrum. It is therefore the type of light that corals and invertebrates that live at greater depths are accustomed to around the real Reefs.

Our best chance at success would therefore be to find a bulb, or fluorescent tube, that offers a spectrum that includes the colors that our corals and invertebrates are accustomed to, and that offers the right intensity at the same time.

It turns out that such a spectrum (really white with a high degree of blue) exists. Such bulbs are made both in the fluorescent form, and in the HQI form (halogen quartz iodine). They are the metal halide lights already mentioned earlier.

As the output of the bulb includes more blue and less yellow and red, the color becomes whiter. This is very much like the rating given to diamonds. The purest and most expensive ones are the white-blue.

In fact, jewelry stores usually display their merchandise under very high Kelvin degree lighting too, and use these HQI bulbs as well.

High Kelvin degree lighting is also what you would measure under noon time, strong sunlight 5000 K and better depending on sky conditions and exact location, are likely to be found.

It is of course not possible to visualize what a particular spectrum looks like. You would need to refer to charts that give you the spectral analysis of the bulb you are interested in. These charts can be obtained from lighting distributors.

Moreover, you could also refer to a chromaticity chart. This is yet another way of describing what a particular light source looks like. More on this later in this chapter.

Such charts canbe obtained from Lighting manufacturers, or you can probably go look them up in your local library if you cannot get hold of one in any other way.

It turns out that the higher the Kelvin degree rating, the better the light renders the true colors. Yellow Tangs look real yellow, and not greenish yellow. No eerie effects are present as is the case when you use too much actinic 03 light.

This is of course what we want, and our fourth criterion is met if the color rendition index is high. This is because it makes the tank look much more "natural".

Keep in mind though that lights can be bought that have a high color rendition index, but that do not have the high intensity that we are looking for. These lights do not qualify because they only meet one of the criteria, not both.

Several manufacturers make high Kelvin degree fluorescent tubes, and high Kelvin degree metal halides lights.

Some of these include :

Metal halides	Fluorescent
Osram	Osram
Philips	Philips
Sylvannia	Duro-Test
Venture	Sylvania
Energy Savers (5500K)	Day-Light

The choice is large, but once you start applying the criteria we have set forth, you will find that it narrows itself down very quickly.

Here are some Kelvin degree and color rendition index ratings for typical "fluorescent" tubes :

	K	CRI	Watt
Cool White	4100	67	40
Cool White de luxe	4200	89	40
Daylight	6500	79	40
Colortone 50	5000	92	40
Colortone 75	7500	95	40
Cool Green	6100	70	40
Ultralume 85	5000	99	40
Color Classer HO	7500	97	60

It appears from that chart that the best fluorescent lights to use are the high output Color Classer ones made by Duro-Test, and rated at 7500 Kelvin degrees.

These bulbs come in 4 and 6 foot lengths, giving respectively 60 and 90 watt of light output. As already indicated, they do need special endcaps and special ballasts.

Using these bulbs in pairs, e.g. 4 or 6 or 8 of them, allows us to install ballasts, also called transformers, that can run 2 lights each. We would therefore need either 2,3 or 4 such ballasts.

Color Classer 7500 Kelvin degree high output bulbs are available through electrical distributors, or from good pet stores, and from my own company as well.

Getting into higher intensities, and staying with the same spectrum is not possible at this time. The highest Kelvin degree H.I.D. rating on the market, is the famous Osram HQI Power Star NDL bulb, which can be obtained in 70, 150, 250 and even higher wattages.

This particular bulb is rated for 5000 Kelvin degrees, and the 150 watt version emits 13500 Lumen, average over the life of the bulb, which is 15 000 hours (at 12 hours a day, that is nearly 3.5 years of usage). For exact specifications on the bulb, contact a local electrical distributor, or the manufacturer.

It is, in our opinion, and in the opinion of many German experts, the bulb that is best suited for Marine Reef Aquariums. There is absolutely no question about it.

Some bulbs come close, but the Power Star really stands out. It is unfortunately an expensive bulb. It also requires a ballast, an igniter, and a capacitor to run, which all adds to the cost further.

Although it does not make much sense to use wattage as a guideline, there is obviously a direct relationship between lumen output and wattage. As a result higher wattage lamps will give off more lumen. And higher lumen output will result in higher lux measurements in the tank.

From an economy standpoint, a bulb with a high lumen output per watt (divide the lumen output by the wattage) is an efficient bulb and costs less to operate.

To attain the kind of intensities that are necessary for corals, invertebrates and macro-algae, very high total lumen -total output from all the bulbs used- is required.

This can only be achieved by throwing away your old ideas about lighting. Indeed, even if you decide to use high intensity discharge lights such as metal halide HQI types, you will need from 3 to 5 watt per gallon of water to achieve high lux readings in all areas of the tank.

Over a 150 gallon tank this means from 450 to 750 watt of high intensity light that meets all the criteria that we have already outlined. This is obviously quite a bit more than most Hobbyists are accustomed to place over their tanks.

This can easily be achieved with Osram Power Stars (sometimes also referred to as Halo Stars) or similar lights, but is much harder with fluorescent tubes because of the limited space above the aquarium.

Using HO fluorescent tubes instead of regular ones, will require less bulbs, as each bulb has a higher lumen output and may solve the problem on smaller tanks. On larger tanks however ...

Tungsten halogen quartz bulbs, which can be bought in do-it-yourself stores, are filament-type bulbs, not double vacuum high intensity discharge bulbs since they do not require a ballast. They operate from a direct wall outlet. All you need to do is plug them in.

Although it may appear to you that this is an adequate way to go, we caution you that such light is very yellow, and that these bulbs are not suited for Marine Reef Tanks. If they were, life would be so much simpler, because these light can be bought for 30.00 to 40.00 dollars a piece.

You may think that the light is white, but when you compare it to the output of a Color Classer, or a Power Star, you will be convinced in a second that their light is really very skewed towards the yellow end of the spectrum (notes on test in Lab book n°12, Thiel, 1986)

15.5. Heat Transfer

Providing you use "pendant" type lights that hang 15 to 18 inches from the water surface, heat transfer is not a factor to consider. It just does not happen.

If the lights are enclosed in a wall you will have to extract the ambient heated air from the area, otherwise it "will" transfer.

If you are using a housing that lies on top of your tank, make sure that it has a good strong and quiet fan to extract the heat, and that it has vent holes to let some of that warm air escape by itself. We have seen several units on the market that do not fit this criterion. The ones that do are, for instance, the Energy Savers Coralife lights, especially the ones with the new 5000 Kelvin degree bulbs. We tested a pre-production model of this light, and the results we obtained were extremely good.

15.6. How many Lumens ?

Here are some examples of lumen output that is achievable with both fluorescent HO tubes and metal halide lighting :

Using the 4 foot tubes, 6 bulbs would give you 360 watt of light, and 8 bulbs would give you 480 watt.

Since these bulbs are rated for about 6250 lumen each, that equals respectively 37 500 and 50 000 lumen total. As a comparison, the sun at noon, can be measured at 150 000 lumen at the surface of the water.

Three Osram HQI Power Stars, @ 150 watts each, would give you around 40 000 Lumen. That is considered the minimum amount to be put over a 150 gallon (600 liter) tank in Germany. In fact many hobbyists use even more light.

If past German experience is any indication, it is highly likely that Hobbyists will, over time, up-grade to the Osram Power Star bulbs, or similar types when available, as that is exactly what happened there.

It took slightly over two years for that to happen, and there are now at least 6 manufacturers that make housings for such lights. This includes Dupla, Preis, Tegeler, and a few others. There are no U.S. manufacturers we know of at this stage that make aquarium versions of this light, but they can be found in industrial finish.

15. 7. Longevity of Spectrum

Lighting is not a simple subject, and it seems that there is always something else that will have to have to be taken into consideration.

Although we have already defined several criteria that need to be met, there is one more, and it is an important one, from the financial stand point : how long will the spectrum of the bulb last ?

How long does the bulb that we have selected maintain its Kelvin degree rating ? Indeed, if we spend several hundred dollars , on a good light, for how long can we expect it to give us the kind of light that we paid for originally?

Fluorescent tubes are notorious for losing their spectrum rather quickly. That is the reason why you will often find recommendations on changing them every six months.

Power Stars lose only 6 percent of their spectrum over the life of the bulb, whicht is about 3 to 3.5 years, and that is extremely good.

Most fluorescent tubes need to be changed every 5 to 6 months. High output Color Classers need to be changed about every 9 months.

The latter bulbs are also made in VHO (very high output) but the reason we did not recommend them is because they do not meet the longevity criterion. You would have to change them about every 3 to 4 months.

So our two choices, HO Color classers and Osram Power Stars, meet this criterion as well. Our third choice, the new 5000 Kelvin degree bulb that was just being introduced by Energy Savers at the time of this writing, has proven to be an excellent choice as well.

In fact, with these 3 types of bulbs, every Hobbyist should be able to come up with a solution for his or her tank, that is both efficient, and within budget.

Keep in mind that we are not interested in any specific make, but that we are looking for a Kelvin degree rating. It may very well be, and more than likely is, that other companies make fluorescent high output tubes of a similar spectrum. You may of course use those as well.

15.8. Philips Actinic Lighting

Actinic lighting, especially the 03 type, which is the one most commonly used, is not an aquarium light.

Although it is not supposed to contain UV, it does. A quick look at its spectral chart will convince you. You must therefore use it with a UV shield, or you may risk burning corals and other lifeforms (this applies to the Power Stars as well. They need an ultraviolet filter).

If you are interested in the "blue" portion of that light, you can use any of the 3 lights that we have recommended so far. They contain a large portion of blue in their spectrum.

Looking at a chromaticity chart will convince you of that.

Chromaticity is another way of describing the color of a bulb or light. Two figures are given, an X value and a Y value. You plot their intersection on a chart, and you can visually determine in what region your bulb's light emittance is.

These charts can be obtained from both manufacturers and from electrical supply places.

A 7500 Kelvin degree spectrum for instance, corresponds to an X of 0.299 and a Y of 0.313. If both numbers were 0.200, you would have blue light.

An X of 0.300 and a Y of 0.300 is a white light with a very high degree of blue in it, and would have a Kelvin degree rating in the vicinity of 10,000°.

There are several types of actinic lighting, and for more information on them, we refer you to The Marine Fish and Invert Reef Aquarium book, in the lighting section.

Although some Advanced Hobbyists, and authors such as for instance John Burleson, recommend actinic lighting strongly, we remain of the opinion that the blue portion of the spectrum that we need is best obtained by using bulbs that give off this blue as part of their spectrum, and not by using bulbs that concentrate just on that color.

And to those of you who are using these bulbs I am not saying "you are wrong", but I am saying "you can do better".

Time will tell how the majority of the hobbyists will end up ligthing their Reef tanks, and my personal feeling is that it will be by a much greater use of high intensity discharge bulbs, with high Kelvin degree ratings.

15.9. The Proposed Ideal Lighting Set-up

Here is what we feel would be the best way to light your tank, without going to extremes, but still fulfilling all the requirements that we set forth :

1. Use high intensity discharge metal halides,

2. Use as many lights as required to obtain Lux readings of 16 000+,

3. Use only bulbs with ratings of 5500 Kelvin degrees or more,

4. Select bulbs with very high color rendition indexes,

5. Stagger the on and off of the bulbs,

6. Make sure that no heat transfer occurs,

7. Use ultraviolet shielding if necessary,

8. Run your light for a total of 12-14 hours per day,

9. Vent the light hood -if you are using one,

10. If your system includes fluorescent tubes, change them regularly.

15.10. An Experiment in Lighting A Reef

As already mentioned in an earlier section, we recently ran a test on a 150 gallon Reef Tank using much higher light intensities than are normally recommended.

We used metal halides in the 4300 Kelvin degree rating, for a total of 1250 watts of light (We now use 5500 K bubls from Energy Savers).

All lights are on a staggered on and off computorized system, with dimming. Lights are on for 12 hours a day, with the full 1250 watts being on for at least 8 hours.

Notwithstanding this extremely high lighting, not a single coral was "burnt". The reason we mention this, is that there have been both rumors and articles circulating that metal halides burn your corals.

We can confirm that this is not, we repeat not, the case. Of course all our light have protective glass in front of them to shield the animal life from dangerous UV lighting.

We are not using a single watt of actinic lighting !

Within a matter of hours of making this change, we could both see, and measure, the amount of oxygen being produced as a result of increased photosynthesis.Bubbles were rising from many locations.

Here are some numbers indicative of how well this tank now runs :

- Dissolved oxygen 11+ mg/l,
- pH 8.0,
- carbonate hardness 20,
- redox potential around 390 mid-day, higher inthe the morning,
- nitrates 0.00 ppm,
- phosphate 0.05 ppm or less,
- Temperature 75 degrees Fahrenheit.

No significant outbreaks of micro-algae have been observed. All macro-algae however grow in a manner we have never observed before. Ulva lactuta is not only as large as a small lettuce, but it is sprouting up in many other areas.

Codium species are growing all over the tank. In fact from non-existent, or not visible, the algae are now from half to three quarter inches long and a quarter inch in diameter.

Valonia species have spread to at least 14 different locations in the tank, and the size of thebubbles is nearly that of a golf ball.

Many types of as yet unidentified macro-algae are sprouting up from rocks all over the tank.

The so-called sea-mat algae, that usually dies after a few weeks in your tank, had grown from about 4 inch long strings, to some that are at least 18 inches long. You can in fact see them in the photograph on the cover of the book.

Elegance corals, anemones, rock anemones and other such, are larger than we have ever seen them.

It is really fascinating to see the changes that occur and the new lifeforms that appear.

We thank Leo Wojcik for undertaking this experiment. We will be watching what happens.

Thepicture of the anemome on the front cover of the book, was taken while we were running this high intensity light.

We will keep reporting in **Marine Reef** how the tank evolves.

Coralife frozen food in handy and easy to use cube pack

Part Two

Instrumentation

and

Equipment

Pendant light for fresh and saltwater aquariums
by Energy Savers Unlimited

NEW! Coralife 50/50 Fluorescent lamps

50% 6000K daylight, 50% Actinic.
Internal reflector. High intensity.
Uses standard 20, 30 and 40 watt ballasts.
Standard BI-PIN connectors.
Brings out the colorful beauty of corals and fish.
Available in 24", 36" and 48".

1. Observations before we begin

1.1 Equipment

It is highly likely that you too will be using a considerable amount of equipment and instrumentation on your tank. You will therefore need to think about :

• the physical space required to install the equipment, and mounting space for the instruments,

• the timing of acquiring all, or part of it. Whether or not you will be buying all of it at once, or in a staggered fashion,

• making provisions for installing some of the equipment at a later date, if that will be the case. Indeed this seems to be what most Hobbyists do, and understanbly so, because of the expense involved,

• making sure that any holes, or water inlets and outlets, that will be required in the tank, and in the filter, are drilled at the time you set up your tank, as once it is running, only taking it down would allow you to do so. Even then it will not be all that simple, as you may have to cut pipes, dismantle some equipment, and so on,

• ensuring that enough electrical wall outlets, and a large enough circuit are available for all the equipment, pumps, and other implements that you will use.

Think this through carefully, as you will need more outlets than you think. Pumps, instruments, airpumps, lights, power heads, heating, in short, anything that needs electricity to run will all require an outlet.

This could be anywhere from half a dozen to a dozen or more outlets, depending on the sophistication of your system,

• acquiring the knowledge necessary to operate and run all this equipment and the instrumentation,

• and understanding what needs to be done when things go wrong with them. E.g. pH meter with an erroneous reading, what do you do?

Consider the following instrument array, all of which can be meaningfully used on a reef tank :

• Reactors to remove Phosphates - Dephosphators
• pH metering and controlling equipment
• Redox potential metering and controlling equipment
• Conductivity measuring equipment (to determine salinity)
• Lux measurement (light intensity in a given spot)
• Dissolved oxygen metering equipment
• Foam fractionnators, protein skimmers
• Carbon dioxide reactors
• Oxygen reactors and diffusers
• Activated carbon reactor
• Fine filters
• Micron Filters
• Sub-micron filters
• Reverse osmosis filters
• Ozone generators and
• Ozone reaction chambers
• Carbon dioxide dispensing equipment
• Automatic water changers
• Dosing pumps to add fertilizers, trace elements, etc
• Peristaltic pumps to add small amounts of water
• Metering pumps
• Air flow meters
• Water flow meters
• Photo meters (determines the exact color of a test solution after you added chemicals, digitally indicates a number, refers to a chart which

interprets that number to give highly accurate results (this is a very advanced piece of equipment)

- Denitrators
- Carbon chambers
- Advanced trickle filters
- Solenoid valves
- Electrically actuated ball valves
- Timers
- Gauges for CO_2
- Gauges for oxygen diffusion
- Float switches
- Various types of valves, includes Ball, check, chemical, needle...
- Power heads
- Pulsators,
- Water return alternator, sometimes called a wavemaker
- Electronic, digital low voltage heating equipment
- Cooling units
- Turbulence makers
- Refractometer
- Diatamaceous earth filters
- Molecular absorption filters
- Resins in cannisters or bags
- Ion specific filters
- Tangential flow filters
- Salinometer
- De-ionizers
- Ion specific Electrodes
- Ultraviolet light
- Data loggers
- Computer software monitoring conditions
- Various types of lighting, e.g. fluorescent (including high output), metal halide, and perhaps actinic lighting
- A wide range of tests, inlcuding less common ones, such as carbon dioxyde, dissolved oxygen, residual ozone, phosphate, iron, biological oxygen demand etc..

Quite an assortment as you can see ! And there are likely to be more of them as time goes on, and technology improves and brings us more equipment to enable us to keep our water quality at higher and higher levels, until we can some day computer control the aquarium and duplicate the biotope around the real Reefs completely.

That day is not far off, as the technology is already available. In fact we know of at least two Hobbyists in our immediate vicinity who already do so. Leo Wojcik, one of them, has in addition included a software package he wrote himself, to automatically raise his lights in the morning and dim them at night, over a period of several hours.

1.2 Cost

It is probably neither feasible nor desirable to spend the required funds to acquire all these instruments right at the start, except perhaps, if it is a professional installation in a restaurant, or in the lobby of a building or similar place.

You may however want to make some projections, and decide up-front which ones you are likely to use, so that you can make the necessary provisions now.

This will allow you to install that equipment without too much effort at a later date, and without having to dismantle all, or part, of your tank when you eventually get ready to modify your system.

A spreadsheet approach would be a good way to do this. If you own a PC, or a Macintosh computer, it will be that much easier. The more up-front planning you complete, the less likely you are to have surprises later on, when such surprises will be tough to deal with.

Setting up a basic Reef Tank, one outfitted with just the basic equipment , will cost more than you think.

Consider too, that many pieces of equipment require additional implements, for example pumps, and the cost rises fast beyond what you had estimated it to be.

Get prices for the items that you feel you want to start with, get prices for the other items too, and then lay out a course of action. What will you buy and when ?

Some of the equipment is necessary right from the start :

- a tank
- a stand
- a trickle filter
- with packing material
- a pump
- a float switch
- heating
- lights
- and valves and tubing or hard pipe, glue, cement etc..

Other equipment, perhaps the more advanced type, can be acquired later, e.g. a foam fractionnator, a redox potential controller, an ozonizer, a dissolved oxygen reactor, water current alternators, etc...

In our experience, carefully planning all what is needed for your tank, and the expenses associated with buying and setting up that equipment, is the most sensible way to go and results in better type systems.

1.3 Conclusion

Plan carefully now. Buy some equipment, install it, then acquire some more pieces and install those, etc...

Doing so will be easy if you have drilled the holes that will be required, installed fittings that may be necessary, and placed unions and tee-connections where you will need them at a later date, once you acquire more equipment.

All you have to do for now is cap off those that are open, that you are not using , with standard PVC fittings.

Once an aquarium is running it is very difficult to make modifications to the tank and the filter, especially if the modifications required are below the water level.

This is one more reason for careful, advance, planning. It is also the reason why I insist so much on this subject. Believe me, I too learned the hard way.

We would not worry, at this point, about which fish and which invertebrates that will be placed in the tank. As long as it is a Reef tank, you will find enough recommendations in this (Advanced Reef Kee[ing II due out later in 1989 ISBN 0-945777-02-7) and other books.

And we are still far away from actually placing animals in the tank anyway. Later parts of this book deal with those, and Advanced Reef Keeping II, which will be out later in 1989, will cover those subjects extensively.

To be able to plan correctly, you must of course understand the purpose of the equipment that will be used, know how it works and how it is hooked up into the system.

A few phone calls to the manufacturers of that equipment, or a visit to pet stores who carry it is therefore certainly recommended.

A second, or first perhaps, look at the videotapes that we produced seems indicated as well, as all the equipment that is discussed in this book is actually shown, and its function explained.

Following is a suggested approach :

• Decide on the size of the tank.

• Select a filter and get its dimensions.

• Make a drawing to scale. The larger you make it, the easier it will be for you to determine what extra parts you will need to complete the installation.

• Lay out the filter and the equipment on that drawing.

• As you draw representations of the equipment, make notes of the pieces of pipe, valves, fittings and so on that you will need. Keep a cumulative total on a separate sheet.

• During the design, decide on where the water intakes and returns for that equipment will have to be located. This will enable you to drill all the required holes in advance.

• Allow for one extra water out take from the filter. Include one additional bulkhead fitting and a PVC cap to shut if off. You may not need it now, but as you improve upon the system, or decide to add some new item, you will be glad the hole is already there.

• Go through the design at least twice to reconfirm that your notes are correct.

• Only then get the filter and the parts.

• Lay everything out on the floor in the way that is will be installed. Buy any missing pieces.

• You should now be ready to install all the pieces without having to run back to the store to get more items; or have to stop working till the following day because you found out you needed an extra piece after store closing time.

Float Switch Mechanical

Tri-Pure™ High Absorption Filter
The Tri-Pure™ processes 50 gal. per day with **NO WASTE** water up to 3000 gallons before cartridge replacement. Removes organic contaminates, pesticides, phosphates, nitrates, heavy metals, chlorine and chloramines.

2. Overview of the Equipment

2.1 Introduction :

It is not the intent of this book to cover all the equipment that can be used in real detail. For that we refer you to "The Marine Fish and Invert Reef Aquarium" book (Thiel 1988 Aardvark Press).

The latter is in its fifth printing at the time of this writing and is still meeting with a very large demand. It is also available from Aardvark Press, publishers of this book and Marine Reef, the Newsletter.

That book and "Advanced Reef Keeping", are two companion books that describe just about everything that you will need to know about Reef tanks.

We will review the various pieces of equipment that we will use, both in this part of Advanced Reef Keeping and in Part Four, when we are describing how we are using them to set up our 150 gallon tank.

We remind you that you can also visually follow the exact way that this is done by acquiring the videotapes that have been produced. For information on how to get those you can call Thiel•Aqua•Tech, or

Aardvark Press (see Appendices for useful telephones and addresses). Four of seven planned tapes had been released at the time this book was written. The last three should be out by March 1989.

Although we are using as much equipment as we felt was necessary and helpful - equipment that made sense we mean- that does not mean that you have to install all of it to be successful with your Reef.

A lot of it is required, e.g. filters, skimmers, ozone, air dryer, but there are other pieces that are optional; whether you use them or not depends mainly on your budget and planning, and how sophisticated you want your system to be.

That is something only you can decide. This book gives you all the options, you select the ones that you feel you want to install and incorporate in your own Reef. Your budget will determine that.

You must also keep in mind that we have tried to automate as much of the functions as we possibly could. This required additional instruments, relays, solenoids and reactors. This may not be what "you" want to do. Indeed a number of these functions can be performed manually for far less.

Most Hobbyists will probably want to go that route, especially in the beginning, and may wish to introduce more automation at a later date. Doing so will not diminish the efficiency of your system, providing that you actually "perform" whatever manual function needs to be performed, and do so whenever it needs to be performed.

2.2 Filter : Wet dry system, Trickle Filter :

Labeling the newer type of filters "Wet - Dry" is a misnomer, as far as I am conerned. Tell me where the "dry" part is, and I will change my mind! All parts are wet, in fact, trickle is not even the correct name either.

In sewage treatment, where these filters originated many many years ago, they are called either ammonia towers, or trickling filters.

It should be pretty obvious from what you have read so far, that we will be using such a trickle filter. As far as Reef Keeping is concerned, that is the best type of filter presently available.

Only BioMesh™ filters come close to their efficiency. These filters are described as well, later in this part of the book. We also described them in rather great detail in The Marine Fish and Invert Reef Aquarium book and in Marine Reef.

We will use the model sold by Dupla Usa - Thiel•Aqua•Tech, and manufactured for them, by Summit Aquatics of Fulton Missouri.

This acrylic unit, developed by Mike Helton and David Nikodym, has given satisfaction to many many Hobbyists. It is not a filter however made by Dupla Germany, but it is based on the German filtration technology of Nollman Aquaristik, who also manufacture for Dupla Aquaristik, since Dupla does not make its own filters.

It is very professionally built, slow cured in the oven for extra strong bonds, using special bonding agents, not off the shelf solvents which have no long time resistance to the pressure that build up inside the acrylic material.

It is based on the German technology, but at an American price. It is undoubtly the best filter on the market, and comes in 3 versions, holding respectively 10, 15, and 20 gallons of Bioballs, or other packing materials.

The unit we are using has 2 removable compartments to hold packing material for biological filtration. Each compartment can hold up to 10.5 gallons of material, for a possible total of 21.00

In our case we will be setting the unit up with one container filled with Bioballs™, and one compartment set up with another medium, one that is not commercially available yet.

It has approximately the same surface area as Bioballs™, meaning around 80,000 cm² per 20 liter of Bioballs™, but is about 25 percent less expensive, and will be sold, as far as we have been told, under the name "Bio•Techs". It will be introduced to the market sometime in 1989.

We are using that new material in conjunction with Bioballs™, because we want to demonstrate that this polypropylene packing can give superior results too, and test at the same time how it affects the biological filter and the oxygenation of the tank water.

Our filter will thus contain a total of 20 gallons equivalent of packing material, for a total usable biological filtration surface area of around 585 square feet. This is divided 50/50 between the two materials.

The picture of the filter on the other page demonstrates its basic characteristics. It has two sumps, which are connected in the middle by an extra compartment, with 2 areas for foam pads, and space to place a container of carbon on the top.

We will not worry here about the amount of carbon, as we will be running a separate carbon filter (see further for more details), as well as a different type of chemical filtration : nl. a molecular absorption filter housing, made by Poly Bio Marine® of New Jersey.

The unit is 20 inches wide, approximately 22.5 inches tall -including the top fittings- and about 35 inches long. It should fit under most stands that are made for 150 and larger tanks. Check before buying, as some manufacturers make narrower stands.

We already pointed out the need to plan carefully, and this is one area where you need to be particularly attentive, or you may end up with a filter that does not fit under your stand !

Although we are using this particular filter, you may use one the many filters that are now offered for sale. And there are many !

Some of these include the filters sold by :

• Summit Aquatics
• Energy Savers
• Reef Lake Systems
• MTC Marine Technical Concepts
• Sea Reef
• BioReef Enterprises
• Route 4 Marine Technology
• Oceanarium
• Ocean Reef Stystems
• DLS Aquatics
• Poisson Filters and Accessories
• The Reef System
• Sea Kleer Reefs
• Acrylic Creations
• Amiracle
• and others still   (names used refer to manufacturers, some may be trade marked)

Although we have listed quite a few manufacturers, this is not meant to be an endorsement of any specific filter. We have worked with and tested the following, which we can recommend : (no specific order of preference)

• Dupla Usa Inc.

- Thiel•Aqua•Tech
- Route 4
- Energy Savers
- Sea Kleer Reefs
- Summit Aquatics
- and the German Dupla - Nollmann filter which, as far as we know, is no longer imported.

When selecting a filter from the very wide range that is now available,

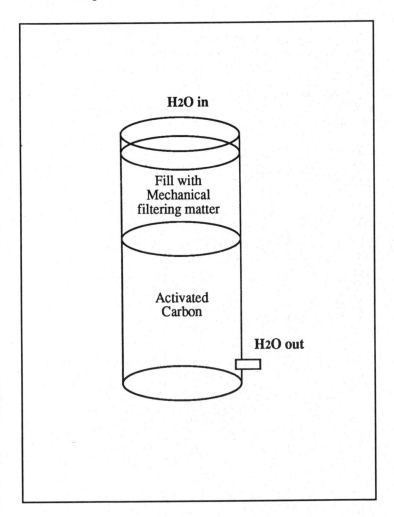

look for the following important features :

• the filter must be large enough to hold all of the material that you will be using as packing for biological filtration. The Marine Fish and Invert Reef Aquarium book explains in detail how to go about this.

First you determine the amount of surface area you will need for your tank, then you select a material, then you select a filter. You may want to refer to pages 69 to 73 in that book. There are also photographs in that book of other filter models.

• look at the quality of the workmanship. All bonded joints should be clean, without air bubbles. The acrylic (if that is what the filter is made of), should be cut to the exact sizes, without sharp edges, etc...

It should be a quality unit. And good quality is something that you can see immediately. If attention has been paid to detail, you know that the important parts have been taken care of too.

• and most important : the sump must be large. You will need to place various other items in the sump. Larger sumps will make adding pieces of equipment that much easier. Plus that additional water increases the overall size of your system, and this can be important. 5 to 6 gallons is probably a minimum to look for.

• the water inlet into the trickling part of the filter should be at leat 1 inch in size. This will allow you to run the kind of water flows that are required through trickle filters and Marine Reef Aquariums in general.

• the water outlet (the areas where you attach the pump) should be at least one inch in diameter too. This will allow you to use strong pumps such as for instance the Iwaki pumps sold by T•A•T, or the Aqua Pump manufactured by Aquarium Sales and Services, and now distributed nationwide.

If you run a large tank and plan to use more than one pump, you may have to add additional holes yourself by drilling appropriately sized holes in the acrylic sump, or in the glass.

Few such filters in glass exist though. Dupla Aquaristik used to sell one several years ago; Dupla USA was importing it from Germany but no longer does.

In fact, with the number of filters now manufactured in the United States, you should not have any problem finding one that suits your need, and tank size.

2.3 Pumps required for the System :

What we describe hereafter are the items required for the set up that we are demonstrating in this book and in our Videotapes.

You may not need the same number, and of course not necessarily the same sizes. This is for you to decide, and you need to adjust, both the quantity and the strength of the pumps based on the aquarium that you have, or will, set up yourself.

We will need pumps for the following functions :

• Main pumps for returning water to the aquarium : two Iwaki model TH55, as modified by T•A•T, to make them salt water safe for long term use.

We will use these strong pumps to return water to the aquarium, but also to create a direct return to the top of the trickle filter, by means of a Tee-fitting that is equipped with ball valves on either side.

This a by-pass assembly that we will not use in the normal course of running the tank, but that can be used when we want to recirculate water from the sump back to the top of the filter, and then back to the sump, by-passing the tank altogether.

This could be the case if we wanted to do some major work in the tank, and needed to disconnect the filters. Running the filter, on itself so to speak, would then ensure that we do not lose our biological filter while we do the work.

• Protein Skimmer : Aqua Pump , a greatly modified Grundfos pump, now totally saltwater safe. We are using the three speed model that can develop up to 1100 gallons per hour. Since we will not need that much water to go through the skimmer, we will run that pump on its second speed.

• Reserve vat for automatic water changing : Eheim Hobby pump, submersed in a polypropylene vat, 35 gallons in size and sold by Walchem, in Waltham, Massachussetts.

For the various reactors that will be installed we require :

• CO_2 reactor   : Eheim Hobby pump
• Oxygen reactor   : Eheim Hobby pump
• Carbon reactor   : Eheim Hobby pump

• Internal alternating circulation is obtained by means of a timer, made by Grasslin, and a relay that switches from one pump to the other every 2.5 minutes. This will become clearer as we progress through setting up the tank.

• Top-off of sump of trickle filter : one small top-off container, placed above the trickle filter. This device functions on the same principle as water dispensers in offices do. More on this later.

• Addition of trace-elements, vitamins and fertilizer : metering pump, Tech•Doser model. The mix is drawn from a 15 gallon vat, which gives us a supply of about 4 weeks of the mixture.

For an explanation on how to prepare this mixture, refer to the Marine Fish and Invert Aquarium book. It is reviewed there in great detail. In our own tank we use Tech•Macro•Algae food, Tech•VitaTrace•Complex vitamins, and alternatively Dick Boyd's Vita Chem mix (Marine). The mixture also contains Tech•Reef KH•Builder and Tech•Reef•Elements, a trace element mix.

• X-Nitrate™ reactor : by-pass off the main pumps, by means of Tee-fittings. We try to push as much water as possible through this reactor, as this is the way that X-nitrate™ works best.

If you install such a reactor you must push a lot of water through the X-nitrate. If installed properly it will bring your Nitrates down to about 2 to 3 ppm. This product, sold by Thiel•Aqua•Tech, comes in units that treat 50, 200, 500 and 1000 gallons of water. More on this later, in the section where we are actually installing this unit.

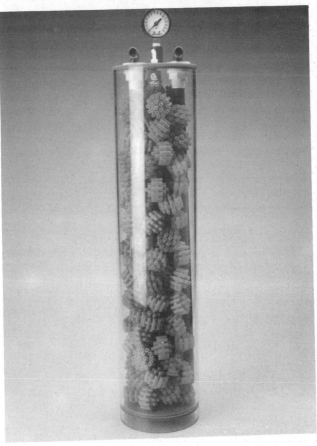

O2 Reactor

• Cooling unit : run with its seperate pump, the same one as the one that returns the water behind the coral rock formation in the tank. This is again a modified Iwaki Model TH 55. The unit is made by Aquarium Sales and Services.

• Two Hagen Aquaclear 800 Powerheads. One on each side of the tank.

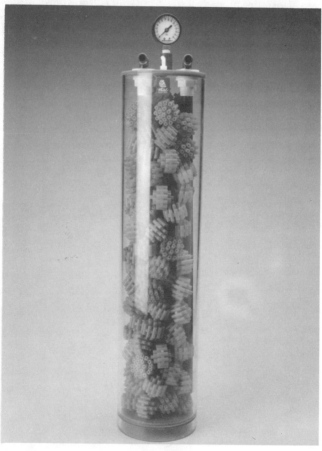

O3 Reactor

Both do not run at the same time. We use a solid state switching device, a turbulence maker we call it, made by Thiel•Aqua•Tech.

One Powerhead runs for about 2 minutes, then the turbulence maker switches the current over to the other one, which runs for two minutes, etc...

This device is also outfitted with an over-ride switch which can cut both Powerheads out, but automatically switches them back on - you decide how long the pumps are off. The maximum off time is 10 minutes.

We use that feature during feeding. We add the food, push the button, and we can walk away, knowing that in 8 minutes (that is what we set if for) the powerheads will start running, and alternating again.

• Besides the above pumps, we use by-passes on two water return lines to run our denitrification units. We run two units, not because two are needed, but because we are testing several units as well as several nutrient formulas.

This has allowed us to perfect the existing, traditional, models somewhat, to make them easier to use and maintain, and take some of the guess work out of operating them.

Leo Wojcik has done some ground breaking work in this area, and we wish to acknowledge his work and contributions here.

2.4 Float Switches :

Several float switches will be required to make the system both safe and efficient to operate.

Hobbyists have not really used float switches extensively, but in Reef systems and with trickle filters, they definitely should.

• two float switches control the main pumps to prevent them from sucking the sump dry, or running dry altogether.

These are float switches for low level control. We will be using the Dupla mercury switches and the Thiel•Aqua•Tech switches. There is really no difference between the two, except that they are made by different companies, and that the latter is made in the USA. Both are of the very reliable mercury type.

• one float switch controls the addition of water from a vat with fresh water, and functions as the top-off function.

We will use reverse osmosis prepared water, hooked into the main house water line. Every time someone uses water in the house, some R.O. water is added to the reserve vat (as indicated earlier, we de-ionize some of that water to prepare our additive mixture)

The submersible pump kicks in when the water level in the sump goes down by more than 3/16 of an inch, adds some freshwater to top-off and compensate for evaporation, and then shuts off again when the water level is back where we want it to be.

• one float switch controls the automatic water changer. It shuts off the pump should the level in the sump of the trickle filter rise too high, due to clogging of the drain pipe.

This particular float switch obviously controls a high position of the water, and not a low, as the other float switches do.

• we will not use float switches on the pumps running the various reactors, as the switches controlling the main pumps will ensure that there is always enough water in the sump of the trickle filter to run those pumps/reactors.

• we have also installed a T•A•T float switch on the water changer, on the vat that is, to prevent it from running dry. That switch is attached to a audible alarm, which tells us, should we have forgotten to look at it, that the vat needs to be replenished.

• depending on how you set up your own system, you may need more, or less, float switches. The key is to think your system "through", and install float switches in each line that may either result in pump damage if anything went wrong, or may cause water to overflow if a pump was not stopped in time.

As we set the tank up, and explain what we are doing, this will become clearer to you.

2.5 Materials used inside the sump :

Besides the Bioballs™ and the similar packing material that we are using, in the biological filtration area (Bio•Techs), the following is required in the filter :

• fine filter pad, attached to pump intake mechanism (grey material in photo of trickle filter). This is a round foam cartridge type assembly through which all the water that gets into the pumps has to go.

This needs to be cleaned regularly, as it traps dirt, and will restrict the water flow and lower dissolved oxygen levels if you don't.

• one sponge filter compartment : we will use natural sponge. This will need to be cleaned at least once a week. This removes particulate matter from the water before it enters the actual front part of the sump, and gets into the pumps, through the foam cartridge described in the previous paragraph.

• one tray with activated carbon (Cora and/or Dupla) over which we will flow the water coming back from the protein skimmer (Thiel• Aqua•Tech) because we will be using ozone on this tank.

• the various electrodes that are attached to the meters that will be installed. This includes a pH regulator, a redox potential controller, an oxygen meter, and a conductivity meter.

We are in fact using several such meters, as will be explained later in Part 4 of the book.

• in your own system you may have more items that need to be placed in the sump. That is of course fine.

You will just have to make provision for this, and plan your work in such a manner that if holes are needed, you drill them before you actually set the system up, or at least before you start it up and fill it with water.

Additionally some Hobbyists place submersible pumps in the sump of their filter, and space for these has to be foreseen as well.

2.6. Tools and such that you will need :

You do not really need a lot of tools to set up a reef tank. You will however need a number of specialized items.

It may not be worth buying them; check whether you can possibly rent them from places that do such business.

Here is a quick overview :

- a set of regular flat screwdrivers,
- probably a set of Philips head screwdrivers,
- silicone and a silicone glue gun,
- acrylic bonding paste, e.g. Weldon 4 or PS 30 (Cadillac Plastics),

- a plexiglass cutter,
- a T-square
- a good tape measure
- a glass drill, if you plan to drill your tank. Tube drills and the drilling compound (grit) are also required of course.

It is not recommended that you drill your tank yourself, unless you have experience with drilling glass. Practice on scrap glass before actually drilling your own. Get advice from someone who has already done it. Get help if you can. And remember "tempered glass" **cannot** be drilled, it will shatter.

How to drill was illustrated in detail in Tape 1 of the series of Videos that we produced on how to set up your Reef Tank.

- you will also need hole saws to drill through acrylic. Hardware stores carry such saws in sets.

- hose clamps if you use flexible tubing, so that you can tighten the tubing in place.

- several rolls of Teflon™ tape.

- PVC glue and primer if you use hard pipe.

- plumber's wrenches,

- a lot of paper towels to wipe up excess glue, cement, etc...

- an electric drill,

- a pair of glasses to wear while you are working, and if you are allergic to chemicals and gasses, a special mask (silicone contains acetic acid, PVC cement contains MEK, both are irritants),

- of course, depending on how you set up your aquarium, there may be more.

I have found that the best way to ensure that you can continue working while setting up the tank, -even on a Sunday, when you can't quickly run out to get that missing piece or tool- is to think the procedures through and write down what you will need, and get everything before starting.

This was not meant to be an exhaustive list, but just a quick overview of the more important tools you will need, the latter being influenced mostly by how you set your tank up.

Drilling :

Still the best way to proceed when drilling, is to first lay out all the holes you will need on a piece of paper, and then draw them on the glass, so you know exactly where to drill.

Make sure that you have enough space between the side, or/and the back of the tank, to slide your fittings through, and then tighten them. Fittings indeed extend over the edge of the actual hole.

Measure real carefully. Once the hole is there, you are stuck with it. You could always reclose it by glueing a piece of glass over it, but a little planning will save you a lot of aggravation. Besides, the end result will be much nicer looking.

It is not really possible to describe, clearly, and in an easy to understand way, all the steps that are involved in drilling a tank. We therefore refer you to Tape 1 of the 7 tapes that we have made, as it shows you in great detail what needs to be done, and how to do it.

If you do not want to buy the tapes, you may be able to rent them from one of your local Pet Stores.

We have, at the end of Advanced Reefkeeping, included a special discount coupon for buyers of this book. This will let you order our tapes for $ 35.00 less than the regular price, or a total of $ 124.99, for tapes one to four.

2.7. Valves and Fittings

Keep in mind that the nominal size of the pipe, or the sizes of the fittings, are always smaller than the actual hole that needs to be drilled. This is because of the thickness of the pipe, respectively fitting, is not part of the size description. Only the internal diameter (I.D.) or the nominal pipe thread (N.P.T.) is given.

What we mean is that to install one inch pipe, you will need a hole in the trickle filter, that can take a one inch bulkhead fitting. The hole required for such a fitting may be one and a half inch to one and five eights inch, depending on the manufacturer of the fitting.

This applies to whatever you are trying to do. Always make sure that

you know the ID -internal diameter- and OD -external diameter- of the
fittings or pipe, or flexible hose that you are using.

• We will need several water out-takes for the various reactors that we
are running, in fact, one for each. We drill a hole to hold a half inch
bulkhead fitting : (a fitting that goes into the hole in the filter, on one end,
and then is tightened by means of a ring : see "The Marine Fish and Invert Reef
Aquarium" for a detailed explanation of all these fittings).

Drilling in acrylic is really easy. All you need is a good electric drill and
a few hole saw bits. Best for you, would be to get a whole set, as that will
probably be the least expensive way to buy them.

Also, since you may need to drill several holes of different sizes, you will
probably need more than one size anyway.

• An additional hole for the water returning from the skimmer : make
that at least one inch or better. This way, any backing up of water inside
the skimmer will be prevented. The latter is a "real" requirement, as,
if the skimmer backs up while you are away, it will probably overflow.

• Of course holes for the one inch main pump bulkheads are required
as well. Since we will be using two pumps that alternate, we will need
two such holes. As we explained elsewhere already, this can be done
with just one hole and a Tee-fitting but it is better to use two holes.

• If you are using an automatic water changing and an automatic top-
off system, you will need one hole for each of those too, although you
can technically just use hose and guide it in the sump, from the top of
the filter, without making a hole.

Again this will become clearer when we describe, in more detail, how
we are actually setting the whole system up, in Part Four.

• Look carefully at the filter, and you will discover that we have also
made one hole each for the two float switches which are in the sump.

Before drilling holes, measure the fittings that you will use. Not all
fittings have the same outside diameter (O.D.). Different manufacturers make different thicknesses (this is unfortunate, as it would be much
simpler if they all used standard sizing).

In each of the holes a fitting is placed and then firmly screwed in to
make it water tight. Hose and pipe that go from these fittings to the
actual pumps and reactors will be installed later.

2.8. Meter - Controller for pH

We all know how important total stability of all water quality parameters is for saltwater tanks, and more so for Marine Reef Tanks. One of the key factors in that stability is the pH level.

Besides keeping the pH at a **constant** level, we also need to maintain it at the **right** level.

Generally recommended pH levels are between 8.00 and 8.25. This is achieved by using a good quality salt, and subsequently monitoring the pH and adding buffers, as required, to maintain the pH where we have decided we want it to be.

Buffers -and the alkalinity- are those compounds that neutralize the acids (e.g. organic acids from the breakdown of protein - amino acids and others), and result in the pH going down slowly over a period of time, as the buffering capacity of the water, meaning its ability to neutralize acidity, gets depleted.

This happens as soon as you place animals in the tank, and there is no real way to avoid this. The buffer has to be replenished continuously, and although this can be achieved, in part, by regular water changes

Dual Controller by Sandpoint sold by TAT

it is better managed by adding special compounds to the water on a regular basis.

This can be risky, especially if you are not exactly sure about what the compounds you are using can do to the water's pH and chemistry. You must therefore make sure that you buy "KH" building fluid or tablets, and not products that contain hydroxides or pure carbonates.

It is also known that during the cycling period of the filter, the pH will have a tendency to go down because of bacterial activity, which generates carbon dioxide as a by product.

This is normal and you should not worry about it. As a result, pH and carbonate hardness adjustments should be made only after the tank has had a chance to cycle.

To increase the buffer, you could add a mixture of powdered carbonates and bi-carbonates of calcium and magnesium, but that is both cumbersome, and not as easy to accomplish as it sounds.

Indeed, even though these compounds can easily be bought in health food sotres for example, the fact that they are in powdered form makes it difficult to introduce them into the water without clouding the tank.

Neither of the compounds dissolve easily, or only minimally if the pH is brought down, or they may raise the pH too much, too rapidly, and as already indicated will cloud the tank's water and put unsightly deposits on all rocks in the aquarium.

Pure calcium carbonate and magnesium carbonate do not dissolve easily at all. Sodium carbonate, which does dissolve very easily, will raise the pH very quicky (to 10.00 or more), even by adding only small amounts).

Calcium hydroxide, although it will raise the buffer - the carbonate hardness - rapidly and a great deal, will also cause your pH to rise over 10.00 which makes it impractical to use, of course. You could treat it first with carbon dioxide, to lower its impact on the pH of your tank, but the procedure required to do so is not something most Hobbyists want to get involved with.

Bicarbonates on the other hand, although they dissolve more easily, will still cloud the water, except for sodium bicarbonate (baking soda).

It is much simpler to use commercially available products, such as the

KH Generator sold by Dupla, Route 4's Carbonate hardness builder, Marine Buffer by SeaChem, and the newer, and highly efficient Tech• KH Builder sold by Thiel•Aqua•Tech (a liquid which can be added using a doser pump, on a continuous basis, full strength or diluted).

There may, additionally, be other products available in your area, and if this is so, you should check their composition before using them.

They should preferably not contain any colloidial products that break the surface resistance of the water, as that will result in excessive foaming which, in turn, will result in constant adjustments to your protein skimmer (foam fractionnator) being necessary.

Still other ways exist : e.g. liquid buffer solutions are sold that contain some form of Hydroxide. This will temporarily solve your problem, but cannot be considered a long term treatment .

Additionally all hydroxides will rapidly raise your pH. Caclium hydroxide for instance should be treated with carbon dioxide first, to bring the pH down to acceptable levels.

Calcium carbonate, calcium hydroxide and CO_2 form calcium hydrogen carbonate when water is present. The latter dissolves easily, and will not raise your pH to much too high a level.

To know what the pH is, and to be able to follow how it is behaving, you will need a monitoring device of some sort. A pH meter or a pH controller is the answer.

The latter, as we shall see later, will also allow you to automatically dispense carbon dioxide into the tank, without danger, for the benefit of the macro-algae and the corals and their zooxanthellae.

Although these meters/controllers are much more expensive than some other instruments that are now offered for sale in hobby magazines, they are definitely worth the money.

In fact, most of the so-called pH pens are no more accurate than your good old chemical reagents. Those "pens" were developed for general measurement, to indicate a general range, not to make precise measurements, which is what you need.

A general measurement is of no use. It may be off by as much as 0.2 pH. You may as well use the reagent type tests which are a lot less expensive.

If you are prepared to invest in a pH meter, consider spending the extra money to get a pH controller, as that is what you will need, if you decide now, or at a later point, to use carbon dioxide as fertilizer for plants (macro-algae), and for the corals and their Zooxanthellae.

We will be using such a controllers (as you can see from the photo of instruments mounted on the panel).

2.9. Meter / Controller for Redox Potential

Although not all of you will want to spend the money for this unit, it is a must if you are using ozone. It gives you the security and total control that is needed to prevent the addition of excessive amounts of ozone to the tank's water.

Several redox potential controllers are now offered for sale :

• Dupla Model MP (announced for February or March 1989)
• Sanders (available now)
• Energy Savers (soon to be released)
• Thiel•Aqua•Tech (available first quarter 1989)
• Route 4 Marine Technology (available now)

The main benefit of using this instrument is that it gives you the ability to use ozone safely, providing you follow the instructions that come with it. It basically allows you to automate the control of the water quality by the addition of ozone to the skimmer.

For more information on how these units work together with a protein skimmer, and with an ozonizer, please also refer to The Marine Fish and Invert Reef Aquarium, and Tape 4 of the series that we produced - there is a one hour discussion just on redox potential on that tape.

Redox potential measurement is an important addition to tank maintenance and to water quality control; probably one of the more important ones to have entered the hobby for a long time to come.

It has been used successfully in Europe for quite a number of years now, but has only appeared in the United States since articles started being published in magazines such as FAMA in the last 12 months.

Although Sanders has had excellent redox potential units in commercial availability for several years, they have not been easy to find and may command a price not everyone is ready to pay.

My own company, Thiel•Aqua•Tech is therefore pleased to have introduced a unit that is made in the USA, and is about half the price of what the other ones cost. You should be able to get such a unit from your local marine pet store, starting the second quarter of 1989.

The quality of your Reef's water should be your major concern, and money invested in equipment that makes such control easier and more accurate and consistent, is money well spent.

The german Dupla unit, which will be available in February or March 1989, is a microprocessor based unit, highly accurate and reliable, and of the quality that you have become accustomed to from that German company.

Of course, as the use of redox potential instrumentation increases, look for more units to appear on the market and the prices to come down.

Most important is that the electrode that you use is one that is meant to be immersed permanently, that it can be used in salt water, is of the

There are many additives for saltwater and reef tanks.
Here is an overview of the Coralife products

"fast response" type, is easy to clean, and contains both a sensing and reference junction.

The better electrodes are referred to as Platinum, silver, silver chloride electrodes, and do not contain Calomel - mercurous chloride - which may leach in the water, is toxic (although exact quantities are not known), and is dissolved by alkalies in the water.

Of course the unit should switch your ozonizer on and off, perhaps have a few more features to it, such as controlling the maximum rate of change per day, or some other feature that is of help in assisting you in monitoring the water quality.

Look for units with a BNC jack, as most of the electrodes you will find advertised in the hobby use that type. Conversion plugs to go from US standard plugs to BNC types can be obtained, but they are expensive.

2.9.1 On using Ozone

Since the publication of The Marine Fish and Invert Reef Aquarium, we have recommended procedures to readers of **"Marine Reef"** on why ozone should be used, and how to use it, even if you do not have a Redox potential controller.

We thought that it would be of benefit to include these recommendations in this book too, for the sake of being as complete as we could be.

Later in this book we will cover ozone and how it should be used very extensively again.

The more you know about ozone, the better off you will be and the less likely you are to shun this highly efficient method of cleaning your aquarium water (improving the water quality).

One of the reasons for low water chemistry is the build up of organic material in the aquarium water. It has many sources, and it is continuously produced and added.

Feeding, dying-off algae and small life forms, fish excrements, uneaten food, dead fish, etc. all contribute to this condition.

This organic material breaks down, and via a long chain of chemical reactions and events, and some biological activity too, NH_3 and NH_4 are produced. Both these are then further broken down by the bacteria in our biological filter.

This whole process is explained in many books on marine fish keeping. Some of these include : Marine Tropical Aquarium Guide by Frank de Graaf, TFH Press; Seawater Aquariums, Stephen Spotte, John Wiley InterScience, and many others, including The Marine Fish and Invert Reef Aquarium, by Albert Thiel (1988). Check the bibliography at the end of this book for more recommendations and titles.

The whole process can be short circuited by using a" foam fractionnator", or protein skimmer, to remove some of these organics and other materials too, before they can actually start breaking down and pollute the water.

Because ozone is such a highly oxidative gas, with a redox potential of over 2000 mv, its chemical properties can be used to further enhance the performance of the foam fractionnator, or protein skimmer.

Ozone added to the air stream that bubbles up through the foam fractionnator, oxidizes - burns out so to speak - some of these materials, and thus prevents them from adding undesirable elements to the aquarium's water. This is a much more complicated process however.

What is always a problem for most hobbyists, is the quantity of ozone that needs to be used. And a problem it is, because there is no real correct answer.

Try understanding the following line of thought :

• if a lot of organics are present, and if such organics are produced on a continuous basis, you will need a lot of ozone to counter-act them, and break them down so they are removed by the skimming process,

• if you use a lot of ozone, and the quantity used is such that an overall reduction of organics occurs, the amount of ozone that you will need to use will gradually diminish as well, as less residual organics require less ozone,

• this leads to ozone use in diminishing quantities, until a balance is found between the amount of organics produced, and what it takes to remove them, when all other conditions in the tank remain equal of course,

• the latter means that this reasoning only applies for a given state of the tank. If you add fish or invertebrates, or feed more than usual, or algae die off, (and these are just a few reasons), you will again need more ozone.

As you can see, it is not really possible to suggest : use "x" mg per liter, or per gallon. One has to resort to other means of determining what the quantity to be used should be.

Since the water quality improves when ozone is used, and since this quality is measured as the Redox potential (at least that is a very convenient way of doing it), we can use the relative change in the millivolt reading (the redox potential) as a yardstick.

Proceed as follows :

• Install a redox potential controller. Set it for a 350 mv turn on-off level (setpoint).

• Wait sufficiently long to get an accurate reading. This may be several hours, depending on the instrument and the electrode that you are using.

Some meters may contain a buffering device to prevent the numbers on the display from jumping around, or from reacting too quickly to small changes. You must therefore give the meter sufficient time to react to the true redox potential of your tank.

• Note the millivolt reading. If your reading is already high, e.g. over 350 mv, you probably do not even need the ozone. In all likelihood however it will be lower, and the addition of ozone to the foam fractionnator will be beneficial.

• Switch on the ozonizer at the maximum setting, but not more than 1.5 mg per real gallon of water in your tank. For instance, a 150 gallon tank never really holds 150 gallons, especially if you have a lot of rocks and live rock in the tank.

This recommendation is necessary to make sure that, should you be using a very strong ozonizer, you do not make the redox potential change too rapidly, or over-ozonize and end up with residual ozone in the aquarium water.

• Let the system run for a while, and watch the effect of the ozonization on the redox potential. If you are using too little ozone the redox potential will either not go up at all, or it will go up extremely slowly.

• If this is the case, increase the amount of ozone you are using. If you are already at the maximum setting and the redox is still going up, you will just have to be patient as, over time, the redox potential will go up to the level that you need to achieve in a well running Reef tank.

• If you are at the maximum setting and the redox potential does not go up, your unit is too small for the amount of pollution that your tank generates. You will need to get a more powerful ozonizer.

• If you were not at the maximum yet, and you raised the output of the ozonizer further, check the redox potential regularly to determine if it is still rising, and how fast.

Additionally, perform a residual ozone test. Indeed, whatever the quantity of ozone that you use is, there should never be any residual ozone in the tank's water, as it is very detrimental to both fish and invertebrates.

Residual ozone testing is very simple. All you need to do is add a few drops of a liquid to a small sample of tank water and look for a color change. If yellow appears, you have residual ozone, and you will to take action (this remark applies to test using O-tolidine).

• Keep checking until you are satisfied that, on one hand the redox potential is rising, and will reach the desired level on the other (the one you set on your redox potential controller, following the manufacturers's instructions). Also make sure no residual ozone is present in the water.

What is that desired Redox Potential Level ?

There are many theories, but it is safe to say that it should be between 300 and 450 millivolt, and that one should not induce rapid changes when attempting to raise the redox potential. If your redox potential is for example 230 mv, do not raise to 370 mv overnight.

Do not change the millivolt by more than 70 to 80 mv per any 24 hour period, unless you really understand all the principles, and are there to observe what the effect is on the fish and other tank inhabitants.

We had earlier suggested lower numbers; further testing leads us to revise the numbers upwards since no apparent harm if done at this new level (Research on mv. Lab book n°14, 1987).

It also appears, and this is important, that the higher the redox potential already is, the smaller the daily increase should be.

If you are now running your tank at for example 350 mv, and you want to raise it to 420 mv, you should not do so in 24, but in 36 to 48 hours.

Using ozone is therefore relatively easy and straightforward, providing you own a redox potential controller. The problems start when you do not have such a controller, as the ozonizer will keep running and may push the redox potential above the limits that you had in mind.

This will then result in the water having such a high oxidative power that it may harm the fish an the invertebrates. Mind you, for that to happen you would have to push the redox potential over 600—650 mv for quite some time.

It is also likely that at such high numbers some residual ozone will be present in the water. This fact can therefore be used to monitor whether or not you may be exceeding the desired and recommended ORP levels.

Although the technique described hereafter is not foolproof, it gives those who do not, or do not yet, have a redox potential meter some control over the process.

• Measure the dissolved oxygen level of your tank's water and write the number down. This is important, as you will need to refer to it several times.

• Take a second sample of water, in a bottle that you can fill completely, making sure that no air is trapped in side. Store that bottle in the dark for 24 hours. Take that second sample right after taking the first one.

• After 24 hours take the second bottle and perform another dissolved oxygen test.

• You will find a difference between the two (the one you performed 24 hours earlier, and this one). This is due to the fact that your water has an organic load, and that the breakdown of these organics have caused the amount of oxygen dissolved in the water to go down.

This second measurement is sometimes done after 48 hours, rather than after 24. This would be the case if you use the Dupla dissolved oxygen test.

• Write the second number down, determine the difference between the two, and write that difference down as well.

• How to perform these tests will depend on who the manufacturer is. We cannot give you a standard routine. Most tests seem to be based on the Winkler method which requires the use of 4 or 5 reagents. Dissolved oxygen tests are as a result longer and a little more involved to perform.

• Now switch on the ozonizer. Run it at about half the setting. To do this, turn the ozonizer's regulating knob all the way over clockwise, and then come back half a turn on meters that do not have a set scale.

On meters that show a percentage-of-output scale, set the knob for 50 percent output.

Since output is dependent on both the dryness and the dust-freeness of the air, the scale does not really mean very much. It is usually only an indication of how much electric current you are sending to the transformer inside the ozonizer, more than it is an indication of ozone output.

• Let the unit run for about 15 minutes, and test for residual ozone. This is a very important step ! You must determine whether the quantity that you are using now is safe. If all is ok, let the unit run at that setting.

If you detected residual ozone already, you must turn the ozonizer's output down further by rotating the regulating know counter clock-wise, another quarter turn.

Then wait 45 minutes and perform yet another residual ozone test. You should more than likely no longer detect any residual ozone. The reason for the long waiting time is to allow the ozone that is present in the water to break down.

If you still detect ozone repeat the previous step, and turn back one more eight of a turn.

Whether or not residual ozone will be detected, and if so for how long, depends on the following :

• the size of your tank,
• the amount of pollution in your water,
• the strength of your ozonizer,
• whether you are blowing the ozone in a foam fractionnator, or in an ozone reactor,
• whether you are using an air dryer,

• and whether or not you are using an air filter (particles of dust inside the ozone generating tube greatly reduce the output).

For the balance of this explanation we now assume that the ozonizer is running, and you detect no residual ozone.

• Let the unit run for 3 hours, and re-test for residual ozone. Follow steps above if you do find some.

• If all is in order, wait 24 hours, and then perform another dissolved oxygen test, and again take a second sample which you will test in 24 hours.

• Write the result of the first test down , and after you have done the second one, write that result down too. Remember to make sure that no air is trapped in the container used to store the water for 24 hours.

Air contains oxygen, that oxygen will transfer to the water and falsify the results of your test.

• The next step involves comparing the sets of values that you now have. You should have 2 numbers for dissolved oxygen, and also 2 numbers for what is refered to as the BOD, or biological- biochemical oxygen demand (the difference between the DO on the first day, and the second test you did).

Example :

	(1)	(2)	
D.O. 1	6.5	7.0	(1)...before you used ozone
D.O. 2	4.0	5.0	(2)...after you used ozone
BOD	2.5	2.0	...the difference

The B.O.D is the difference between the two numbers.

These are just arbitrary numbers, used to explain the reasoning that follows. Repeat the process with your own numbers :

• We notice that D.O. has increased between the two tests. This is a result of using ozone, which has removed organics, which in turn take oxygen out of the water, and therefore reduce the DO over time.

The more organics (pollution) the higher this depletion is. Since the ozonnization reduced those organics, less oxygen will be removed from the water, and the end result should be a higher number for the DO.

• Only if your ozonization was being done at a rate that exceeded the continuous rate of production of organics will your DO have increased.

• This can in fact be demonstrated by comparing the second set of values. If there are less organics in the water as a result of the ozo-nization, the BOD will be lower, as less organics remove less oxygen of course.

What this means is that you are on the right track. Your level of ozonization is improving the water quality, and you should continue doing what you are doing, and at the same rate.

Because of what we said earlier, that as time goes by and the water quality improves, less ozone is needed to maintain that same water quality, you must check regularly for residual ozone, as that will be the indication that you need to start turning your ozonizer down to a lower setting (if you are using a redox potential regulator this does not apply to you).

Always make sure that your residual ozone (R.O.) test is still chemically active by performing the test on regular tap water.

One of the chemicals in the test reacts with chlorine too, and will make it turn yellow, green, red or blue, depending on the quantity of chlorine in your tap water.

For the example above, we have assumed that BOD went down. If this was not the case for you, you need to slightly increase the ozone input, and repeat the testing steps.

You will need to do so until your BOD is down to around 1.5 to a max of 2 mg per liter (or ppm- since it is practically the same - for those interested the exact formula is : ppm = mg/l divided by specific gravity).

Monitor residual ozone regularly. It is very important that you do, as it will prevent damage from over use of ozone.

By measuring DO, BOD, and RO, you can get to a stage where you can be fairly certain that you are ozonizing enough, on one hand, and that the amount is not too high on the other.

It is of course a rather involved way of doing things, but if you do not have a redox potential controller, it is the only method that I have been able to suggest that is 90 percent safe.

It is not 100 percent safe, for the simple reason that between two testing sessions something could still go wrong.

Both dissolved oxygen, and residual ozone tests are short lived test chemicals. Follow the manufacturers' recommendations closely to ensure that you are working with tests that are still chemically active.

If your tap water does not contain chlorine, add a few drops of household bleach to 10 cc of water and then test your residual ozone test. The color change should occur very quickly and will be very pronounced.

Both tests are expensive because both contain rather expensive chemicals. You may think of a 20 or 30 dollar test as an expensive test. Keep in mind though, that a good phosphate, or a good nitrate test, real accurate ones, can easily set you back more than $ 50.00.

Because of the need for high accuracy when testing for residual ozone, it is important that you buy a good and reliable test. Saving $ 5.00 or so on a cheaper test, but losing animals, will cost you a lot more money. Think about it.

Note : By their nature ozone tests contain toxic chemicals. You must handle these tests with care. Never add the tested water back to the tank. Never add the test reagent to the tank. Do not ingest the chemicals, and keep the test away from children.

Although we have elected to insert this recommendation in the ozone test section, it applies to all tests that you use.

2.10. Doser Pump (fertilizer, trace elements and such)

Again, stability of water chemistry is at stake. Adding fertilizer and trace elements once a week may make sense to you, but it does not bring about the kind of stability that you may want in your Reef's water.

For example, once a week treatments create a condition where on the day that you add the liquids their level in the water is high, and then drops hour after hour, day after day, until you again put your weekly dosage in.

If you graphed the concentrations, this creates a sinusoidal curve not a straigth continuous line.

Additional stability can be achieved by using a dosing or better even, a metering pump that can dispense a precise amount of the compounds or fluids that you add to the tank, at short and regular intervals. Such pumps can inject real small quantities continuously.

An in depth description of how to do this can be found in The Marine Fish and Invert Reef Aquarium book, pages 96-97-98, where we describe how to use the dosing pump sold by Dupla Gmbh.

There are however other units that can be obtained from scientific supply houses, although they are not advertised in Hobby magazines. In fact such supply houses sell a wealth of instrumentation that can be used around Reef Tanks.

You should, for instance, check the catalogues of companies such as Cole-Parmer, Chicago; Markson's, Phoenix; Omega Engeneering, Stamford Connecticut, and a few others.

Doser/metering pumps are a definite positive addition to your aquarium. If you are trying to increase the stability of all conditions in your tank consider getting one. It will allow you to dispense liquid fertilizers, trace element mixtures, and KH increasing fluids very evenly into the water.

You could also set up a continuous drip system and not buy a metering pump. To do so you would have to dilute what you are adding daily or weekly, in such a way, that the total amount contained in the frops added in 24 hours corresponds to what the tank really needs.

The following steps are necessary to install such a drip system :

• Count how many drops per hour such a drip system dispenses.
• Collect the output in a graduated container.
• To be accurate, do this for 3 hours.
• Check the output in milliliters, or in ounces.
• Multiply this by 8 (3x8 = 24 hours).
• You now know how much fluid the drip system will add to your tank every 24 hours.
• Decide on the size of the drip container.
• Determine how many times the daily drip quantity fits in that bottle or vat.
• Let us assume for this example that you decide on a five gallon water bottle, and that the daily drip rate was about 0.25 gallons.
• This means that your bottle can easily hold a 5 : 0.25 = 20 day supply of drip fluid.
• Fill the bottle with distilled, reverse osmosis, or de-ionized water (best), leaving space for about half a gallon.
• To that water add 20 times the quantity of additives that you normally would add very day.
• Top off the bottle with more distilled, R.O., or D.I. water to the 5 gallon mark.
• Set up your drip system.

You can of course use smaller bottles or containers. Just substitute the numbers (quantity of fluid of the actual container used) and you will have a workable drip system for a relatively low price.

This method can be automated, and rather than using a drip method system, which can be hard to control because the drip may slow down as a result of small particles in the fluid, you can use a fluid metering pump.

Such pumps run continuously, but only add very small quantities of fluid to your tank.

The Tech•doser pump is such a device. It will deliver 280 ml of fluid per 24 hours (= 0.075 gallons per day). If you then mix the amount of additives that you normally add every day, to that 280 ml, you will have a one day supply, a supply that will be dispensed evenly throughout the day by the Tech•doser.

To have more than one day's supply, all you need to do is use a larger container and mix in that solution in multiples of those 280 ml. For instance, a 5 day supply would require 5 x 280 ml of distilled water, and 5 times the additives you normally add every day.

The principles are the same as what we explained for the drip method. The difference is that you now have an automated system.

2.11. Using Conductivity to measure Salinity

Recently, in Germany, Hobbyists have started measuring salinity in a different way than is traditionally done. We already touched upon this method in our previous book, and it seems that this method is gaining rapid recognition.

Conductivity, expressed in microsiemens, is used to measure the exact salinity, as the higher the salinity, the more salts are present and the higher the conductivity measurement will be, and vice-versa.

As more information on this new method becomes available, e.g a chart with microsiemens values that correspond to different salinities in ppt (parts per thousand), this method should prove to be worthwile for continuous monitoring of tank conditions.

We have not been able to find such a chart, and have not been able to conduct enough experiments in time for publication.

What we do know however, and what we have applied to our own tanks, is the 33.5 to 35 ppt salinity conductivity equivalent in microsiemens, which is between 51 500 and 53 000 at25 Celcius, or 77 degrees Fahrenheit.

We will however keep our "Marine Reef" readers informed as more information becomes available, and as we conduct our own testing.

For those not familiar with Marine Reef, it is a Newsletter, published every 3 weeks, by Aardvark Press (see Appendices for address and telephone).

Should you attempt to make such measurements yourself, you will need a meter that can display and measure conductivity readings in the range of 40,000 to 60, 000 microsiemens.

Since most of you will continue to use more traditional methods, we want to include a few words about salinity in ppt and about specific gravity.

Because s.g. is temperature dependent it is not a very accurate way of measuring, and ppt is much to be preferred. This is however not a test that is available in the hobby, and in fact it is not even an easy test to perform under laboratory conditions.

Rather than testing for salinity, one tests for chlorinity, because of the relationship that exists between the two. This relationship was described by Wooster in the Journal of Marine Research, and his findings basically state that salinity in ‰ (ppt) is equal to 1.81 Cl. in ‰.

This can then used to test for Cl, and then convert the result using the above factor of 1.81. This is not practical for Hobbyists who therefore have to rely on specific gravity.

Charts on how temperature affects specific gravity have been published, the most usable one being the one that can be found in Martin Moe's Marine Aquarium Handbook, on page 50, and also in Stephen Spotte's Seawater Aquariums, in the Appendices.

Those and other similar charts allow you to make the necessary adjustments to your specific gravity measurements.

For our purposes we will keep the salinity at 35 ppt, or expressed differently at a s.g. of around 1.023 at 76/77 degrees Fahrenheit.

The main reason for this is that the water around the coral reefs always has 35 ‰ (ppt) salinity, at least the Indo-Pacific reefs where most of the animal life that Hobbyists keep comes from (remember that the exact number is not as important as the stability that you maintain. 33.5 to 35 ppt is generally considered safe).

2.12. Lux meters

If you are concerned about the corals and macro-algae that you keep, one of the factors that you will need to consider is the amount of light that you use over your tank.

More than likely you may want to measure the intensity of that light, and to do so, you would use a Lux meter.

Although this is not at all something that is required to make your Reef tank operate efficiently, it is one of those additions that gives the lighting process a more controlled approach.

You should however delay acquiring light and lux meters until you have installed all the other equipment that contributes directly to how well the tank runs, as that is far more important than measuring light intensities.

You could always borrow a light or lux meter from a friend, or rent it from a camera shop, if you decide that you want to measure the light intensity over your aquarium.

Since the lights you use are a rather permanent part of your aquarium set-up, measuring its intensity once will give you the information that you want to know and there should be no need to constantly remeasure, obviating the fact that you do not really need to buy a Lux meter.

What we presently recommend and use is : (see also Part 2, section 15)

• Metal halide Power Stars from Osram (5000 Kelvin degrees)
• High output fluorecent tubes from Duro Test (7500 Kelvin degrees)
• and we can also recommend the 5000 Kelvin degree metal halides recently introduced by Energy Savers which should be available by now.

We do not advocate the use of actinic lighting, we never have . This is contrary to what others may tell you to do. We know. We have never had any reason to use such lights because the bulbs that we recommend, and have used for over 4 years now, even in very high wattage ratings, give off more than enough light in the blue spectrum.

We have never had any long term success with actinic bulbs, and have had many comments from Hobbyists all around the country to that effect as well. Many report increased problems with smear algae as well.

Perhaps the use of Actinic O3 requires water quality parameters that are not within the reach of most Hobbyists. Although I do not wish to make adamant statements that these lights do not work, it would appear that the majority of Hobbyists can do better.

In our own tanks we maintain extremely high water quality levels, with dissolved oxygen above saturation, redox potential over 400 mv, temperature around 75/76 degrees Fahrenheit, dKH of 15-18, extremely low nitrate and phosphate levels. Excessive micro-algae growth was never a problem when using Actinic O3 lights.

We did however not notice any significant difference in the appearance of our corals and invertebrates when using such lighting, compared to what these same animals look like under metal halide bulbs.

As is often said, "many roads lead to Rome", we have chosen the metal halide way and can report superior results with these lights, especially when using the Osram brand.

2.13 Protein Skimmer - Foam Fractionnators

The use of protein skimmers is discussed in many books but, notwithstanding all that, their use in the USA is not very widespread.

This is hard to understand, because what a protein skimmer does is so obviously beneficial that the reasons for their lack of popularity are hard to pinpoint.

Could it perhaps be that their price, and also the fact that their function is not well understood, makes hobbyists reluctant and stops them from buying them ? We do not know.

What is encouraging however, is that in the last couple of months several manufacturers have started offering foam fractionnators made in the USA. This brings their price down and makes them more available at the same time.

Several models are being offered. This includes regular columnar skimmers, turbo skimmer (motor driven) and Venturi skimmers. Some of these companies are :

- Route 4 Marine Technology with their M.T.C. brand
- Tunze, through Sea Klear Reefs Inc.
- Thiel•Aqua•Tech
- Coralife - Energy Savers Unlimited
- And of course Sander, which has been around for many years.

Marine Reef, the newlsetter dedicated to Reef Tanks recently published an article on foam fractionnators. Because we think that it is of interest, and pertinent, we have included it here, with permission :

Protein Skimming as it is more commonly called, is a process that, to put is simply, removes organic and other materials, from the water before they have a chance to break down and pollute the water in our aquariums.

This is of course a very desirable action, and it is therefore surprising that so few Hobbyists and Stores resort to it. The heavier the load of fish and invertebrates, the more this form of filtration is needed.

The problem always seems to be either availability, or lack of knowledge on how to size the protein skimmer.

Since the size of the bubbles, and the contact time between the bubbles and the water are the two major criteria for skimming efficiency (Spotte, 1979) (Hueckstedt 1967), we obviously need to optimize both these factors, if we are going to be successful at running our skimmer at its maximum efficiency.

- Obtaining small bubbles is probably the easiest of the two criteria to solve. Limewood airstones in columnar skimmers, or Venturi valves with Pitot tubes in so-called Power skimmers, both give extremely fine bubbles.

Keep in mind though, that to maintain the bubble size at that optimum level you will need to change your airstones regularly. Three weeks is probably the average length of time a limewood airstone will last. Insist on "limewood". They will give you the best result.

If you are using a Venturi skimmer, make sure it is equipped with a Pitot tube; a bent tube that enters the venturi, and is placed in a very specific way to ensure that maximum advantage is taken from the differential pressure created inside the pipe where the Venturi is located.

Venturi skimmers without a Pitot tube will not work as well as skimmers that have such a tube. When you look at such a tube it will seem fairly simple. Believe us it is not. Thickness, length, exact position etc.. are all important to ensure optimum results.

Contact time, or how far and how long the bubble has to travel through the water before it reaches the top, is another problem altogether.

There are more variables to deal with, e.g. the rate of water flow through the skimmer, the length of the tube (column height), how the air and the water flow through the column, all influence the contact time.

Increasing the contact time can be solved rather easily : the air flows upwards and counter flow (against the water flow), and the water inlet is made in such a way that the water rotates downwards, rather than going down straight. Most skimmers that you can buy nowadays are already built in this fashion.

It should be clear that we want to move a fair amount of water through the skimmer at all times, but on the other hand, moving it through the skimmer too fast reduces the contact time. So the right balance must be found.

You could, in fact, experiment with this easily yourself by changing the rate of flow into the skimmer and measuring the redox potential of the outflowing water.

As you slow the flow rate down, the redox potential will go up somewhat, perhaps an extra 35 to 60 mv, depending on the rate of change in the water flow that you made and the amount of ozone that you are using (or whether you are using it at all).

The change in redox potential will be greatest if you are indeed using ozone and are pumping it into the skimmer.

The reason for this is that the oxidation is more effective because the contact time is longer. As a result the ORP will increase a little more.

You cannot keep slowing the water flow down ad infinitum, because no new water would enter the column, or it would enter too slowly.

There are two ways to find the correct flow rate:

• accept the commonly suggested flow rates as a guideline, and set your pump's output accordingly.

• Test yourself, and determine the ideal flow rate based on its impact on the redox potential.

This is not difficult, but it takes time and equipment : 2 redox potential meters and, ideally, a flow meter in line with the outflow of the skimmer to the sump of your filter, or back to the aquarium.

Proceed as follows :

• Use one redox potential meter to measure the ORP of the tank water,

• Use another ORP meter to test the redox potential of the skimmer water, right at the outflow.

• Let the meters adjust for about 3 hours,

• Take both readings and write them down. Also note the water flow rate through the skimmer.

• Reduce the output of the pump going to the skimmer by 25 gallons per hour. Note the change in the redox potential of the outflowing water and also of the tank water. Since changes take time to manifest themselves, you will need to wait about one hour before taking a redox potential reading.

• Typically, both the skimmer's ORP and the tank's ORP will have gone up by anywhere from 10 to 50 mv.

• Reduce the skimmer throughflow some more, e.g. reduce it by another 20-25 gallons per hour, and after one hour take the same readings.

• You keep reducing the amount of water going through the skimmer, for as long as the ORP of the tank keeps going up. When that no longer happens, the amount of pollution created is greater than what the skimmer can remove, and you need to increase the flow through the skimmer.

• Once you have established your tank's ideal level for the amount of fish and invertebrates in that tank, at the time you did this experiment, either write the GPH down, or make some sort of a mark on the valve that you used to control the flow, (the latter in the event that you did not use a flowmeter to do this test).

Whenever you change the amount of fish and/or invertebrates, you will have to re-adjust the flow , as this affects the amount of pollution that is generated, and the overall water chemistry.

This will be evidenced by how the ORP behaves. If it goes down for instance, you will have to speed the flow through the skimmer up again.

Foam fractionnators are great for improving the water quality, there is no doubt about that. They do however need to be monitored, and adjusted from time to time.

Installing a protein skimmer, and expecting it to run optimally, without making any adjustments and measurements, is like buying a new watch, and not setting it to the correct time. It may run extremely well, but you will not be using it very efficiently.

Unfortuantely, this fact has not been stressed enough in hobby literature. As a result, many hobbyists fail to adjust the skimmer they operate, regularly. This lowers its efficiency and reduces its usefulness. If you are now using a skimmer, or are planning to, keep these remarks in mind.

Sizing a Skimmer :

Based on experiments we conducted on a 30, a 55 and a 125, and a 150 gallon tank, we would like to suggest the folowing guidelines for selecting a skimmer :

• Width of the tube : 0.40 inches per 10 gallons of water, up to a maximum of 6 inches

• Heigth of the tube :

up to 40 gallons	1.5 feet + height of the scum cup	
up to 90 gallons	2.0 feet	"
up to 125 gallons	2.5 feet	"
up to 150 gallons	3.0 feet	"

these are what we consider minimum heights, using a few inches extra is always beneficial and increases the contact time further. (based on research 1987 and 1988. THIEL Lab books n°8-9)

2.14. Refractometers (for salinity in ppt)

This may be one of the best acquisitions you can make. The meter is very simple to operate and gives very accurate information. Just place a few drops of the water to be tested on the front of the meter, close the lid, look through the visor, and get a direct reading of what the salinity is, in parts per thousand. Simple enough ?

This may seem too simple to be true. It is not. That is all there is to it. You get an immediate reading, in parts per thousand, using only 3 to 4 drops of aquarium water.

Such meters can be ordered from scientific supply places. The one we use, was ordered from Markson's in Phoenix, Arizona, and cost $ 285.00

The advantage of these type of meters, over different types of salinity measurements, is that you are not measuring what the salt does to the water (it increases its density, or specific gravity), but you are measuring exactly how much chloride etc. (salt) is in the water.

Because specific gravity is influenced by the temperature, and because salinity is not, the latter measurement is of course more accurate, and to be preferred.

If you are trying to get all water chemistry parameters defined "as accurately as possible", then the salinometer is obviously the better way to go. I personally use it all the time. Because it is so simple to operate, you will also be more likely to check your salinity more often.

2.15. Cooling Unit - Chiller

From my days in the freshwater hobby, I remember that we were always trying to concentrate on "heating" the tank, to make sure that the temperature was all right, especially when I was keeping Discus.

In the Marine hobby, it would appear that most people have to concentrate on keeping the temperature "lower".

An ideal Reef Set up runs at 75 to 76 degrees. That probably means that you do not have to heat the aquarium, rather, you have to concentrate on keeping the temperature down.

In the Marine Fish and Invert Reef Aquarium book, we explained how to use a second hand refrigerator, or freezer to do this. Refer to pages 201 and on for that information.

If, however, you need to bring the temperature down by more than 2 to 3 degrees, that method will not do, and you will need a regular cooling unit.

A good cooling unit may cost you 500.00 or more dollars, but it is a wise investement. And it will bring the temperature down to where you want it to be.

Aquarium Sales and Services sells several units and you will have to size the one you need to the gallon content of your tank, to the temperature in the room, and to the temperature fluctuations that will occur in that room.

It is a fact that most of the life forms that are kept in Reef Tanks do better at these lower tempatures. Include a chiller in your budget when you plan your expenditures.

If your tank is in an air-condionned environment, you will more than likely not need a chiller providing that the lights that you use, and the pumps, do not significantly increase the temperature of the water. This is one more reason to select the pumps that you will install, carefully.

Buying the right pump, and the right kind of light fixtures, even if they cost you a few dollars more, **may in the long run save you the cost of a cooling unit.**

On a 150 gallon tank you will probably need a 1/4 horse cooling unit. On a smaller tank, you can probably get by with a fifth or a sixth of a horse power unit.

2.16. Brine Reserve Vat

This small vat which can be operated with a relay, or which can be operated manually, allows you to adjust the salinity quickly.

Any container will do. Fill it with strong brine -water with a very high salt content- and use it as required.

In our case we have such a vat (it holds 2 gallons, but smaller will do just as well), hooked up to the relay which is part of the conductivity controller that we use. The set point on the controller is at 51 500 micro-siemens.

When the salinity goes below that number, the relay triggers a small solenoid and opens it. Brine then flows into the sump of the trickle filter.

This causes the probe of the conductivity controller to read a higher microsiemens number, which in turn causes the solenoid to close when it reaches the set point number.

This automated process will keep your salinity very to any constant number that you decide on.

If you do not use this method you should check your salinity at least twice a week and make manual adjustments. After a period of time you will know how your system behaves, and you can then adjust based on that information.

That may be infrequently, or more frequently, depending on how much the salinity varies in your particular tank, and this is were having a refractometer/salinometer comes in real handy.

Fluctuations occur because of evaporation, salt creep, and also because of water changes. Indeed you may not add water of exactly the same salinity every time you change water. Over a period of time these variations may then affect the salinity more than you would have thought.

The amount of brine to be added is really small. The stronger you make the brine, the less it will take to re-adjust the salinity.

Small solenoids can be obtained as spare parts for many household tools. Richdel (Carson City, Nevada) is probably the largest supplier of such solenoids.

2.17. Fresh water Reserve vat

Along the lines of what was just said about adjusting the salintiy upwards, it may be necessary, at times, to adjust it downwards.

This is done in the same fashion, by triggering a solenoid hooked up to a vat of fresh water, preferably distilled, reverse osmosis or better still de-ionized. The quality of reverse osmosis water is usually good enough for our tanks. Most of the nitrates and most of the phosphates will be removed, and so will many other impurities. It is however not as good as triple distilled or de-ionized water

Controllers with two relays, which is what you will need to do this, can be obtained from, for intance, Extech, in Waltham, Massachusetts.

You can do this manually as well, by regularly checking the salinity and adjusting as is necessary.This is obviously a lot less expensive.

Checking the salinity twice a week is certainly a good idea. Do not make drastic changes as many lifeforms in the tank are very sensitive to rapid changes in salt content.

This applies not only to fish and invertebrates, but to macro-algae as well. Caulerpa species, for instance, are notorious for not tolerating such fluctuations well at all.

2.18. Measuring Redox potential in two areas

Measuring redox potential (and other values for that matter) in two different areas can be of real value. This can be done in various ways

• use 2 redox potential meters,
• or install an electrode switching device (Thiel•Aqua•Tech $75.00) that lets you use 2 electrodes with only one meter or one controller.

It is a small electronically wired device to which you can connect two probes on one side; the other side connects to your meter/controller

By tripping a switch you can view the redox potential of one area or the other, as the instrument switches the read-out from one electrode to the second one.

We use it to measure the redox potential of the water that is going back up to the tank, and also the water coming down from the tank into the top of the biological filters.

You can do this by placing the electrodes next to the pump intake for the redox potential of the water going up to the tank, and right by the inflow from the water coming down form the tank, to measure the other.

Alternatively, and this is a better way of doing it, you can place the electrodes in line withthe water flow, by using a specially outfitte T-fitting, which can also be obtained from Thiel•Aqua•Tech.

Knowing both these numbers gives you an even bettter control over what is happening in your tank.

Experience has proven that a difference of 60 to 70 mv between the two is ideal. Mind you, the magnitude of the difference changes because of many factors and there is of course not "one" ideal number.

Larger differences probably mean that organic material in the tank is decomposing and is pulling your redox potential down too much.

It may also mean that your syphon box filter, or your corner overflow box filter needs cleaning because it contains decaying organic matter that reduces the redox potential as a result of that decay and the pollution it creates.

Determining why the difference is large, if that happens to be the case, is of course something that you will have to look into and remedy.

Instead of measuring the redox potential in two areas of the tank, or in the sump of the trickle filter and the tank, you could measure the ORP of the water coming out of the skimmer, and the ORP of the tank.

Knowing how the quality of the effluent skimmer water behaves will tell you whether your foam fractionnator and ozonizer are performing optimally or not. As the redox potential of the skimmer's water drops, so will the tank's, and such should be an indication that your skimmer needs regulating, or that your drying compound needs changing (or both of course).

2.19. Measuring pH in two spots

What we have just said about Redox Potential applies to pH as well. The principle is the same, and providing you are using BNC jack electrodes the same unit can be used for both. All you will need is a second electrode.

The price of the electrode, added to the price of the device, is still considerably less than acquiring a second good quality pH or Redox Potential meter or controller.

Although measuring pH in two different locations may not make sense to you, think about it in this way :

• you measure the pH of the water going up to the tank, which tells you what the condition of the water in your vat is (the sump of the trickle filter)

• you measure the pH of the water in the tank, which tells you what condition exists in the aquarium itself.

The difference tells you a lot about the metabolic activity, and organic breakdown in the tank.

The closer together both numbers are, the better off you are in terms of water quality and tank living conditions..

It should be clear that you must make sure that your electrodes are properly calibrated, and that you clean and recalibrate them regu-

larly. This will ensure maximum accuracy and allow you to interpret
the numbers meaningfully.

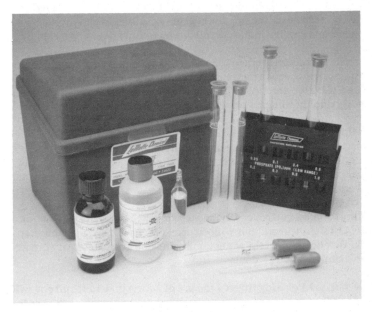

Phosphate test kit

2.20. Ozonizers

In section 2.9.1 we briefly touched on the use of Ozone and explained
the concepts underlying its use.

If you are planning on keeping a Reef Tank, this is one piece of equipment that you will definitely need. No ifs, buts, or whats.

There has been a lot of controversy surrounding this instrument but it
is, in my opinion, an absolutenecessitty if you are planning to keep a
successful Reef Tank.

You must buy an ozonizer that can deliver, in mg/liter, at least 1.5

times the actual water content of your tank. For instance, if you have a 150 galon tank, you will need a unit that can produce at least 225 mg of ozone.

The reasons for this are numerous, and are not always that obvious.

As the amount of pollution in the tank increases, because of overfeeding, or because of die-offs that occur (e.g. algae, small vertebrates and invertebrate lifeforms, fish etc..) your water quality goes down rapidly.

For the filtration system to cope with this pollution you "may" require a great deal of ozone for a short period of time. If your unit is properly sized, this high amount will be available and the result will be that your water quality will get back in line.

If this were not the case the loss of, for instance, one fish or one anemone may bring down the water quality so much that other animal life is affected as well, dies, and pollutes the water even more. This may lead to more losses, etc... and a rapid downward spiral of the water chemistry, resulting in a so-called wipe-out.

If the ozonizer can cope with the pollution created by the first loss, and at least stabilize conditions, albeit at a lower level, this snowball effect-like deterioration of the water quality may be averted, and no irreperable damage will be done.

Section 2.9.1 already covered the use of Ozone in detail, and you will find still more recommendations elsewhere in this book (Check the Index). So many in fact, that we feel confident, that you will understand the concept of ozonization completely, and be able to use it safely and without fear or apprehension.

2.21 Drilling Holes in Glass

If you have never drilled holes in glass, it is strongly recommended that you try it out on scrap pieces of glass before you actually start drilling your tank.

We know that we have already said so, but we would like to repeat it once more, as we want to avoid broken tanks.

In the Series of Videotapes that we produced we show you exactly how that is done. Before drilling, you may wish to refer to Tape 1. You will see the tools that are needed to drill, and how they are used.

You will need a glass drill, tube drills of the proper size, and the grit that is used to grind through the glass. Get the fine grit variety. It makes a much cleaner cleaner hole. Do not attempt to use other equipment, e.g. hand drills; you are looking for trouble.

And if you are not sure of what you are doing, get help from somebody who does. Somebody who has drilled glass before.

It is not really complicated but, if you have never done it, it requires a little "guts", especially if it is your own tank.

It is nice however to be able to position the holes for the water returns exactly where you want them, make them of the proper size, and end up with a Reef Tank that is easier to operate than the ones that run with automatic overflow surface skimming syphons.

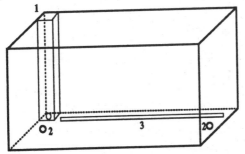

1. The overflow corner box with a hole at the bottom from where the water flows to the trickle filter
2. Water returns, one on each side of the tank. 3. Water return and perforated pipe behind the corals.

Notes on the drawing :

2. The water return hole behind the coral rock. This is a long pipe with holes perforated in it. See text for more details   1. The water returns on each side, which can be alternated if desired   3. The corner overflow box filter, or the space where your automatic syphon is positionned. The two holes labeled 1 can return water at the same time,

or could be alternated by means of a timer and a relay, by means of one or more solenoid valves, or best by using a device such as the Ocean Motion Maker.

One could also use a 3-way electrically actuated ball valve, or two 2-way ones, and a timing device. These two arrangements, although possible, are intricate to set up and rather costly, because of the high price of electrical actuators and the special ball valves needed to make the proper installation. Standard ball valves cannot be fitted to the actuators.

Whichever way you set your particular system up is dependent on the size, and of course the equipment that you are willing to invest in.

The drawing on the previous page shows you a tank that has been drilled in 4 different locations.

There is a hole for the water going down to the trickle filter, at the bottom of the overflow corner box.

There are two holes for the water coming back to the tank, one on either side, one on the right and one on the left, and there is a fourth hole in the back of the tank, but through the bottom, to bring water back from the filter into the tank, but behind the coral formations that you will be placing in the reef tank.

This all ensures that there is good, and even, water movement in all parts of your aquarium. All these returns prevent the formation of dead spots, or spots where the water is stagnating, resulting in lower in dissolved oxygen content, and possibly anaerobic activity.

Such a set up also helps in preventing detritus from accumulating in certain areas, and decaying, thus reducing the amount of dissolved oxygen as well.

We already know that that is totally undesirable, and we want to do everything possible to avoid it.

More on this in Part 3 of this book..

Note : many items of importance are covered several times in this book. This is not to be repetitious, but to classify each item in all the categories where it belongs, and look at each from a slightly different perspective. We apologize to those of you who do not like this format. We have however found it be beneficial in the past, especially in several teaching assignements I was involved with.

2. 22. Drilling Holes in Acrylic

This is a lot easier to do than drilling holes in glass. All you will need is a good electric drill, the hole saw drills we mentionned in the tool section, and a lay-out of where exactly you will need to drill holes.

If you have not drilled through acrylic before, you may wish to try it out on a few pieces of scrap first. This will ensure that you understand how drilling through acrylic actually "feels", and how the acrylic material behaves, as you drill through it.

Special drills for acrylic exist, but they are realtively expensive, and you may not have any other uses for them but drilling a few holes in the filter, and possibly in the tank.

Drill slowly, and back off the drill regularly, to let the accumulated chips of plexiglass get out of the groove that you are drilling. This will result in a cleaner and nicer looking cut, and will prevent chipping.

Ease the pressure, especially as you nearly get all the way through the material. That way you are not putting any stress on the filter, and there is less of a risk of cracking, and chipping.

Although carbide drills may be the best drills you can buy, do not use them when drilling acrylic. They have a tendency to seize right at the moment they go through the plexiglass, and this may crack the filter or the tank if you are not used to working with these drills.

It is best therefore to use all-purpose drills, or the special acrylic drills. Drill slowly, and back off the drill from the acrylic regularly.

Use new drills, not used ones. They will go through the acrylic too slowly, and heat up because of the rotational speed and friction. This causes the plexiglass to melt and re-harden in the groove, and makes for an unclean and difficult cut.

Do not exert a lot of pressure on the drill either. It is not necessary and you may crack the acrylic. After all the holes have been drilled, sand the edges with fine grit wet/dry sanding paper to smoothen all edges.

When installing the bulkhead fittings, proceed in exactly the same manner as was described when we explained how to do so in glass aquariums. Silicone will make a water tight seal, is easily removable if you needed to, but will seal nevertheless.

2.23. Automatic Water Changers

We refer you to pages 101 through 105 of The Marine Fish and Invert Reef Aquarium book, where we explained how to set up such a water changing system at length. It is also covered later in this book in the section on drip and water changing systems.

Any method can be improved upon as time goes by, as newer techniques are tried, and as newer equipment becomes available.

We will be implementing some of these in our set up :

• we will be using a polypropylene vat to contain the reserve water. This vat can hold up to 35 gallons (Walchem, Waltham, Mass.) and our Tech• Doser pump can be mounted right onto that vat, as both are made by the same company.

• we are also using a similar vat to store freshwater for at least 72 hours before it is used. As already indicated, this vat is refilled by the output of a small reverse osmosis unit that is hooked into the main water line of the house. That reverse osmosis water is then run through one of the Thiel•Aqua•Tech de-ionizer units. Since R.O water is already of quite good quality, the life of the D.I. units is prolonged considerably.

Every time someone in the house uses water, the system adds some R.O. water to that vat as well. This is efficient, and minimizes the amount of water that is lost. Reverse osmosis units indeed waste a lot of water, some use as much as 4 gallons of tap water to end up with one gallon of treated water.

• A newer submersible pump by March, which we treat with silicone dip to cover some stainless steel screws.

• A short interval digital timer by Micronta (Radio Shack), that allows on-off cycles of 1 minute increments. This enables us to add small quantities to the sump, and keep our water changer down to the quantity that we decided on.

•A mercury float switch assembly to prevent the reserve vat from running dry.

All in all, an automatic water changer is not that difficult to install, especially if you can evacuate the water that is being removed to a drain.

Setting such a system up when you do not have a drain was also explained on pages 101 to 105 of The Marine Fish and Invert Reef Aquarium.

If you want to improve upon this system even further, you could use one of the Tech•Doser pumps and set it to deliver, daily, the amount of water that you want to change.

The Tech•doser pump can deliver from a minimum of 280 ml, to a maximum of 5 gallons per 24 hours.

2.24. Activated Carbon Reactor for Air

The air that is blown into the biological filtration area of your trickle filter may contain lots of undesirable gasses and other elements, and you may wish to filter it first by blowing it through a small activated carbon reactor.

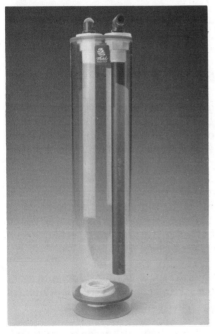

We use our own units, 19 inches tall and 3 inches in diameter. They are filled with activated carbon, and are placed in-line, between the air pump and the trickle filter.

This is a long term set-up. We only change the carbon every 10 to 12 weeks.

This unit ensures that possibly noxious compounds do not get into the filter, respectively the water.

These compounds include for instance :

• nicotine from smoking,
• perfume scents,
• kitchen fumes from stoves etc.
• aerosol spray of various kinds

• cleaning product, e.g. furniture polish
• and others, e.g. ozone escaping from the skimmer.

While we do not consider this a crucial addition to your system, it helps and we certainly recommend doing it, especially since its cost is relatively low.

One of the possible sources of air contamination we mentioned is ozone. This should be a real concern if you often smell ozone around your filter, and if the air pump that drives air into the biological part of your trickle filter is in that same space.

Ozone coming out of the top of your skimmer may be pulled through the air pump into the biological part of your trickle filter. If such is the case, you may be losing a fair amount of Nitrosomonas and Nitrobacter, and you may find that your water always contains small amounts of ammonia and nitrite.

Using a small air purifying carbon reactor will alleviate this problem. Additionally you may wish to place an ozone trap on top of your skimmer.

2.25. Activated Carbon Reactor for Water

Although we are slowly going away from the use of activated carbon, in favor of Molecular Absorption filters (M.A. filters) such as Poly Filter pads and discs in special cannister housings, activated carbon is still required for those instances where ozone is used, either in a protein skimmer, or in an ozone reactor (see ozone reator).

Carbon reactors can be as simple as a cannister filter completely filled with activated carbon, to some of the more special reactors sold by Thiel•Aqua•Tech and Route 4 Marine Technology. For more details on these, we again refer you to The Marine Fish and Invert Reef Aquarium book and other sections of this book (check the index).

Another method still, if you have the space in your sump, is to make the water that returns from your skimmer flow into a compartment of the filter that is filled with good quality activated carbon.

This does not need to be a special compartment, but can be any container that you can place in the sump and fill with activated carbon. Let the water flow in at the top, let it run through the carbon, and let it come out at the bottom of whatever container you are using.

Empty Reactor

An old cannister filter housing that you are no longer using will do. You may have to modify it slightly though, to make sure that the water flows out easily from through the bottom of. This usually requires drilling more holes.

Of course, depending on the type of carbon that you use, you will have to set it up in such a way that the carbon cannot get out of the device and end up in the filter itself. Fine carbon is difficult to remove, quickly migrates towards the pump intakes, and results in a messy situation overall, including having small particles of carbon spread all over the aquarium.

Some trickle filters come with such units installed already. This is the case for instance with both Dupla USA, Summit Aquatics and T•A•T units (all three companies offer 3 standard models, plus custom ones as well).

Remember to change the activated carbon regularly to ensure that all ozone is indeed being removed from the water. This is an important maintenance step.

You will want to use a Residual Ozone test (Thiel•Aqua•Tech) on a regular basis. This test is very simple to perform and is described in more detail in Part Three. All you need to do is add drops of a reagent to some tank water and look for a color change.

It is difficult to recommend how much carbon needs to be used to effectively remove all ozone. You will need to test by trial and error. One could of course use a few pounds, and play it safe. This is however not necessary. Start with a few ounces, and keep increasing the amount until no more residual ozone is detected after the water from the skimmer has passed through the carbon chamber.

2.26. X-nitrate™ Reactor

The principle behind all reactors is the same. Water is forced through a long cylindrical acrylic tube, and has to travel through a compound inside that cylinder, before it can exit and get back into the sump of your trickle filter, or in the main water stream.

This particular reactor is filled with a compound that removes nitrate from the water and brings it down to acceptable levels.

We have tested this X-nitrate™ and found it to be able to reduce and maintain nitrate levels to the 2 to 4 ppm level. The compound exhausts itself and needs to be changed. It cannot be regenerated, that is not the type of compound it is.

If your nitrate levels are high when you first start using X-nitrate, the product will last for several weeks. Subsequent lots of X-nitrate will last for months.

To monitor how X-nitrate affects your nitrate level you must accurately test for it. This is best done by performing the test on diluted water and then multiplying the result by the dilution factor.

For example, if the water you are testing contains 25 percent aquarium water and 75 percent diluting fluid (e.g. Tech•Diluting solution), you must multiply the result by four.

The reactor is installed in such a way that water is drawn from the sump, or from the aquarium, and returned either to the tank, or back to the sump.

X-nitrate works best when you push a lot of water through the compound. Just flowing water over it will not give you as good results as if you flow water through it.

The reactor we use is 6 inches in diameter, and about 26 inches tall including the height taken up by the fittings.

Smaller custom-made models are also available, but do not take as much X-nitrate. If your tank needs several "units", you will probably need the standard model.

2.27. Carbonate Hardness Reactor

This reactor is similar to the previous one, except that it is filled with pieces of coral rock. A small amount of carbon dioxide is injected from the top, and the whole cylinder is kept under slight overpressure.

This is another acrylic cylinder. The T•A•T reactors are 26 inches tall and six inches in diameter.

Water is injected from the top and can only escape through a pipe that runs from the top of the cylinder, to within one inch of its base. (see illustrations).

How do these reactors operate ?

Water is injected through (3), which in our case is a half inch PVC pipe fittinginto which you can screw a barb and attach flexible tubing.

In the tank we are setting up the water comes from the sump of the trickle filter by means of an Eheim Hobby pump, used in submersed mode.

(5) is the actual reactor, which is 26 inches tall and six inches in diameter. The cylinder is filled with pieces of broken coral (not shown). If you do not have broken coral use any other calcareous material.

(1) is the inlet for CO_2 as to run this type of a reactor you will need a supply of carbon dioxide. How much depends on the amount of water you are flowing through the reactor.

(4) is the half inch tube that runs to nearly the bottom of the cylinder.As water is pushed in the reactor, it will rise from the bottom up and try to fill the reactor.

Since however, you are also pushing carbon dioxide in the reactor through (1), internal pressure starts building up. This will result in the water rising in tube (4) until it starts coming out of the top, and flows back into the sump of the filter. You must of course attach hose or pipe

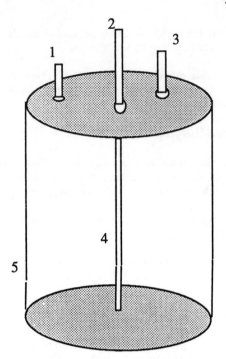

to the outflow of the reactor and guide it to the sump or to the tank.

The key in making the unit run properly is to adjust the amount of water and the amount of CO_2 in such a way, that there is always about 1 to 1.5 inches of water in the bottom of the cylinder.

Because the water inside the reactor is lower in pH than the water in your tank, your must make sure that you do not acidify it too much, lest your overall pH will drop too much. This is done by using either the automated or manual carbon dioxide addition procedures described elsewhere in this book (see index).

The flow through this type of a reactor is therefore usually pretty low, unless you are using a mix of air and CO_2 in which case it can be higher. Fifty gallons per hour is usually plenty.

The principle is simple: the carbon dioxide that you are using slowly dissolves some of the coral, and adds carbonates and bicarbonates to your tank thus helping in maintaining the carbonate hardness.

As these units get perfected, e.g. by making them self-leveling, they will gain in use. They are easy to install and do not require a lot of maintenance, except for making sure that you have enough carbon dioxide and refilling the bottle whenever necessary.

Carbonate hardness reactors have been used in Germany for over 5 years and are quite popular. They make maintaining higher carbonate hardness levels easier and semi-automatic.

2.28. Oxygen Reactor

Oxygen reactors works on the same principles described in 2.27.

Instead of being filled with coral pieces, it is filled with approximately 2.5 gallons of Bioballs.

Water flows into the cylinder and is spread out by a drip plate at the top, similar to drip plates on top of trickle filters.

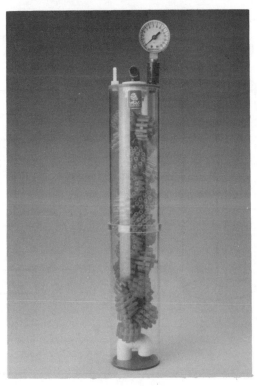

Modular reactor

Instead of carbon dioxide we use air, or a mixture of air and oxygen (enriched air) to run the unit and maintain the overpressure inside the reactor.

Depending on the amount of water you flow through the reactor, you may or may not need a strong air pump.

We will run the one we are setting up with a Eheim Hobby pump, in submersed fashion, in the bottom of the trickle filter. The air pump used is a Whisper 900.

Water is taken from the sump of the filter, and returned to the same sump in the immediate vicinity of the intakes of the main pumps that return water to the aquarium.

Since air contains a great deal of oxygen, and since the reactor runs

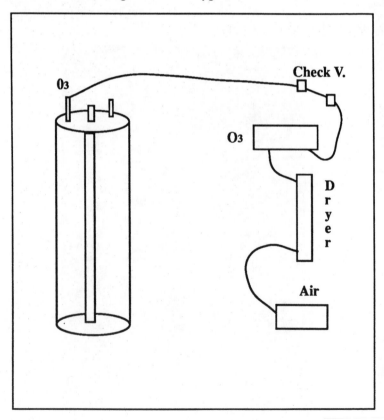

under over pressure, oxygen is "forced" into the water and the overall result is that the dissolved oxygen levels increase.

In a recent test, we raised that level by 1.4 mg per liter, using a highly accurate YSL oxygen meter adjusted for both temperature and salt content of the water. That is a significant increase, especially in salt water (Lab book THIEL 1987 n°12).

In fact, the increase is even higher in waters where low oxygen levels exist to begin with. In our test the D.O. level was around 90 % of saturation before we started.

Since the unit is not really large it can easily be placed next to the aquarium, or even a a distance, providing you use an appropriate water pump and piping.

My own company is planning to introduce a self leveling unit in February/March of 1989. That will make its use even easier, since you will no longer have the adjust the inflow of water and the air pressure to arrive at the desired water level of 1 to 1.5 inches at the bottom of the reactor.

The unit comes with a solid state assembly in which you can plug in your air pump, or your oxygen supply coupled with a solenoid.

2.29. Automatic Metering Pump

Metering pumps are pumps that have a known daily and hourly output which can be adjusted by changing a few settings on the pump.

This is a very interesting type of pump as it will allow one to dispense any liquid in exact quantity, and very evenly, over a 24 hour period.

We are using such a pump on our tank to add fertilizer, vitamins, and some other additives, all strongly diluted, but in the right proportions, so that one gallon of water per day contains all the elements that we want to add to our system in 24 hours.

It is similar to what a dosing pump does, but metering pumps dispense small amounts continuously, which increases the evenness of the addition even more.

This type of pump is not only more efficient than a peristaltic dosing pump, but it is also more reliable, as metering pumps do not rely on compressing a small diameter hose, the way peristaltic ones do. The risk of additives getting into the motor when the hose bursts is thus eliminated. A dosing pump may add drops of a mixture every hour, or every two hours; a metering pump on the other hand, runs continuously and dispenses fluid at very short intervals.

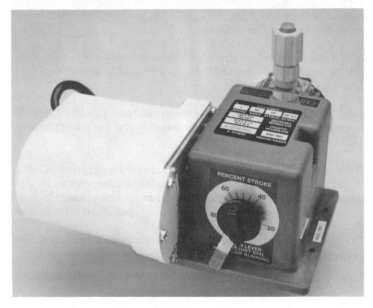

Dosing/Metering Pump

2.30. Ozone Reactor

Ozone reactors operate on the same principle as oxygen reactors. In fact the reactors are identical, and both are filled with Bioballs.

The only change is in the fact that instead of air, a mix of air and ozone is used to create the overpressure.

The water coming out of the reactor **must** be run over activated carbon to remove any residual ozone. This is very important, as we have already pointed out several times when discussing the use of ozone.

Setting such a reactor up is really simple. Instead of blowing plain air into the reactor, you first blow the air through a dryer, then through an ozonizer, and then into the reactor. You may also want to use an air filter and you must use ozone resistant tubing between the ozonizer and the reactor.

You will want to maintain about 1 to 1.5 inches of water, at all times, at the bottom of the reactor, to maintain the over pressure.

Remember to flow the water coming out of the Reactor over activated carbon, as it will definitely contain a great deal of residual ozone.

Use your residual ozone test regularly to test whether your activated carbon needs changing. There should not be any residual ozone in your tank's water at any time. And remember to test your test. We explained elsewhere how to do this (see also index).

2. 31. Poly Filter Cannister Assembly

Poly Bio Marine, manufacturers of Poly filters, the pads that many of you may have, or are using, also manufactures a cannister assembly which can be placed in-line with the main water return to the tank.

A typical Reef set up, using this filter, would therefore be (in succession of how they are piped) :

• Trickle filter
• Check valve
• Pump
• Some form of flow control, for example a ball valve
• A Poly Filter cannister
• more pipe, which ends up in the tank and returns the filtered water.

Because molecular absorption filters are so highly efficient, we strongly recommend that you consider including them in your Reef set up.

We have 3 such assemblies installed on our own tank. One in each of the three water return lines that bring water back to the tank.

Based on about 5 month's experience, we have been changing these Poly Filter discs about every 3 to 4 weeks, giving us, based on the pumps we are using, in excess of 1 million gallons of water cumulatively going through the filter cannisters before the discs need replacing.

If we followed the manufacturer's instructions completely, we could push even more water through the discs but the pumps we are using cannot take that amount of back pressure.

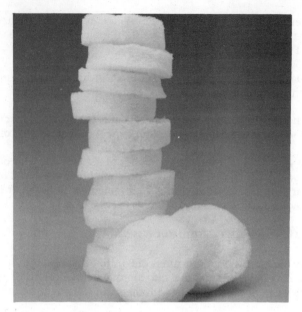

Molecular absorption discs

Indeed as the discs absorb more compounds, they produce more back pressure, and that requires stronger motors.

The cannisters can house 12 discs, but you can also operate the unit with 6 discs and 6 spacers. This is probably the method that most hobbyists with tanks of less than 100 gallons would want to use.

Leo Wojcik reports that he has been able to extend the life of the discs by washing them in reverse osmosis or distilled water about every two weeks. This removes detritus, and eases the throughflow of water, thus extending the life of the Poly filters.

The discs should only be changed when they are really dark brown to black in color, even after you have washed them several times.

2. 32. Micron & Sub-Micron Filters

The same company also markets micron and sub-micron filters and housings which can also be placed in-line with the main water circulation back to the tank.

The principle is simple. The water must go through a medium (a form of bag made out of special material) that is rated not to let through particulates that exceed the bag's rating.

Several such bag ratings are available, resulting in this type of filtration being able to remove particulate matter as small as 0.2 micron. This really means that just about anything that is not dissolved can be filtered out, including free floating parasites.

The unit would be piped right after the molecular absorption filter, if you are using one, or just in the water line returning to the tank if you are not.

Each assembly consists of two bags. The first one removes larger particulate matter and ensures that your micronic or sub micronic bag does not plug up too rapidly.

The internal bag -the one that traps the larger matter- is referred to as a sacrificial bag, as you will probably replace it more often than the finer one (usually a ratio of 2:1).

Our system includes 3 of these units, piped in right after the Poly filter molecular absorption units.

Since most hobbyists may not have as many water returns as we do, adjust the number to reflect the requirements of your own system.

2. 33. Bio-Mesh™ Filters

We have covered this form of filtration in detail in The Marine Fish and Invert Reef Aquarium book, pages 41 to 45. You may wish to read those pages again. It was also discussed in several articles in our newsletter Marine Reef.

What we wrote elicited so many comments and telephone calls, that we would like to describe the filter a little more in detail.

Bio-Mesh™ filters are sold by Thiel•Aqua•Tech, and are biological filters that are more efficient than undergravel filters, but not really as efficient as full-fledged trickle filters.

They are presently available in two sizes: small and large. The small unit can handle tanks up to 70 gallons, and the large unit tanks up to 150 gallons. Custom models are available as well.

It is based on the principle that when water flows evenly and continuously through a series of fibrous plates, each one offering a very large surface area for biological growth, you will end up with a highly efficient filter.

Bio-Mesh™ filters can be operated in several ways :

• hanging off the side or back of the tank,
• sitting underneath the tank, inside the cabinet,
• even inside the tank.

Compartments for activated carbon, Poly Filters, and X-nitrate™ are provided, and so is space for a submersible pump to run the unit.

You can operate the filter using strong Power heads, for instance the Aquaclear models 400 or 800. This is in fact the best way to run the filter when it is hanging from the side or the back of the tank.

The surface area offered is very large : Jung™ calculated that the mesh

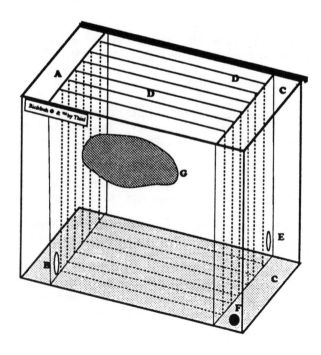

on the plates offers 64.8 square feet of surface area per square foot. A typical filter has 6 to 8 square feet of mesh, or somewhere from 389 square feet of area for biological filtration, to around 518 square feet.

All that in a rather small package that can be run with a good power head.Quite impressive, and worth looking into if you need additional biological filtration.

The filter is extremely easy to install too. Just hang it from the side or the back of your tank, sink a power head in the compartment provided, start the prime on the syphon on the other side, and plug the power head in.

Your filter is now running and all you need to do is add whatever water treatment products that you will be using. This can include activated carbon, Poly Filters, X-nitrate™, and perhaps others. Space for them is provided.

The filters have four or six plates, depending on their size. If you pre-filter the water going into the Bio-Mesh filter, by placing filter floss or foam in the compartment that is provided, all your plates will act as biological filters.

If you do not pre-filter the water, the first plate will act as both a mechanical and a biological filter plate. This plate will, as a result, need to be cleaned from time to time (we suggest about once a week). It is therefore much better to pre-filter the water.

The plates should never have to be cleaned, as they act as biological filters only, especially if the water entering the Bio-Mesh™ is pre-filtered.

Many hobbyists use this filter as an addition to their existing filtration. This is an especially good idea if your present filtration is not large enough to handle the load of fish and other animals that you keep.

It is probably an easy way to up-grade both your undergravel, or too small a trickle fiter, without running into a great deal of expenses.

You will end up with a biological filtration quality that will let you keep a decent Reef Tank without a major investment in trickle filters and accessories required to run them.

Most importantly, you can add this type of filter to your system any time, and without too much difficulty. We highly recommend it, and have run such a filter on a 180 gallon tank of ours for the longest time.

2.34. Installing Electrical Actuators

Actuators are part of ball valves, at least in the application that we use them for. They are in essence nothing more than a motorized shut on and off device.

You will need both the actuator and the special ball valve that fits the actuator you are buying. They come in many sizes to fit anything from half to over one inch pipe.

What are the uses of such a device? There are several possible applications that can be considered :

• shutting off the outflow of your skimmer when a power failure occurs. This will prevent the skimmer from emptying itself, and possibly overflowing the sump of the filter. This requires a straight two-way valve and an actuator.

• diverting water from one water return line to another one at regular intervals. This was discussed when we mentionned alternating the water return into your tank from the right to the left, and doing so every couple of minutes. In this application you will need a 3-way valve and an actuator.

• acting as a check valve. When the power fails the valve closes. When the power comes back on, it re-opens.

Electrical actuators come in NO -normally open- and NC -normally closed- versions.

Normally closed actuators will close the valve when no electrical current is sent to them. Normally open actuators do the opposite.

For the two applications we mentioned, we need NC, normally closed actuators.

•• As long as current is going to the pump that runs the skimmer and to the actuator, the latter will be open, and water will flow from the skimmer to wherever you are returning it to.

If the power fails the actuator closes, and no more water can get out of your skimmer. This prevents floods especially if your filter's sump is small and not attached to a drain.

When the current comes back on, and the skimmer motor starts run-

Coralife 5500 Kelvin degree 175 watt bulb, also available
from Coralife in 250 and 400 watt

ning again, the actuator re-opens the ball valve and water flows both
in and out of the skimmer.

•• The three-way valve actuator changes the direction of the water flow
based on whether current is reaching one set of contacts, or the other.
Changing that sequence must be done with a timer that is referred to
as single pole, double throw timer. Such timers can be ordered from
electrical supply shops, or from specialized catalogues.

Installation :

The ball valve part of the assembly is piped in the same manner as any
other ball valve, with primer and PVC cement. The electrical wiring is
done as indicated in the instruction sheet that comes with the actuator.

We cannot give you a detailed set of instructions as they vary depending on who the manufacturer of the actuator is.

The actuator we use on our skimmer output line is made by Hayward
Industrial Plastics. The cost of a two-way valve and an actuator is
between $150.00 and $250.00 depending on the brand and the material
they are made of.

The installation of single pole double throw (SPDT) timers and of the
three-way actuator is not simple, and may require that you enlist the
help of an electrician.

Both these valves introduce more security in the manner in which your system runs and may therefore be an addition worth considering, especially if you live in an area where power outages occur regularly.

Three-way actuators are yet another way of implementing the alternating water current principles that we discussed earlier in this book.

Their cost, combined with their more difficult installation procedures, are perhaps reasons enough to opt for our own Ocean Motion device, or Route 4 Marine Technology's Wavemaker.

2.35. Pressure Switches

A number of switches that operate on the pressure principle can be used around aquariums as well.

The one of most interest to us is a switch that is piped in line with the water return. It senses the pressure produced when the pump pushes water through the pipes.

If, for some reason, that pressure diminishes or falls to zero, the switch de-activates the pump and prevents it from running dry.

Thus it serves the same purpose as the float switches we already described earlier in this book.

Pressure switches can be used to control other devices, for example an air pump. This is exactly what we have done in our self-leveling oxygen and ozone reactors.

They can also be used to activate pumps, e.g. a water top-off system. If the pressure in the vat being monitored becomes too low, the switch kicks in a pump that will add water to the vat.

Many such specialized applications exist but are beyond the scope of this book.

Part 3

Water Chemistry

and

Water Analysis

A1 Aluminum

A1 Oak

A3 Aluminum
Retrofit

A2 Acrylic

Examples of Energy Savers Unl. Hoods, available in oak, acrylic and metal
shown here in two versions, one with fluorescent tubes and one with metal
halide 5500 K bulbs and two actinic O3 bulbs.

1. Introduction

Equipment and instrumentation is in many cases a requirement to allow us to run our tanks properly. Some is necessary and some is optional, as we have already pointed out.

Some equipment makes one's life easier and takes some of the tediousness out of keeping Reef tanks, other equipment one needs to be able to keep the tank going.

What this really means is that such equipment, and such instruments, allow us to modify and maintain the water quality to such an extent, that the animals we wish to keep stay alive, and hopefully grow.

What really happens to aquarium water after lifeforms are introduced is two-fold :

• Constituent elements that are beneficial are being depleted all the time and need to be replenished continuously, e.g. trace elements, iron, manganese, vitamins, carbon dioxide, oxygen, fertilizer, etc...

• Other elements, noxious and unwanted ones, enter the water continuously, and need to be removed. These include ammonia, nitrite, nitrate, phosphate, amino acids, nitrosamines, organics, albumin, urea, etc...

To this effect we install equipment and biological, chemical, mechanical and other types of filters, reactors and water treatment devices.

The mere fact that we install them does not tell us whether the water quality is improving, staying stable, or getting worse. Filters just perform their function but do not tell us anything about how efficient they are performing this task.

We may be able to visually determine that the tank "looks good" or only "so-so", but that is not a very professional approach.

We therefore resort to a whole battery of tests to determine what the water chemistry parameters are, and we then initiate some form of action to take care of whatever problems there may be.

This part of Advanced Reef Keeping I deals with these tests, lists the parameters that you should strive for, and also suggests methods of improvement.

We had already covered this subject in great detail in The Marine Fish and Invert Reef Aquarium book, but the many questions and phone calls that we receive at Thiel•Aqua•Tech tend to make us think that we were perhaps not as clear as we had hoped, at least not for certain tests.

We will therefore re-explain all the test that we feel are of value to a Reef Keeping Hobbyist, suggest the values that you should strive for in your tank, and what action you can take to correct any discrepancies.

Some tests are covered in more detail than others, especially the ones that are not commonly taken by most Hobbyists, e.g. phosphate, carbon dioxide, dissolved oxygen, and residual ozone.

Others, the ones that you are familiar with, are only touched upon briefly, mainly to give you the maxima allowed, and how to deal with excessive amounts of these compounds.

Additionally, we will cover redox potential, its meaning, and how to use it as a guideline of how your aquarium is doing. This is a most important new concept (to the hobby anyway), and is finding its way in more and more literature.

Often it is not explained correctly, or writers fail to understand what its use exactly should be. As a "number" we cannot do much with it, but if we look at how it behaves over time, the picture becomes totally different.

Besides redox potential, we are also covering the subject of ozone in a little more detail. Protein skimmers, or better, foam fractionnators, were already discussed in Part Two and in The Marine Fish and Invert Reef Aquarium.

Since different manufacturers may use different chemicals for their tests, you must always read the instructions that come with these tests carefully, before getting to any conclusions.

Because in this book the same subjects are covered in different parts of the book, on purpose and in an effort to shed more light on them, while looking at them from different perspectives, you may want to refer to the index for the pages where you can find information on the subject matters that you would like to re-read because they are of particular interest to you.

2. Residual Ozone Test : Recommended level : 0.00 ppm

This test is obviously only of use to those of you who use ozone to begin with. But as we have indicated in Parts One and Two, ozone is a water treatment method you will need if you wish to raise the water quality to the levels of redox potential that are now being advocated for Reef tanks.

We will be using the Thiel•Aqua•Tech Residual Ozone test for this explanation. The principles are the same even if you use another brand.

The only changes may be the amount of water you need, to perform the test, and the number of drops of the reagent that you need to add to that water to determine whether or not any ozone is present.

If using someone else's test, read the instructions carefully and make sure that you know what color to look for, and whether it should be just a faint color or a strong pronounced one.

• Take 10 cc of aquarium water, in any vial that is graduated and can show you that you have exactly that amount.

• Add 10 drops of the reagent.

• Wait about 10 seconds. Look at the sample. If it is even slightly yellow you know that you have residual ozone in your tank.

• If you are undecided as to whether or not your water is yellowish after testing it there obviously is very little ozone in the water, if any.

As a double-check, re-do the test with 5 ml of water and 10 drops. You could also get a second opinion, but if it is that difficult to identify the yellowing, the amount present is at worst very small anyway.

The deeper the yellow the more ozone is present. In the worst of all cases the color will be greenish, or even bluish. This would mean that you have an extremely high amount of ozone in the water.

If that were the case you would probably have lost all, or a great deal, of the life in the aquarium already. You would also be able to smell ozone above the tank and in the air.

What should you do when residual ozone is present?

• Start by turning your ozonizer off completely. Residual ozone should have disappeared in about 45 minutes to an hour. It has a real short lifespan in water.

Its half life is around 45 minutes. This means that if you had, for example, 0.1 mg of residual ozone in the water, 45 minutes later that would have been reduced by 50 percent to 0.05 mg/l.

• Change your activated carbon or use more . If you were not using carbon, you should now add some, if you plan to continue using ozone. Activated carbon removes residual ozone very efficiently and is easy to place in the sump of the filter.

• This is really all you have to do if the fish and invertebrates were not affected. After all residual ozone has disappeared, turn your ozonizer back on, but at a lower setting, and check for residual ozone after about 15 minutes.

If you still find ozone in the water, you must turn your ozonizer down further. It could also be that the water returning from the skimmer or the ozone reactor, is not flowing over the carbon properly.

• Change the way you have it set up to ensure that the water goes "through" the activated carbon, and not just "over" it.

This is important. Indeed, if you are using carbon in a fine mesh bag, the bag may restrict the throughflow of water too much and as a result ozone is not being removed efficiently. This leads to some of it entering the main water stream and getting into the tank.

Carbon bags become coated with slime and other detritus which impedes the throughflow of water, or stops it completely. This results in the ozone only being partially removed, or not at all, which will be evidenced by residual ozone in the tank's water.

Check the potency of your test regularly.

The chemicals used in the residual ozone test are unfortunately short-lived chemicals. Tests do not necessarily last till the bottle is empty, they only last for a long as the chemicals are still reacting.

There is nothing that anyone can do about it. That is the nature of those chemicals. They are also very susceptible to light and should be kept in the dark

To test the potency of your test take some tap water, but before taking the 10 cc, let the water run for about 3 minutes, so all the water that was in the pipes, is gone. Add 15 drops of the ozone test reagent to the 10cc of tap water.

Since tap water contains chlorine, the tested water should turn yellow or even green.

If you are in a building where the water is treated and does not contain chlorine, proceed as follows :

• Take 10 cc of regular tap water
• Add 5 drops of household bleach
• Add 15 drops of the test solution

The tested water should now be yellow or bluish. If it is not, your test has lost its potency and you need to buy a new one.

Do not let expired test lie around, dispose of them and do not re-use the container. The two test we know of both use noxious chemicals.

Keep the test out of the sun, keep it in the dark if you can. The test deteriorates under the influence of light too.

Never add the tested sample back to the tank. It will kill off most of the animal life in the aquarium and will do so in a matter of hours. Fish in particular will be affected.

Rinse the test cylinder or vial that you used several times, to remove any traces of the test reagent. Or better, label that vial, and use it for ozone testing only. That way, no trace of the test reagent will ever get into your aquarium.

Keep the ozone test away from children. It contains toxic chemicals. If you get test solution on your hands, wash your hands carefully.

3. Carbon dioxide : Recommended level 3 to 4 mg / liter

Carbon dioxide is important if you keep macro-algae, and also if you keep corals and other invertebrates with symbiotic algae. If you don't, you need not worry about CO_2.

We only know of one test for carbon dioxide made by an aquarium products company : the Dupla Exklusiv one from Germany marketed by Dupla USA.

We have also tried a test marketed by Cole-Parmer and found it to be both accurate and inexpensive.

Here is how to proceed (when using the Dupla test) :

• Take 100 ml of aquarium water in any graduated container. Take the reagent, open the bottle, and get ready to add drops to the 100 ml.

• Add one drop of the reagent. The water will turn slightly purple to pinkish, but that color will disappear very quickly. In fact, the CO_2 in the water neutralizes the reagent, and the water being tested goes back to its original color very quickly.

• Add a second drop, and watch whether the pinkish color stays or goes away. If it goes away rather quickly, e.g. within 15 to 20 seconds, you will need to add another drop of the reagent.

• If it stays, you have added 2 drops so far, and your Carbon dioxide content is 4 mg per liter.

• If the pinkish disappeared, add a 3rd drop, watch the color, if it stays you have 6 mg per liter. If it does not stay, add one more drop.

You keep doing this until the pinkish color stays for a least 45 seconds.

The mg per liter of CO_2 is equal to two times the number of drops of the reagent that you added.

You can also perform this test with 200 ml of water, in which case each drop represents only 1 mg of carbon dioxide per liter.

The result will be more accurate as you can get intermediate readings, e.g. 3 or 5 mg/l, but you will of course use more drops of the reagent.

If you have too much CO_2, which is unlikely, all you would need to do is aerate the water somewhat and you would chase excess CO_2 out of the water very quickly.

In all likelihood you will not have enough CO_2 and your color may have stayed pinkish after one or two drops.

This means that you do not have enough carbon dioxide in the water and you will need to consider adding some, either manually or automatically, with pH control.

The manual system usually suffices for a marine aquariums, since we are not looking at adding a great deal of CO_2.

You can acquire such a system for around $175.00. For information on how to hook it up, which is really quite simple, check The Marine Fish and Invert Reef Aquarium book.

It is not complicated; the manual system is marketed as a starter set and includes all the parts you need to be up and running with carbon dioxide is less than half an hour.

If you are into automation you can acquire such a system too, but you will need :

• a pH controller with an electrode,
• a solenoid valve,
• a set of pressure gauges and a pressure reducing fitting,
• two small check valves,
• a small reactor to mix the CO_2 efficiently with the water,
• a few feet of carbon dioxide resistant hose. This is usually flexible silicone or flexible PVC hose.

Do not use the clear acrylic hose (airline tubing) as it will harden and crack, causing you to lose carbon dioxide and constantly have to refill your carbon dioxide container at a welding supply place, or other authorized establishment.

An automated carbon dioxide addition system will probably run you around $ 1,500.00. This is of course a lot of money, but do not forget that your set-up will include a highly accurate pH controller at the same time.

Good units read two digits passed the significant digit, e.g. 8.18, which is much better than the read-out of many other instruments.

In our experience, most hobbyists can easily get by with a manual CO_2 system. You can always upgrade it to an automated one at a later date.

Keep the test reagent in the dark, it will last you longer. This is in fact a recommendation that applies to just about any liquid or dry reagent.

To test for the reagent's potency, first bubble CO_2 in a glass of fresh water, and then test. You should get at least 5 to 6 mg of Carbon dioxide per liter.

If your result is lower, your test is still chemically active but can no lon-ger give you an accurate result. If the result you obtain is zero mg/l, or much higher than 8 mg/l your test has expired.

The liquid contained in the Dupla test is purple and easily stains. Be extra careful when using it. It "is" a very good test, however.

Besides Dupla, other dealers .of CO_2 systems include Route 4 Marine Technology, Coralife and Poisson Filters.

4. Phosphate Test : Recommended : 0.1 to max 0.5 ppm

The lower the amount of phosphate in the tank, the better off you are. Algae, in particular, thrive on phosphates, and its presence is often to blame for frequent outbreaks of micro-algae all over the tank that nothing seems to be able to control.

Testing for phosphates should be a regular undertaking, as once phos-phate builds up, micro-algae will soon appear.

Such algae are very difficult to control as most of you have probably found out already.

We will be using the Dupla phosphate test. Others tests exist but not in the aquarium market. Chemetrix makes an excellent test as well.

Take 6 ml of water in a graduated cylinder. Add 2 drops of reagent A and then 2 drops of reagent B. Wait a few minutes until a color change occurs. This may take up to 2 minutes.

The tested water will turn a shade of blue. The bluer it turns, the higher the concentration of phosphate you have in the water.

Check the color of the tested water against the colors in the Dupla comparison color fan, and read off what the phosphate level is.

If your concentration exceeds the recommended levels, immediate action is required. Excess phosphate is always prone to lead to problems with invertebrates besides all the micro-algae problems that PO_4 will bring about.

Water changes, several small ones, must be made on successive days. Use water that does not contain any phosphates. This must be continued until phosphates are below 0.5 per million, or 0.5 mg per liter, depending on which test you are using.

Make sure that you test your tap water first to ensure that it does not contain more phosphate than your tank does.

This is often the case, and you can obviously not use that water. You must find another source. Perhaps de-ionized reverse osmosis, or triple distilled water is the avenue for you.

Small reverse osmosis units, even the ones that produce only 5 gallons a day, will do for most people. We already described them in Part Two.

You must however test the water coming out of the reverse osmosis filter for phosphates. Depending on the membrane used, not all phosphates may be removed. This is, for example, the case with a 5 gallon a day unit that we are using ourselves. Residual levels of around 0.07 were determined using a highly accurate photo-colorimetric method. The answer here is to re-treat that water with a de-ionizer unit.

Adding more macro-algae is another way to reduce phosphates but it is a slow process, and only to be recommended to keep levels low once you have reduced them by water changes.

Thiel•Aqua•Tech is working on a filter that will remove phosphates from your water, and bring their level down to zero ppm. This filter should be available late in the second quarter of 1989.

It consists of two parts, one that is permanent and needs only to be cleaned once in a while, and a second part, a small cartridge type unit, that needs to be replaced whenever it is exhausted.

How long the second unit lasts depends on how much phosphate is produced in your tank. Every tank is different in this respect.

In some cases your PO_4 levels may be so high that you cannot determine from the test color what they actually are. The color is darker than the darkest color of the comparison chart.

If that is your situation, you must first dilute the tank water before testing. Instead of taking 6 ml of water from the aquarium, take only 3 ml and add 3 ml of distilled or another type of phosphate free water.

Then test and read off the result. Multiply the result by two, since the amount of aquarium water represented only 50 percent of the total.

Similarly, if you had to dilute more to get a color that you could compare to the colors in the color fan, you will have to multiply by another number again. For instance if the aquarium water represented only 10 percent of the total, multiply by ten.

Or if your aquarium water represented 25 percent of the total test sample, you will have to multiply by four. This would have been the case if you used 1.5 ml of aquarium water, and 4.5 ml of distilled water.

Don't use tap water to dilute as it may contain phosphates already. That would falsify your test result. Use non-contaminated diluting solutions such as the Tech•35 ‰ Diluting•Solution.

Keep in mind too that the quality of your tap water varies. Seasonal variations are to be expected, and variations after strong rain are very common too.

Testing it only once may therefore give you the impression that your tap water is all right. Because of the many changes that can occur, it may however not be all the time.

Other methods of purifying water exist. This includes the ion exchange cartrigde filters. They are extremely efficient, and are an addition to your system that you should seriously consider.

An ultra pure water treatment unit consisting of 3 cartridges, will run you ± $200.00, and about $35.00—40.00 for each cartridge when replacement is needed. Two cartridge systems cost around $ 150.00 ; both types are available from T•A•T.

5. Nitrite Recommended level : 0 to max. 0.1 ppm

There are many Nitrite tests on the market and they are all fairly simple to use. We will not go into how to perform these tests. Read the instructions carefully.

Usually you add either a few drops of a liquid reagent to test water and compare with a color; or you immerse a little paper in the water, some of the paper changes color, and you again compare that with a set of colors to arrive at a number.

Nitrite is one of the noxious compounds that always needs to be kept as low as possible, preferably zero, and that is done in your biological filtration system. In our case, inside the trickle filter.

Nitrobacter, the bacteria that break down nitrite to nitrate, are always far less in number than the bacteria that break down ammonia. But notwithstanding that, filters that run well can, and will, take care of the amount of nitrite that is continuously produced.

It is also known that ozone breaks nitrite rapidly down to nitrate. As a result, if you are using a good ozonizer, run it with a dryer, and perhaps an air filter as well, you should normally not find any nitrite in your system.

Nitrite is noxious because it interferes with oxygen uptake of the blood, and as a result it stresses the fish, and leads to death because of lack of oxygen, or stress that makes the fish less resistant to other diseases and parasites.

Nitrite is very toxic. If you measure excess quantities you must make immediate water changes and bring the levels down as far as you can, and quickly.

Persistent low levels of nitrite in your tank are indicative of a bacterial upset in your biological filter. This is a reason for concern. You need to find its source and remedy the situation. The reasons can be multiple but are often attributable to high bioloads in the tank. As a result the filter is not able to deal with all of the nitrogen breakdown products, one of which is nitrite, and problems will ensue.

Make sure that the water you use to make water changes is of the same temperature and salinity as the tank. Your fish and invertebrates are already stressed from the excess nitrite, so stressing them even more is to be avoided at all cost. Rapid temperature and salinity changes create great and unneccessary stress.

Once in a while reports emerge that such or such animal is nitrite resistant, and therefore better suited to cycle the tank. Don't believe it.

If nitrites are high, any of the fish that we normally buy from pet stores will die. It is all a matter of degree and length of exposure. Nitrite kills.

6. Nitrate Rec. level : as low as possible - 2 to 3 ppm

Nitrate, as the end product of the nitrogen breakdown cycle, is not as noxious as ammonia and nitrite. In fish-only tanks we usually do not even pay attention to it. In reef tanks, with lots of corals and invertebrates, we must try and keep nitrate as low as we possibly can.

It is definitely a form of pollution to be reckoned with. Reef aquariums with high nitrates will not look as good as tanks with very low levels. Low means definitely less than 5 ppm, and preferably even lower. Ideally you should not be able to detect any nitrate at all. That is however unlikely, even if you use a denitrification unit. Even then, you will probably find nitrate levels to be in the vicinity of 1 ppm.

You can lower nitrates down to zero ppm using a denitrator and stronger lighting. The nutrient up-take by algae is greatly increased when the lighting is very high (e.g. over 6 watts per gallon), which combined with the reduction brought about by the denitrification filter, brings total nitrates down to zero.

We use X-nitrate in our tanks and have managed to bring nitrate levels down to around 2 to maximum 3 ppm. We run about twice the water con-tent of the tank through the reactor in which we have placed the X-nitrate, each hour.

Many corals, both soft, stony and leather, just seem to do a lot better when the nitrate levels are real low. We have experienced that in tank after tank, and have heard so from many hobbyists as well.

When nitrates are low, your redox potential will be much higher as well, an indication that the water quality is much better.

There are numerous tests and you are probably familiar with how to perform the one you own, so we will skip the testing procedures, especially since there are so many different tests.

Since we are interested in measuring really low levels of nitrate, you must acquire a test that allows you to do so.

Most tests we know of measure in the high range only, and although you may need it in the initial stages, before you have managed to lower nitrate levels, you will soon require a test that measures in the very low ppm range.

If you already have a low range test, and your water has a high nitrate content and you cannot get a direct reading, you must first dilute it with distilled water. We described the procedure under the heading phosphates.

Once you know the nitrate content, and if it is higher than the recommended levels, you must start working on reducing it immediately.

There are several methods, and usually a combination of several of them will work best. Here are some of the tried ones :

• Add more macro-algae to the tank. Macro-algae remove some nitrate, but prefer other nitrogen compounds (e.g. ammonium).

• Make water changes, several small ones on consecutive days, with nitrate free water. Reverse osmosis, de-ionized and distilled water are your best choices.

• Use X-nitrate compound in your filter, in a reactor or anywhere in the water circulation, to allow a lot of water to flow through it.

• Use a denitrification unit, but be prepared to monitor it just about every day.

Denitrification units work. They do remove nitrate from the system, but they need constant attention; otherwise, you will find that they produce either nitrite, which is undesirable, or hydrogen sulfide, which is even worse.

If you run water through such filters too fast, they will start acting as normal biological filters, since they will be operating under aerobic conditions. That is of course not the purpose for which you installed them.

Getting a tank with high nitrate levels down to acceptable levels may take several weeks. Using X-nitrate, for instance, will require at least a good 10 days before you start seeing results.

Nothing is instantaneous, the key however is to initiate some procedures that allow you to improve the water quality, and stick with them until you have the desired results.

You must also know what your test is measuring : nitrate or N-nitrate. There is a big difference. For those interested, N-nitrate = 4.43 NO_3 and conversely, NO_3 = N-nitrate times 0.23

Our recommendations for low nitrate levels refer to NO_3 not to N-nitrate. 3 ppm of NO_3 is lower than 1 ppm N-nitrate, in fact it is only around 0.7 ppm, very low indeed.

Where does nitrate come from ?

• Besides entering your tank's water as part of the biological filtration process, nitrates also result from oxidation of nitrite to nitrate by ozone, e.g. in protein skimmers and ozone reactors.

• Any decay of organic material adds nitrates to the tank (remember this includes dead and dying off algae, fish, vertebrates and invertebrates, excess and uneaten food, undigested food etc.)

• Other soureces include the water that you use for water changes and top-offs, e.g. tap water or well water,

• the salt that you use. It may contain nitrates too. You can check this easily by performing a nitrate test on distilled water to which you have added some of the salt you question.

• so can the fertilizers that you add, e.g. products to speed up the growth of macro-algae. You can check in the manner just described above. Often, however, these products are more likely to contain phosphate and not nitrate.

• Certain water additives contain large amounts of nitrate as well.

As we have just demonstrated, nitrates gets into the water in many ways, often from sources you do not expect. Be careful, therefore, when selecting products that you add to your Reef Aquarium. Testing small samples of them may save you a lot of trouble later on.

7. Oxygen Recommended level : saturation, or higher

We have covered dissolved oxygen somewhat, previously in this book, and extensively in The Marine Fish and Invert Reef Aquarium.

Many hobbyists have called us about the test and testing method that we advocated there : the Dupla Aquaristik one from Germany. Perhaps our explanations were not clear enough; we will give it another try here. It is indeed a rather lenghty test.

Let us begin by saying that your dissolved oxygen levels should be at the saturation point, or higher, for the temperature of the water. As explained, at every temperature, water, and especially salt water, can only hold a certain amount of oxygen.

That maximum is referred to as the saturation level. At 100 percent saturation, you would be at exactly that number.

At lower temperatures, the saturtion number is higher than at higher temperatures, another reason for keeping the temperature of your Reef tank towards the lower recommended 75 to 76 degrees Fahrenheit.

We already gave you a chart listing the saturation levels at various temperatures. You may want to refer to it see inex if needed) after you complete the test, to compare the value you found with what it should be at the temperature of the water that you are testing.

Let us look once more at the actual Dupla dissolved oxygen test.

You will need :

• a Dupla test cylinder or any vial that can hold 20 ml, but not more. It needs to be exactly 20 ml of water, as we cannot have any air trapped in the cylinder, or vial, while performing this test.

• Test reagents A, B, C, and D. Reagents A,B and C are sold in one box, and D, the titration solution, is sold separately, as you will run of out reagent D more often than you will run out of reagent A, B, or C.

The procedure to be followed is :

• fill the test cylinder to the overflowing level with aquarium water,

• take the cap off the test cylinder, and take the white plug out of its center,

• push the cap back on the cylinder to close it; water will squirt out through the little hole in the middle of the cap. That is exactly what we want as it removes any air that may have been trapped.

• close the test cylinder by pushing the lid in as far as you can.

• now reopen the cylinder,

• add 5 drops of reagent A,

• add 5 drops of reagent B,

• close the test cylinder, put the plug back in the lid, and shake gently for a few seconds to mix the reagents properly with the water,

• you must now wait about 10 minutes. The addition of reagent A and reagent B will cause a gel-like white to brown sediment to form inside the test cylinder.

The reason you need to wait is to let that white to brown matter settle to the bottom of the cylinder. It will not settle completely, but will sort of hang in the water that is inside the test cylinder, towards the lower part of the cylinder itself. It basically sinks, but slowly.

• after 10 minutes, re-open the cylinder, and here is where some people got confused or found the test difficult to understand :

↤ If the sediment has settled to below the hole in the test cylinder at the 6 milliliter mark, let all the water above that hole run out. This is done by removing the white plug, and opening the holes on the side of the test cylinder. Excess fluid will flow out, so hold it over a sink or some paper towels.

↤ If the matter that settled is above the 6 ml mark, then proceed as we just indicated, but open the hole at the 12 ml mark, not the one at the 6 ml mark, otherwise you will lose some of the sediment and that is something we do not want to happen.

• now add 5 drops of reagent C, shake gently to mix the reagent with the rest of the water,

• this will change the white or brown sediment to a deep yellow color. If this does not happen, your test has expired, and you need to get a new set of reagents A B C,

• this color change may take up to 5 minutes to happen efficiently. Give the chemical reaction time to take place.

• now start adding drops of reagent D until the mixture turns clear again.

The number of drops that you added, divided by two, equals the dissolved oxygen in milligrams per liter. For instance, if you added 14 drops, you have a dissolved oxygen level of 7 mg per liter. If you added 12 drops, it is 6 mg per liter, etc...

Do not add the tested water back to the aquarium. It is noxious to fish and invertebrates. For those interested in the chemicals, we described the whole test in an recent issue of Marine Reef, our newsletter.

Although the test may seem complicated at first, it is really not. It is perhaps a bit more involved than other tests, and takes more time, but it is not really complicated.

Once you know the result, you can compare that result with what the saturation level should be at the temperature that you keep you aquarium at. If you are at saturation or higher, your dissolved oxygen level is in the right range.

If it is not you will have to start asking yourself why, and take corrective action. The sooner you take such action the better, as continuously low dissolved oxygen levels stress the animal life in the aquarium.

Usually the reasons for low levels of oxygen are :

• Your tank is overloaded, too many fish, too many invertebrates, or more than likely too many of both.

• Your filters are too small. This applies mainly to your trickle filter. It cannot deal with all the pollution that is generated.

• You are using a packing material in your trickle filter that may not be adequate, it may not have enough surface area, or it traps too much dirt which results in decay and lower D.O. levels

• You are not adding air to the trickling filter's biological column. This affects the D.O. level substantially, as demonstrated again recently by George Bepko, of Milford, Connecticut.

• You must clean all your mechanical filters more often. Perhaps you are overlooking some areas that trap dirt.

• There is a lot of dead and decaying material in the tank.

• There is a lot of dead and decaying material in the filters.

• You may be feeding too much.

• and other reasons still, but these are some of the important ones.

Any of the above will result in lower dissolved oxygen levels. Usually the reasons turn out to be a combination of several of them. You must then take steps to alleviate the problem, and increase your dissolved oxygen levels as a result. Better maintenance practices are usually a big help.

If your problems persist, even though you have cleaned all filters, are not over feeding, etc.. you will probably need to install an Oxygen Reactor on your system. This will definitely increase the amount of dissolved oxygen. This is probably one of the best things you can do for your aquarium.

There are several models available, including the one by my own company.

Oxygen levels are very important for the Reef Tank. Much more important than we used to think.

In fact, when we kept fish-only tanks, we did not even pay any attention to them, in "Reef" tanks however we must monitor the levels regularly, and ensure that they are at the recommended levels at all times. Every author on Reef Tanks agrees with that.

8. Ammonia   Recommended level : 0 ppm

This is again one of the tests that you are familiar with, as you have probably been doing it for years. If not, it is explained in greater detail in The Marine Fish and Invert Reef Aquarium book, in the testing section.

What is important, is to ensure that the level is always zero ppm. This is done by installing or maintaining adequate biological filtration, and removing dead or decaying material from the tank and from the filters regularly, and as soon as you notice it.

Trickle filtration will do that very efficiently for you, but you must have the right packing material in the filters.

Anything that traps dirt acts as both a mechanical and a biological filter, and since it filters mechanically it will trap dirt, and will require cleaning. This destroys a good part of the bacteria every time you clean and is, of course, not an optimum type of filter.

The packing material that you use must have a good throughflow, and not trap dirt, while at the same time offering a great deal of surface area. There are several such packing materials on the market :

Bioballs, Jaeger Tri-Packs, Biopax, Biopak, Bio Cube-tubes, Bio Disks, Bio•Techs, and many more.

If you detect ammonia in your system, you must look for the causes. Your biological filter may be too small, and you may have to augment its capacity by using a different type of packing material, e.g. some of the plastic spheres that are widely available.

It may also be that your tank is just plainly overloaded, and that you need to increase the size of your filter. The Marine Fish and Invert Reef Aquarium book described, in detail, how this can be done without too much difficulty. You may want to review that section.

You could also solve the problem by adding some other form of filtration to your trickle filter. We strongly recommend a Bio-Mesh filter. We explained the workings of that type of filter both in this book, and in the Marine Fish and Invert Reef Aquarium book.

Dupla's ammonia test is a 3 part test, measuring total ammonium ion present in the water. At high pH levels, such as the ones at which we keep Reef Tanks, some of the ionic form is converted to gas, and the gas which is very toxic dissolves very easily in the water.

Ammonium ion itself is not noxious, but ammonia gas is, and it will kill fish and greatly stress invertebrates.

You must try to keep the level at zero at all times.

Good husbandry techniques, sizing your filter properly, adding extra biological filtration in heavily loaded tanks, and cleaning out dead material, as well as not overfeeding, are some of the steps that will enable you to keep your tank free of ammonium and ammonia.

Protein skimming is a major step forward in this respect. Indeed, a good protein skimmer (foam fractionnator) will remove a great deal of organics before they can actually break down further, and give rise to ammonium.

We therefore strongly recommended that you use such a skimmer, preferably one that is of a more modern conception than some of the ones that are on the market now.

Thiel•Aqua•Tech offers several modern skimmers for sale, starting a prices of $ 299.00, for units that can easily take care of tanks up to 150 gallons. The same company also offers a Venturi power skimmer, 22 inches tall and 6 inches in diameter, and can even custom build such power protein skimmers.

The standard columnar unit will handle larger tanks up to 240 gallons. A store model of both is available too. The columnar version of it is 7 feet tall, including the collection scum cup. Ozone traps (caps filled with activated carbon) are available for these skimmers as well.

Route 4 Aquarium Technology, Summit Aquatics. and Coralife offer excellent skimmers in the same price range as well. Before making any decisions, check the section on skimmer sizing in this book (see index if needed).

Ammonia may increase as a result of a partial, or total, dying off of your biological filter. This is of course a worst case scenario , as it really means that you will have to go back through the entire cycling process since most or all of your biological filter is lost.

Why does this happen ? Often it is the result of additives that you may have used, e.g. medicine, or dyes, or some other treatment that is meant to eradicate parasites, but has noxious side-effects as well.

It is also the reason why we have recommended that you set up a hospital tank, and only treat fish outside of the main aquarium, and never add medicine of any kind to your Reef Tank.

Biological filters may also die off as a result of noxious elements leaching into the water. These can come from implements that you use, or decorative pieces, or even from materials that you put in your trickle filter.

It was recently brought to our attention that imitation Bioballs™ are being sold on the West Coast. We do not know how they are made, and caution you that if the products used are not entirely safe (and that includes the dyes to color them), some elements may leach into the water and kill off your biological filter, and even your fish and invertebrates.

Perhaps the most misunderstood phenomenon in a reef tank is the dying of algae. Algae can store elements and do so in quantities that far exceed the normal concentrations of these elements in water.

When algae die, they not only release these elements back into the aquarium, but in addition release they phytotoxins. The latter are often the cause of so-called wipe-outs, or the destruction of part of, or all of, your biological filter, fish and other lifeforms.

Should large die-offs occur in your tank, you must make water changes immediately, and remove the dead algal material at once.

9. Iron   Recommended Level : 0.05 to 0.1 ppm

If you keep macro-algae, you must fertilize. We explained this in the section on water additives already, and gave you the reasons why.

To know where you stand in terms of iron content, you must test. Iron testing is fairly straightforward : add a scoop of the test reagent to a set ml of water and watch the color change. At least that is how Dupla's test is performed.

Although the test is simple, Hobbyists have called to find out exactly how much compound must be used. The explanation in the Dupla test does not seem too clear.

The Dupla test cylinder comes with a combination scoop - spatula. In the case of iron testing you want to use a rounded scoopful of the reagent. The scoop side is the side that looks like a small round spoon.

Then again, you cannot really use too much reagent, as only as much reagent will react as there is iron to react with. What this means is that you can use too little, but not too much.

If you used too little, all the reagent would be exhausted before all the iron had had a chance to react with it. There would still be some iron left that had not reacted, and your reading would therefore be lower than it in reality is.

If, on the other hand, you use too much, all the iron will have reacted, your reading will be correct, but you may have waisted a little reagent.

Keeping the iron level at 0.05 to 0.1 ppm requires the addition of a fertilizer that contains iron. Tech•Plant•Nutrient and Tech•Algae• Nutrient are such fertilizers, but there are many others on the market. Tech•Plant Nutrients are made in the USA using USP grade chemicals and EDTA in the chelation process (EDTA is an acetic acid derivative).

Whatever fertilizer you buy, make sure it contains iron in a chelated form. If it does not, the iron will not stay in solution and will not be available to the macro and other types of algae that you may be keeping.

Several types of chelators exist. Many are phosphate based. We do not recommend products that use such phosphate based chelators, as they are not suited for our aquariums.

They will ultimately increase the phosphate load of the tank, which we need to avoid, as excess phosphates are usually already present and are produced continuously.

Adding fertilizers manually, perhaps daily at feeding time, is the simplest method. You can of course automate the process, to get an even and continuous addition of fertilizer, by using a metering or a dosing pump (we have explained how both of these work in Part Two of this book).

How much and how frequently you need to add fertilizer to maintain the recommended levels, depends on whose fertilizer you are using, and what its strength is, as well as how many macro and other algae your tank contains. If you have large amounts of macro-algae, you will obviously need more fertilizer to maintain the desired level.

As a last remark : if you do not keep macro-algae, you do not need such fertilizers and you obviously do not need to test for iron, either.

What do you do if your iron levels are too high ?

Iron levels may be too high for various reasons :

• You may have added too much fertilizer (your mix may be too strong)
• Your dosing or metering pump may have malfunctioned.
• The water you use contains high levels of iron (e.g. some well waters, especially those from deep wells).

Iron can be precipitated by using chemicals, but that is normally not practical in a Reef Tank. Our best approach therefore is to change aquarium water, for several consecutive times, until the level is down to where it should be.

Of course, if the water you are now using contains too much iron already, you must find another source or first run the water through a reverse osmosis or ion-exchange filter. Alternatively, use Poly Filters since they will remove iron as well, especially excessive amounts.

Making large water changes, or changing a lot of water in one session is usually not a good idea because it alters the water chemistry too much. This stresses the fish.

If it is the lesser of two evils, however, you will have to take the chance that you may do so. Whether to change a lot of water, or whether to make small changes, will depend on what the excess iron level actually is.

If the level is lower than 1.5 ppm you can change small amounts for several consecutive times, e.g. every 4 hours. If the level is over 1.5 ppm you will need to change as much as 25 percent, then re-test for iron levels and decide whether you need to make one more large water change, or several smaller ones.

Thiel•Aqua•Tech markets its own iron test, the Tech•Iron test. It is a highly accurate 2 component test, unlike other iron tests which use only one highly hygroscopic powder. It is manufactured from USP chemicals and gives highly accurate low level readings, the ones that we are interested in. Tests for iron content are available from other manufacturers as well.

10. General Hardness dGH   Recommended Level : n/a

The general hardness of a Reef tank's water is always very high. Unless you have a test solution that is meant to test very high general hardness levels, do not even attempt to do so as you will use up your entire test reagent supply and not even come up with a result.

You need not worry about general hardness, as it is unlikely that it is out of balance. It is usually determined by the compounds that are in the salt you use in which they are mixed in the proper fashion and proportion to maintain the right hardness at the manufacturing stage.

It is therefore not a matter of concern to us. It is unlikely too, that you would be adding anything to the water that would increase it further, and as a result it will vary minimally.

Our recommendation is not to test for general hardness. Test only for carbonate hardness, and for alkalinity if you have such a test.

11. Carbonate hardness Rec. Level : 12 min. to 18 max.

Carbonate hardness is that portion of the hardness that can be easily removed, and it consists mainly of carbonates and bicarbonates - also called hydrogen carbonates - of calcium, magnesium and borate sources.

It is an important component of the water chemistry, because it not only determines the stability of the pH, but also provides the corals and the calcareous algae with the calcium they need to survive.

The "buffer" as it is called, is depleted on a continuous basis because of its interaction with the acids that are produced in the tank. These acids include carbon dioxide, organic acids from protein breakdown, and a number of others from metabolic and other processes.

Because a reduction in the buffer will, over time, result in a reduction in the pH as well, we need to ensure that the carbonate hardness is continuously maintained at proper levels.

Various schools of thought exist. Some suggest leaving it at 9 dKH which is about what you would find around a real Reef, others suggest building in a margin, and keeping it at higher levels, for example 12 or more dKH.

Personal experience, and conversations with many Reef Keepers, has reinforced my conviction that, to keep corals and to keep calcareous algae for extended periods of time, the dKH needs to be higher.

We have as a result recommended for the last 4 years that you maintain your dKH between 12 and 18, and we personally keep our tanks at 15. (Lab books 4-5-7 THIEl 1986 1987)

You should test your KH at least once a week, and adjust it whenever necessary, especially if you use carbon dioxide fertilization.

To adjust your tank's dKH you need to add one of the many buffer products that are on the market. Since they all differ in how fast and how much they raise the carbonate hardness, you must read the instructions that come with the product carefully and only then decide on the quantity you will need. Typically adjustments have to be made slowly with regular intermittent testing.

Some products contain elements that break the surface tension of the water. They make your skimmer work harder, meaning foam more. Keep that in mind, as if the product you use is one of those, you will have to re-adjust the skimmer before adding that product, and re-adjust it again after the treatment is completed.

Some of these products include: Marine Buffer by the makers of Instant Ocean, Tech•Reef•KH by Thiel•Aqua•Tech, KH Generator by Dupla, and the newly introduced KH builder by Route 4 of Elmwood Park, NJ.

If your carbonate hardness is too high you can reduce it by injecting more carbon dioxide for a while, or you can make water changes with softer water, until you are back in the right range.

Even if you do not modify a high dKH, the system will take care of itself, as the carbonate hardness will fall automatically as we explained a little earlier.

Users of CO_2 fertilization must check their carbonate hardness at least once a week, as carbon dioxide depletes the buffer which will cause your pH to drop to too low a level.

In an automated system this would be taken care of by itself, as once the pH controller senses that the pH is too low, lower than the setting you decided on, it will stop pushing carbon dioxide in the system.

But in a manual system this does not happen, and you must make sure that the KH is in the right ranges, and keep it there by adding buffering compounds, in quantities required and determined by your testing

The addition of CO_2 was discussed in great detail in The Marine Fish and Invert Reef Aquarium book, both the manual way, and the automated way. Refer to it if it is of interest to your particular tank. It is also covered later in this book, in the equipment installation section.

There are several KH tests on the market, including the ones made by Tetra, Dupla and Thiel•Aqua•Tech's 2 component pH and salt water stabilized Reef•KH test in dropper bottles.

Remember to make all KH adjustments slowly and test regularly to determine what the exact impact of the product that you are using is on your water..

12. Copper Cu   Recommended level : 0 ppm

Though the above suggestion is not entirely correct, as aquarium salt water always contains traces of copper, for all intents and purposes, aquarium copper tests will not be able to detect such low levels, and the reading on your test should therefore be zero.

Copper can enter the system with the tap water you are using, as water travels to the copper piping in the house or building. This is more pronounced if your water piping is relatively new, since more copper ions will move into the water from new pipes than from old ones.

Always let tap water run for a few minutes before using it. This will remove the water that stood in the pipes for a long time, and reduce the risk of adding copper to your tank.

Warm water pipes have more copper in the water than cold water pipes. The ionic exchange process is faster, and greater, at higher temperatures. If you use a mixture of hot and cold water, you must therefore let that run for a few minute too. To be on the safe side, test that water before using it.

Be careful also with some forms of distilled water that you buy in super-markets. Although it is called distilled, it may contain detectable traces of copper . They result from copper distilling installations being used.

Reverse osmosis filtration will remove copper from your tap water. You may wish to use such water for water changes, instead of plain tap. Still the best is de-ionized and triple distilled water.

Copper falls out, precipitates, in water of high pH levels. This means that if you have pieces of coral and rocks that were previously used in a fish tank to which copper was added, some copper precipitates will still be present on those rocks and coral pieces.

You can therefore not use such pieces in your Reef Tank. They have to be treated and soaked in an acid bath several times , to remove the copper.

This is a process that can take weeks, and sometimes even months, depending on the amount of copper that was precipitated on the rocks.

As a safety rule, if you do not know where a piece of coral or coral rock came from, do not put it in your Reef Tank. It is not worth the trouble and the possible damage.

13. Hydrogen Sulfide Recommended level : 0 ppm

Hydrogen sulfide is one of the by-products of anaerobic activity. Methane gas is another one.

When there are areas in your filters or in your tank, for instance in thick substrates, where oxygen is not reaching, anaerobic activity will start and hydrogen sulfide will be produced.

The reason is simple, the bacteria that grow in those areas break down the sulfates in the water and produce H_2S.

This is a gas that mixes very rapidly with water -it diffuses- and is highly toxic to all animal life. It also greatly reduces the amount of dissolved oxygen in your aquarium (Lab book 11THIEL 1886)

If you notice black spots on your substrate, you must stir them up immediately to stop the formation of anaerobics. Better still is to syphon all of it out of the tank, to prevent those noxious compounds from mixing with the rest of the water. The black color is the result of iron in the water combining with sulfides.

Cleaning your filters regularly and making sure that you have good water circulation throughout all areas of the tank, is another way to prevent anaerobic activity.

Hydrogen sulfide can be chased out of the water easily by means of extra aeration. If you run your tank properly however, you should not have any problems with it at all, except if your aquarium has very thick substrate layers through which the water cannot easily circulate.

The finer the material used for the substrate, the more likely you are to see anaerobic activity develop. Sand is therefore the least desirable form of substrate as it "packs", and can as a result become anaerobic very quickly.

Sand is aesthetically very appealing and many Hobbyists would like to use it in their aquariums. Unfortunately, in light of what we have just said, we do not recommend its use at all.

Another source of hydrogen sulfide, still as a result of anaerobic activity, is denitrification filters that are not running properly. Usually it results from water going into the filter too slowly, or from not enough food being provided for the bacteria in the filter.

This is the reason why you must watch the drip rate through the denitrifying filter daily, and make sure too that enough and the right kind of nutrient is available and added regularly.

A metering pump solves that problem easily; it involves an additional expense but is generally considered a wise investment as it automates many tasks that are important for water chemistry stability.

If you are interested in testing for this compound, you can buy an excellent testing kit from Chemetrix, or use the Thiel•Aqua•Tech qualitative hydrogen sulfide test.

14. Phenol - Phenols Recommended level : zero

Phenol and other phenolic compounds can be present in the water when something interferes with the normal breakdown of protein, or if you are using phenolic plastics, or resins, that leach phenols back into the water.

This is not a compound that the average hobbyist normally tests for, but tests are available; again Chemetrix is one source.

The use of skimmers and particularly ozone will prevent phenol from being present or building up. This is another good reason to install a protein skimmer with an ozonizer. Ozone breaks phenols down and eliminates them safely from your system.

There are many types of phenols, in its simplest form it is called just that : phenol (carbolic acid, phenolic acid, benzophenol, hydroxybenzene). Phenols are strong irritants and are therefore noxious.

Phenols in excess of 5 ppm in the air are toxic to humans as well. Cresols, resorcinols, xylenol, and naphtols are all forms of phenolic compounds.

Some occur as by-products of protein breakdown, and if they build up they will cause death of fish and invertebrates, others may enter the system by leachment from equipment that is not tatally inert.

Phenols are removed by regular water changes and good ozonization through a columnar or Venturi protein skimmer (foam fractionnator).If your system includes this equipment you will, more than likely, never find any phenol in your tank.

15. Activated Carbon Test

Those of you who are still using activated carbon, whether granular or in powder form, need to be able to check whether the activated carbon is actually still removing compounds from the tank's water. This is especially important in the case of ozone.

This can be done using the fact that carbon adsorbs yellowing matter. If we use that as a yardstick, we can determine visually whether that yellowing matter is in fact still being removed.

All you will need is a small piece of white plastic on which you make a faint yellow mark or two. Two lines, perhaps half an inch wide, will do. The key however is that the yellow must be really faint and made with a water resistant ink.

Place that plastic card in the tank, and hold it under water. Look at it from about two feet away. If you can still see the yellow on the plastic, your carbon is still active. If you can no longer see the yellow, your carbon needs changing.

What the test means is that if you cannot see the yellow, your water must be slightly yellow itself, masking the faint yellow color on the plastic card. If the water is slightly yellow the carbon is obviously not removing the yellowing matter.

Dupla sells such a test, but you could easily make one yourself. We suggest that you perform this test once a week, especially if you are using ozone .

16. The pH Test Recommended level : 8.0 to 8.2

This is such a classic test, that we do not really want to spend any time at all on it. Many commercial tests are available and are all simple to perform.

Keep the pH of your Reef tank stable; somewhere between 8.0 and 8.2. Stability at any of those levels is more important than any specific "ideal" number.

Invertebrates do not really seem to mind that much at what exact level the pH is as long as you keep the pH stable. We keep our tank at a pH of 8.05, using an automatic CO_2 system.

The latter brings the pH down when it rises, by adding carbon dioxide, and shutting off when our setpoint pH is reached again. A rising pH seems to be the norm in a system that runs with trickle filters, as the improved water quality has a tendency to make the pH go up.

Because of the variety of animals that Hobbyists keep there is not "one" pH number that is right for all of them, since many of lifeforms come from different areas, different depths, different Reefs, and are as a result accutomed to different pH levels.

Even though many of the invertebrates offered for sale in Pet Stores come from the Indo-Pacific, they too come from a variety of reefs that differ in water conditions.

Keep in mind as well that around Reefs the pH changes constantly, within limitations of course, because of low and high tide effects combined with the motion of the Ocean.

17. Cleaning pH and O.R.P. Electrodes

Electrodes are very sensitive instruments and need to be cared for properly and regularly. This will not only extend their useful life, but ensures that your electrodes will give you accurate readings.

As they are placed in your tank, or filter, and are submersed in a liquid that contains many pollutants, organic material, salt, a high degree of carbonates, etc... the tip of the probe and the semi-permeable membrane cover themselves with dirt, usually in a matter of weeks. Sooner if your tank is highly polluted.

This results in inaccurate readings and requires that you clean both the tip and the membrane on a regular basis.

The latter is done by immersing the electrode in a special acidic solution for 15 to 20 minutes, every few weeks. Thiel•Aqua•Tech and Dupla sell such cleaning solutions. You can also obtain them from Scientific supply houses.

Place the electrode in the cleaning solution in a glass or vial, let stand for about 15 minutes, then rinse the electrode in distilled water by swirling it in the container vigorously.

Place the electrode back in the solution for another 10 minutes and rinse again with distilled water. Your electrode should now be clean. After cleaning, your pH electrode should be recalibrated to ensure real accuracy.

Redox potential electrodes are not recalibrated, but just placed back in the tank.

Rredox potential electrode can be recalibrated as well of course, but you will need a meter that allows you to do so, and a calibrating solution. The problem is that ORP calibrating solutions are rather expensive and cumbersome to use.

The one my company sells costs $65.00 (granted, you can do about 15 calibrations with it), and includes 2 reference pH solutions, Quinhidrone, and the all important set of instructions.

Since different pH meters require different calibration techniques , we can not describe the procedure fully.

It involves, however, placing your electrode in reference solutions that have a known pH, reading on the dial of your meter what the pH number is that your electrode is sensing, and if it is not exactly the same as the pH of the reference solution, adjusting the read-out to match that number.

This is usually done for 2 different pH levels, to ensure a higher accuracy (slope and assymetry adjustment).

Redox potential electrode calibration requires you to follow a more complicated procedure. Available tests explain the whole process in quite some detail, making it possible to perform the calibration without too many problems. The whole process usually takes about 15 minutes and requires in addition to the reagents supplied with the test, 2 glass vials or cylinders.

18. Storing Electrodes properly, when not in use

Storing your electrodes properly is perhaps the most important action that you will take to prolong their life.

Electrodes are filled with a reference fluid. Often this will be 1M KCl, or 3M KCl, or some similar chemical compound (one molar and 3 molar potassium chloride).

The liquid that you place in the tip of the electrode when storing it, should be that same reference fluid. This stabilizes the electrode and will greatly preserve its useful life.

When the liquids on both sides of the semi-permeable membrane are the same, the electrode is, so to speak, "neutral" and the membrane is not sensing any reaction between the outside and the reference liquid.

Since good electrodes are expensive, it certainly pays to take the necessary steps to preserve them by cleaning and re-calibrating them regularly. Every 5 to 6 weeks is usually suggested.

Redox Potential electrodes usually contain silver chloride rather than potassium chloride. So should the caps. These liquids can be ordered from scientific supply places, or usually also from the company that you bought your meter and electrode from. T•A•T sells both.

Check, from time to time, whether fluid is still present in the cap when storing electrodes for extended periods of time. If the fluid in the cap has dried out, place the electrode in distilled water for 8 to 10 hours. Refill the cap with the required liquid and place it back on the electrode.

After 2 to 3 more hours your electrode should be operating normally again, but you will need to re-calibrate it before using it.

You may think that we want you to re-calibrate your electrodes very frequently. In laboratories electrodes are re-calibrated every time they are used, or certainly if they have not been used for a few hours, or have been used in different liquids.

Since we only test one liquid, and since the probe stays immersed, we do not need to re-calibrate that often. Every 5 to 6 weeks should do.

Sometimes, when calibrating your electrode, you will not be able to make the digital or analog read-out match the pH of the reference liquid that you are using. If this happens to you it means that your electrode is no longer usable and needs to be replaced.

19. Where should you place the electrodes ?

Values for pH, and especially for redox potential, are not identical in all areas of the aquarium. The differences will not be large, but there will be differences. The more sensitive the electrode, the more you will notice that difference.

You can of course place your electrodes in the sump of your trickle filter, in fact several filters have a place foreseen for electrodes already.

Keep in mind however that conditions in the sump may not be the same as conditions in the aquarium. Case in point :

• if you are using CO₂ and returning the water from the carbon dioxide reactor to the sump, and the electrode is anywhere near that return, the pH reading that you will get will be lower than the actual pH of the tank, because of the direct influence of the carbon dioxide on the water in the sump.

• if you are using a protein skimmer, especially if ozone is used, and your redox potential electrode is near that water return, the redox potential that you measure will be higher than the redox potential of the tank, because the water coming from the skimmer that mixes with the water in the sump, will have a much higher redox potential. Not that it matters very much, as, if you keep those numbers stable, you will be achieving the right effect in the long run.

If, however, you want the true pH and the true redox potential, you should measure it in the tank directly, or you should pipe the electrode in-line with the water coming down from the tank to the trickle filter.

Special Tee-fittings that allow you to do that exist, and cost around $17.50 from Thiel•Aqua•Tech. They are easy to installl, and ensure that the water flows evenly over the tip of the electrode continuously.

Alternatively, the best spot to place your electrodes is right where the water goes into the overflow syphon, or into the corner overflow box. The water flowing into the overflow is representative of the water in the aquarium; the flow is also constant and usually relatively strong.

You could also measure the pH and the redox potential in two locations, by using one of the conversion units sold by Thiel•Aqua•Tech, described earlier in this book (Custom models for more than 2 electrodes are available as well).

This is in fact exactly what we will be doing. Both pH and redox potential will be measured in the water line going up to the tank, and also in the water line coming down from the tank to the filter.

The way this is done is simple. We have installed two of the Tee-fittings that hold electrodes, in both the water pipe going up to the tank, and also in the pipe coming down to the trickle filter.

We then place a pH and a redox potential electrode inside the fittings, one set in each water line.

The reason we are installing the system in this fashion is to be able to determine how much the pH and the redox potential vary, after the water has been through the tank and been exposed to the existing pollution in the aquarium.

This has been a most interesting experiment. Indeed the pH fluctuates by only 0.05 maximum on average, whereas the redox potential varies a lot more (Lab books 15-16-18 THIEL 1987 1988).

The magnitude depends on time of day, and whether the lights are on or not, meaning whether metabolism and photosynthesis are high or low.

In the morning, the redox potential difference is no more than 10 mv on most days. Once the lights have been on for about 4 hours the difference has risen to about 60 mv, on average.

Towards the evening the difference is usually around 25 to 30 mv only. We have not determined yet why the spread narrows again in the evening, but we suspect that it may have to do with a somewhat reduced metabolic rate and the fact that food that was not eaten has now been filtered out and neutralized.

We are obviously continuing this experiment, and will more than likely report on it in **Marine Reef**, our newsletter.

20. Ozone and How to Use It

20.1. Comments

If there is one water treatment method that is often misunderstood, and blamed for all kinds of problems, it must be ozone. It seems that, as soon as hobbyists equip their tanks with an ozonizer, and as soon as anything goes wrong, they will blame ozone for it. Even if ozone is not close to being remotely connected to the problem.

Here is a gas that has a very high oxidative power, that can clean up the tank's water very efficiently, and most hobbyists either do not know how to use it, or are just plain afraid of doing so.

Here is a method of raising the water quality that is not too complicated to incorporate in your system, and Hobbyists shun it.

It is hard to understand why this unfortunate viewpoint and this mistrust for ozone exists; but it certainly does. And it exists not only among Hobbyists; the situation is exactly the same when one talks to store owners.

We must assume that, in the past, people have had bad experiences and that the word has spread, not unlike what carbon dioxide went through, and still goes through, in the freshwater hobby.

I strongly believe that if you understand the item, or product, that you are using, you will not fear it; you know you have control over it. When you reach that stage, you will use it with confidence, and you will be able to get the benefits that it provides.

And here lies perhaps the root of the problem: Hobbyists and stores do not understand ozonization , as a result, rather than using it, they just pretend it does not exist, or claim you do not need it, or that it is harmful and will kill your fish.

The mere fact that, until very recently, only one company had ozonizers available, should prove my point that it was not a popular item. This will hopefully change as time goes on, and as more manufacturers bring good quality and stronger ozonization units on the market.

20.2 What is ozone ?

Ozone is a special form of oxygen.It is refered to as an "allotropic" form. Normal atmospheric oxygen has two atoms, ozone has three.

The chemical formulas for both are therefore only slightly different, O_2 for oxygen, and O_3 for ozone, but what a difference in how they chemically act and affect the water in your tank!

It is a gas of course, blue in color, with a very distinctive odor. You can actually smell as little as 0.2 ppm in the air. If ozone is present you will not fail to notice it. You must however prevent this, as ozone is an irritant to the lungs. This is done by placing a cap filled with carbon on top of your skimmer, and/or activated carbon chamber.

Ozone has a very high oxidative power, expressed as millivolt and redox potential : it amounts to 2076 or 2.076 volt.

It is a much stronger oxidizer than chlorine (1360 millivolt), oxygen, and many other compounds, and is in addition very unstable, which means that it breaks back down to oxygen very rapidly, liberating atomic or nascent oxygen, (O), where it gets its strong oxidative power from.

It is in fact this characteristic that allows us to use it in our hobby. If it were a more stable gas it could not be used, as we would not be able to remove it from the water quickly enough, before that water re-entered the aquarium.

Because it is so short lived, we can put its effects to use and still ensure that it does not end up in the main water mass.

It oxidizes rubber, phenols, cyanides, organics, humins (it breaks them down to CO_2 and water) and many other compounds of course, even steel, although stainless steel will resist ozone for many many years.

Acrylic hose, such as the type you use for airline tubing, does not resist ozone either, it breaks down quickly. It may change color, harden, and eventually crack, causing leaks of air mixed with ozone into the ambient surroundings.

Rubber will break down in a matter of days or weeks, and should never be used in anything that comes in contact with the ozone. Certain plastics are not ozone resistant either.

Rather than rubber or acrylic hose, we should use Norprene (best) or Tygon (second best) as they resist ozone extremely well and for long periods of time. Anything else will deteriorate very quickly, and ozone will be lost to the surrounding air.

As a result your skimmer will not run as well, as less air pressure and less ozone will reach inside the column.

You must also remember that using the wrong type of hose connections causes a strong loss of ozone. The reaction of the hose and the ozone inside the tubing itself, uses up a great amount of the ozone before it reaches the water column in the skimmer.

20.3. How do we use Ozone ?

There are only two ways to safely use ozone in any aquarium set up :

- with a Foam Fractionnator - Protein Skimmer
- with an Ozone Reactor.

Bubbling ozone directly into the tank is totally excluded, and bubbling it in the sump of the trickle filter is looking for trouble.

Indeed, residual ozone will get to the tank, which is dangerous and will lead to problems. Some ozone may even find its way into the back of the trickle filter, escape from the water, and enter the biological filtration column. If that happens, you will have lose your biological filter in a matter of hours, because the ozone will burn out - oxidise, so to speak -the beneficial bacteria in the filter.

That is exactly the reason why we have always been against installing a small protein skimmer that can be run with ozone in the sump of the trickle filter.

If you own such a filter, we suggest that you do not use it with ozone, but resort to doing so in an outside skimmer. Alternatively, acquire an ozone reactor instead.

The safest way is to use in a protein skimmer, whether columnar or Venturi makes no difference, as long as you flow the water that comes out of the skimmer over activated carbon before it actually mixes with the tank's main water mass, and gets back into the aquarium.

Some trickle filters now even have special compartments where you can place a fair amount of activated carbon (Dupla USA, Thiel•Aqua•Tech, Summit Aquatics, are just 3 of the many that are now offered for sale through ads or discussed in the magazines that you should read : FAMA, Marine Reef, Marine Fish Monthly, Tropical Fish Hobbyist, Aquarium Fish Magazine).

 Of course the additional safety factor that we have not mentioned yet is the redox potential controller. Such a meter - controller, takes the guess work out of the whole process. More on that later in this Part of the book (also refer to the index for all occurances of ozone in this book).

20.4. How is ozone produced ?

Most ozonizers work on the very high electrical discharge principle, generating a so-called corona, which breaks the oxygen in the air up, to some extent, in a mixture of oxygen and some ozone.

Very little ozone is actually produced, but to make ozonization efficient we do not needs grams, we only need milligrams.

The chemical formulation is :   3 O_2 will form 2 O_3.

To produce a strong corona discharge, very high voltages are necessary. We are talking about anywhere from 4500 to 7500 volts, depending on the strength of the ozonizer.

As air is blown through the area where the corona is produced, the oxygen in the air is used to make ozone, it is broken up and recombines based on the chemical reaction given above.

Because humid air will not make as much ozone as dry air, you must dry the air first, using one of the several air dryers that are available. Unfortunately, none of the compounds used in dryers last for very long.

You will therefore have to regenerate your drying compound every few days. This not something that we can change, drying compounds will just not last for long periods of time, especially in areas where the humidity is high (the room in which your aquarium is, or the cabinet underneath, probably has close to 80 percent humidity).

Ozone can also be produced using ultraviolet light, but this principle is only used in larger units, especially the ones that run continuously. Indeed, if the ultraviolet bulb is switched on and off too frequently, it will have to be replaced regularly, and that becomes too expensive a proposition.

Dust in the air also inhibits the formation of ozone. Use an air filter in addition to your dryer and your unit will produce more ozone.

Small air filters can be made by placing some filter floss in a tube, in line with the air that goes the ozonizer. The sequence of the pieces is as follows : air pump - dryer - air filter - ozonizer - skimmer.

Better than such a rudimentary filter is the fibrous membrane air filter, you can order such air filters from Thiel•Aqua•Tech. They are not expensive and last for months and months.

20.5. How much ozone should you use ?

There is no real answer to this. We covered this topic earlier in this book already. It is the result of different bio-loads in each tank, and also of differing filtration systems used.

Some filters just work better than others and leave less pollution in the water. That, in turn, then requires less ozone to remove the balance of the pollution.

To recapitulate :

• the more pollution there is in the water, the more ozone you will need to make your redox potential go up,

• as the water quality improves, and as less pollution is present, you will need less ozone,

• this downward trend in the quantity needed will go on, until the amount of ozone used, can deal with the amount of pollution the tank generates on a continuous basis.

That amount is different for every tank. In essence, a state of equilibrium is reached between the pollution generated and the amount of ozone needed to neutralize it.

Once that level is known, all you need to do, is to inject slightly more than that amount, and your redox potential will go up.

The only way to determine the magnitude of that quantity accurately yourself, for your own system, is to have a redox potential meter, or better even a redox potential controller.

You can then, by varying the amount of ozone you push into the skimmer, determine from the readings on your meter where the equilibrium point lies exactly.

This is a trial and error method, but it works. And it will not take you very long to determine where the best setting on your ozonizer is.

You may also wish to re-read "On using Ozone", Part 2.9.1 in this book.

20.6. Who should use Ozone ?

If you keep a Reef aquarium, and you want to achieve real high water quality levels, you will definitely need an ozonizer. There are no real ways around it.

To raise the redox potential to the high 300's, low 400's millivolt, you will need to clean up the water much more than what other types of filtration can do for you.

Sander from Germany makes several models, we have seen at least 3 of them for sale in the USA. Thiel•Aqua•Tech makes one model and it is made in the United States. We pride ourselves of the fact that it is a very safe unit. It even has a heat fuse built into it, in addition to the regular outside fuse.

This is for extra protection.The whole inside is also "potted" with a special resin to ensure that whatever happens, you can never get near wires that may shock you electrically and possibly hurt you.

Additionally, the inside of the tube in which the corona discharge takes place is specially coated to give a better, and much longer useful life, and a higher and cleaner ozone output.

For optimum efficiency we recommend that you always use an air dryer and a small air filter in conjunction with your ozonizer.

20. 7. What will Ozone do for you ?

If used the way we have already explained several times in this book, ozone will allow you to raise your redox potential to just about any number you want, providing you give it the time to do so, and providing your ozonizer is a strong enough model.

The key is to raise the redox potential to the right millivolt range. More on redox potential, and what type of millivolt readings you should try to achieve in your Reef Tank, later in this section.

By allowing you to get your water quality up that high, you will have a tank that looks much better overall, and runs without the complications that so many hobbyists have experienced in the past.

You will also have far less problems with micro-algae, red algae, smear algae, filamentous algae, etc...

Since ozone burns out a lot of the organics in the water -and if run properly a skimmer can be 80 percent efficient- there are less compounds that will decay and bring the water quality down. There will, as a result, also be less noxious by-products of such breakdown processes present, which in itself is a boon and stresses the lifeforms in the tank considerably less.

In fact, the combined action of a skimmer and ozone greatly reduces the stress on the fish, and creates an environment that is much more suited for the animals that you keep, than older type aquariums that do not use this modern technology.

If you have not used ozone up to now, you must start slowly. Not more than 0.25 mg per gallon for at least two weeks. Then you can start increasing the quantity based on the redox potential that you are trying to achieve.

Depending on the amount of pollution in your tank, this may take as much as 1 mg per gallon, for a while anyway. As the water quality improves, this will become less and less. Whenever you use that much ozone, you must test for residual ozone regularly.

Of course when you run your ozonizer in conjunction with a redox potential controller, the whole matter of quantity is no longer so important, as the controller will switch your ozonizer on and off, as required, once the redox potential that you have set the controller for, is reached.

That redox potential will then be maintained. The controller will switch the ozonizer back on and off as needed, and provide enough ozonization to maintain your redox potential at that level.

Only in extreme cases will it be unable to do that. For instance, if a large fish or a sizeable anemone died and started decomposing, your overall water quality would still go down until you remove the decaying material ; then it will go back up.

Model I ozonizer by TAT

Without ozone the quality of the water would drop subsatnatially more, in fact, such a die-off may lead to such bad water quality that more and more animals die, leading to the aquarium being wasted.

20.8. Precautions You must take when using Ozone

There are a few precautions that you need to take to use ozone safely, both for your tank and for yourself :

• Flow the water coming from the skimmer over activated carbon, and make sure that it flows "through" the activated carbon, not just over it, as the latter is guaranteed to lead to residual ozone in thewater in a matter of days.

• Use a test to determine that your activated carbon is still adsorbing and removing ozone and other materials. We have referred to this test as the yellowing or carbon efficiency test.

• Use a Residual Ozone test and check your test on a regular basis to ensure it is still chemically active. We have explained how to do this in section 2.9.1.

• Place an ozone cap on top of your skimmer to prevent ozone from escaping in the ambient air. This device is also referred to as an ozone trap.

• Definitely use an air dryer to allow your unit to put out what it is rated for, and not 30 or 40 percent of that amount. The latter happens when humid air is pushed through the ozonizer.

• When using an Ozone Reactor you must flow the water over and through activated carbon, test for residual ozone, and increase the amount of carbon until no residual ozone is left in the water after it has passed through the carbon chamber or container.

• Never use ozone on "internal" skimmers. It is very difficult to remove residual ozone before the water gets into the tank, and damage will result if such ozone remains in the tank's water.

• Use only ozone resistant tubing, preferably Norprene, between the ozonizer and the Protein Skimmer, or Ozone Reactor. Others types of tubing, especially airline tubing, will soon break down and release ozone in the air. Alternatively, use Tygon.

Keep in mind as well that such tubing, in the process of reacting with ozone, reduces the amount of ozone that actually reaches the skimmer or reactor. This result in a very inefficient use of your ozonizer.

• Never put a stronger fuse in your ozonizer than the one that was in it originally. If the fuse keeps blowing you must have your unit serviced. Putting in a stronger fuse will only lead to greater problems, such as the internal transformer becoming overloaded, and burning out. That will require a major repair job on the unit.

• Never open your ozonizer while it is still plugged in. The high internal voltages are very dangerous. In fact, if you use our ozonizers there is no need to open them at all. We even seal them so you cannot open them. This is not to hide the parts but to make them safer.

• Do never tinker with the insides of your ozonizer. If it malfunctions, have it serviced.

• Place the ozonizer higher than the water level in the skimmer or in the ozone reactor. This will prevent water from being sucked in the unit when the power fails.

• As a further protection, insert an ozone resistant check valve in line. T•A•T and other companies sell such devices.

• If you can smell ozone in the air, a leak obviously exists and must be found. Switch your ozonizer off and look for the leak. Soapy water rubbed over all connections will locate the leak rapidly, as bubbles will form at the spot where the leak is.

Overall these suggestions are not difficult to follow and are very common sense type of recommendations. Get in the routine of adhering to them and you will not have to worry as to whether or not you are using ozone safely.

Of course, since it is an electrical device, you should keep children away from ozonizers and any other such equipment.

20.9. How fast will Ozone work for You ?

Depending on the amount of pollution in the tank, and depending on the amount of ozone that your unit delivers, it will take anywhere from a few minutes, to a few hours before you will see a difference.

In reality, ozone starts working immediately, but if the amount of pollution in your tank is high, changes will occur slowly.

Significant differences may take weeks to take place. By siginificant we mean an increase of, for instance, from 230 mv to 360 mv, or some similar large increase in water quallity that is permanent, and can be maintained with only minimal amounts of ozone being injected into the protein skimmer.

If you have a redox potential controller, or even a redox potential meter, you should see the millivolt readings go up. Slowly if pollution is high, more rapidly if pollution is not that high. But working it is.

The ozone you are adding has to deal not only with the pollution that is already present, but also with the pollution that is continuously generated. If your tank is not in all that good shape to begin with, both these amounts are obviously high and a radical change in water chemistry will take several days, or even weeks, to manifest itself.

You must just be patient and watch what happens to the tank and its water chemistry. Test regularly to ensure no residual ozone is ever present in the water that goes to the tank. Also, monitor how your foam fractionnator is running. Make sure that it is pulling organics out of the water. This is easily determined by checking whether such material is collecting in the cup at the top of your skimmer.

In any event, increases in your redox potential should not occur rapidly anyway. Usually recommendations are 25 to 30 millivolt, per 24 hours, maximum, but we have recently revised our own recommendation to 60-75 mv per 24 hours (based on empyrical evidence THIEL 1988)

20. 10. Ozone tests

There are several way to test for ozone. Since we are not into testing quantitatively, but only want to determine whether ozone is present in the water or not - a qualitative test - standard methods include :

• Litmus paper impregnated with Potassium iodine. It will turn blue if ozone is present at all.

• Starch paper impregnated with Potassium iodine. It will also turn blue if ozone is present.

• O-Tolidine tests. The tested water will turn yellow or bluish, depending on how much ozone is actually in the water. This is the better of the three methods, mainly because it reacts to the smallest quantities, as long as it has been chemically mixed to do so.You can obtain such a test from T•A•T.

21. Silicic Acid

It has recently been repeatedly reported in many German circles that one of the reasons for slimy red, and sometimes black, algae is the presence in the water of silicic acid, or some other chemical forms of soluble silicates (most are not soluble or only minimally).

Silicates are highly insoluble, but silicic acid obviously is not. It is present in some areas of the country in tap water and sometimes also in well water.

Removing silicic acid is unfortunately a task that needs to be done before the water actually gets into your tank. Before you add the salt.

It can be removed from alkaline water, but we have not found any-thing that can safely be used on our tanks.

A two step process that can used, but that is not practical for hobbyists, would be as follows :

• first the water is acidified with a strong acid, e.g. 6N hydrochloric acid or sulfuric acid.

• Sodium aluminate is then used to remove the colloidal, or coagulated silicic acid.

Other methods that have been tried, and give partial results, without noxious side-effects, is to flow the water over calcined magnesia, dolomite or magnesite.

Dolomite, for instance, acts as a sorbent, and removes silicic acid in doing so. This is a much more practical way, providing you can get obtain pure dolomite in granular form. All you then need to do is to place the dolomite inside a cannister, or a reactor, and flow water through it.

Using dolomite, as was done in undergravel systems, will not work because you will need to clean the dolomite regularly (which is not practical) and change it every couple of weeks.

If you wish to remove silicic acid before adding the salt, in essence if you want to treat the tap or well water that you use, you will need an ion exchange unit with the appropriate resins.

Because it is not customary, and not wise, to use only one resin exchanger, cation exchange needs to be added to the system as well. This makes it safe and practical.My own company's de-ionizer contains the resins needed to do so, and is available.

You should aim for a level of zero ppm at all times; this will require that you test your water before using it. T•A•T sells such tests and so do some of the chemical supply houses that sell by catalogue.

Obviously, if you now use resin exchangers that remove silicates from the water, there should be no need for testing, providing you can determine when the resins need to be replaced or re-charged.

22. Reduction Oxidation Potential :

22.1. Defining Redox Potential

Oxidation reduction reactions are a very important part of chemistry, and are not easily explained in layman's terms.

It is probably best to dispense with the explanation as, valences, the strength of ionic bonds, lowest states of free energy, and quantum mechanics are not really of much interest to the Hobbyist.

To be able to apply Redox Potential measurements to your Reef Tank, understanding the chemical meaning of oxidation reduction is in fact not really important at all.

Whether we understand electron structures or not, we can still apply the knowledge we can gain from measuring the ORP, as it is also called - ORP stands simply for oxidation reduction - to better our water's quality.

We need to give you a little background though, just enough so you can get an idea of where the name comes from, and what it represents.

Redox potential is measured in millivolt, or for very strong oxidizing compounds in volts (e.g. ozone : 2.076 volt, which is equal to 2076 mv).

In simplified form, this voltage or millivoltage concept has its origin in the ionization potential of a element, or the force, strength, required to move electrons. Oxidation and reduction both involve the movement of electrons from one element or compound to another.

It turns out that the greater the force required to move electrons, or said in a chemically more correct form, the greater the energy liberated during this process, the higher the oxidative power of the element is.

The actual energy comes from another chemical concept that has to do with electron affinity, but we will not go into that.

All that is important here, is that the higher the volt or millivolt reading is, the higher the oxidative power is as well. And the higher the oxidative power, the more matter can be oxidized.

22.2. What does redox potential mean to us ?

Based on what we just said, higher redox potential numbers correspond to higher oxidative states. Such a state is, chemically speaking, only possible when no reductive processes are taking place.

Reductive processes are those that we know as decomposition, decay, and so on, and basically mean that pollution is present in the water.

If at high oxidative states, which equals high redox potenials, no pollution is present, the water must be of excellent quality. And that is of course what we all try to achieve in our aquariums.

If we measure redox potential, making abstract from its magnitude for the time being, and if higher numbers correspond to better water quality, we should of course do all possible to keep the number high. Let us not concern ourselves yet with the exact number, or range.

Keeping the redox potential high, or ensuring good water quality, is the reason for all the equipment and filtration we use.

Since we now know that good water quality goes hand in hand with a high redox potential, we can use the behaviour of that same potential as a yardstick of how our tank is doing.

We should in fact, not even be concerned with the actual number as much as we should pay attention to the trend that that number indicates.

22. 3. How do we interpret the Mv number ?

Once we have determined the redox potential by using a meter or a redox potential controller, we have an idea of how the water in our tank ràtes, based on the fact that freshly mixed salt water has an ORP of 230 to 240 mv, about 10 to 15 minutes after you mixed it.

We can safely assume that freshly mixed salt water is relatively free of pollution, except for the pollution from impurities in the salt and in the water used.

Anything lower than 230-240 mv, would therefore make us worse off than where we started. That would obviously indicate that something is wrong with your tank; that some form of pollution is bringing the redox potential down, and that something is of course pollution, decay, dirty filters, anything in the water that influence its oxidative power.

The reasoning is as follows :

• high redox potential = good water quality = high oxidative power
• pollution brings about reductive chemical reactions
• reductive processes remove oxygen from other compounds
• this results in the oxidative power of the water being diminished
• which in turn lowers the redox potential.

Having established that redox potential should be higher than 230 - 240 millivolt, what would we consider a minimum number ?

The mid 200's is better than what we started at, and is therefore an acceptable number. It is however not a level of water quality that is good enough yet, as around reefs the numbers are commonly much higher.

At the mid 200 level you should not experience too many problems with your tank, but you may find that micro-algae are still a problem, that anemones do not grow, but have a tendency to become smaller and look drab, and that your fish may still get diseased from time to time. All are signs of limited stress resulting from an unhealthy living environment.

Although not a bad number, it is certainly not a good one either. We need to work at getting the millivolt reading higher, and that requires extra equipment, better maintenance, not overloading the tank, etc...

A protein skimmer, operated with ozone, is a must to get the water quality to improve and the redox potential to rise (which is of course the same, as one it not possible without the other).

Once the millivolt is at the right level, and going up, we need to monitor what exactly happens to it during a 24 hour period.

Typically your redox potential should be higher in the morning, go down slowly during the day, and be at its lowest at night.

During the night, when the lights are off, and metabolism is low, the water is cleaned up by your filtration system and the resultant redox potential in the morning, is therefore high. Or at least higher than it was the evening before.

During the day, as metabolism increases, and pollutants enter the water, the ORP will go down slowly, especially after a feeding session.

Of course, if you operate the skimmer with a good ozonizer, this tendency may be counter-acted, and your redox potential may stay rather stable all throughout the day.

That is the ideal situation, but it does not happen in too many tanks. We have seen it over and over again though, in Leo Wojcik's tanks and in our own.

More than likely yours will go down, perhaps by as much as 150 mv. Considering that 75 mv is about the maximum that you want your redox potential to fluctuate, this will therefore require action on your part to narrow that gap.

22. 4. What to do to increase it ?

We have, throughout this book, indicated many methods to improve your water quality. As the water quality improves, so will the redox potential, as should be clear by now in light of the explanations we have already given.

Let us review a few of them :

• Good maintenance, which includes cleaning all mechanical filters regularly, even the ones that are not that easy to service. Any filter or material that traps dirt is a possible source of decay. Decay uses up some of the water's "oxidative" power, which results in a drop in the redox potential.

You can convince yourself of that very easily. Add some organic material to the tank, e.g. food, let it sit in a spot and decay, and watch how it affects your redox potential.

• Use a properly sized foam fractionnator. Inside-the-tank units only work on small tanks. If yours is over 55 gallons, you will need an outside unit, because on larger tanks internal protein skimmers are too inefficient.

It does not really matter which skimmer you buy, whether it is columnar or Venturi, as long as it skims effectively. Effective skimming means that the scum cap at the top of the skimmer has to fill itself with organic and other matter that it is removing from the water.

If it does not, you must adjust the skimmer level, and you may need to change your airstone(s). Don't overlook the latter, as the size of the bubbles is very important in the determination of contact time, and ultimately the efficiency of your skimmer.

• Use an ozonizer in conjunction with your skimmer. It not only improves the efficiency of the skimming process, but it improves the water quality in other ways too, by oxidizing organics, humins, nitrite, and other noxious compounds that are lowering the water quality.

• Make sure that the biological filter is large enough. You can refer to The Marine Fish and Invert Reef Aquarium book, in the section on "Required biological surface area", to determine how your own filter stacks up.

Often, just changing the packing material that you use may improve the situation a great deal.

• Use molecular absorption filters to "polish" the water even further. These filters, not new to the hobby, are now available in cannister form, which facilitates their installation, and increases their efficiency greatly. We have mentioned them several times already, and personally use Poly Filters from Poly Bio Marine.

They can now be set up in such a way that "all" the water in your tank will go through the Poly Filter disks. Change the disks about every 4 weeks, or sooner if they have turned brown to black in color.

• Do not overfeed. The quantity that you think is "probably not enough", because it looks so little, is probably too much already. Target feed. In that way you know where the food goes, and you know it is getting eaten.

By target feeding we mean place the piece of food on the animal that you are trying to feed. Do not just throw food in the water.

There are of course other ways, but they all come down to ensuring to no pollution enters the water, and that any pollution you see gets removed as soon as you notice it. This applies especially to dying-off algae, uneaten food, and of course and most importantly dead fish or other lifeforms.

22. 5. Watching the Trend

As already indicated, once you have established what the redox potential is, it is important that you get a good idea of what its trend is. This involves writing down the millivolt number for a few days, at different times of the day, together with some other pertinent information.

The trend to look for should of course be either stable, or up. If you notice that it is going down, you must try to determine the cause and correct it.

Keep records in the following fashion (this is only an example):

Day	Time	Mv	pH	°F	Comments
12.01	07.00	432	8.05	76.4	
	11.30	424	8.08	76.8	
	18.00	407	8.04	76.2	
	22.00	401	8.05	76.7	
12.02	07.00	431	8.06	76.5	
	11.30	425	8.04	76.9	
	18.00	408	8.05	76.7	

Measure for a few days, at the same time of day, and then determine what the trend is. Stable is fine. Downwards is not good. You must find out why and take corrective action. Upwards is all right of course.

Differences between morning, midday and evening readings are normal, because of higher metabolic rates once the lights are on. These affect the redox potential downwards, but as you can see, not by very much.

In the example above, by about 30 mv, which about right. 75 mv is about the maximum acceptable difference, and should prompt you for action.

The above numbers were recorded on the dates listed, on a 150 gallon tank equipped with most of the equipment discussed in this book. The set point on the redox potential controller was 430 mv.

22.6. What affects the Redox Potential ?

Other than pollution, which we have already described, redox potential is affected by :

• The pH of your water. When the pH goes up, the redox potential will go down somewhat. You can therefore only compare numbers that are taken at about the same pH levels. Do not compare the redox potential of your tank running at a pH of 8.1, with the redox potential of a friend's tank running at 8.25

• Time of day. This is because, as the metabolism increases in the tank, the activity of the fish and other lifeforms affects the water quality somewhat negatively. Again, only compare numbers that were taken at similar times of the day. Do not compare a redox potential taken at 7.00 a.m., with one taken in the late afternoon.

• The amount of ozone used. Higher ozonization will bring about higher redox potential numbers (levels).

• The bio-load in the tank, especially whether you have a lot of macro-algae or not. More macro-algae will tend to give higher day time readings, because of higher amounts of oxygen that will be released during photosynthesis. It is therefore adviseable to keep high amounts of macro algae in the tank.

This "benefit" is however dependent on whether or not you are providing enough light for the algae to photosynthesize properly.

• Compare only redox potential of tanks with about the same bioload and the same type of filtration.

• Feeding will lower the redox potential for some short period of time. The redox potential should go back up to what it was before the feeding occured within one hour or so.

• Whether you use water additives or not. Most of them will lower the redox potential, some in fact considerably. This will be more pronounced if you add them all at once. Additives are therefore best dispensed using a metering pump.

• Fresh activated carbon will lower the redox potential for a few hours, maybe even a few days. Not all carbons do this, and you should check yours in a small container using your ORP meter, to determine whether the reduction is due to the carbon you are using, or not.

And there are other reasons still. One obvious one for instance, is the addition of new livestock. Keep in mind that although one small fish may not have much of an impact on the redox potential, one large fish will certainly lower the number quite a bit.

ORP electrodes are very sensitive and can sense even very small variations rapidly. Small changes that are not permanent should however not be cause for concern.

What must concern you is if the redox potential goes down, and fails to come back up after an hour or two. Permanent lowering will always require your intervention.

22.7. Recommended levels

There are many schools of thought. Most agree that the redox potential should be over 300 mv, but some go as far as recommending numbers that are much much higher.

We personallly recommend and have used the following levels on our own tanks for quite some time :

Water going up to the tank : around 450 to 460 millivolt
Water coming down from the tank : not less than 380 to 390 millivolt,

at a pH of 8.05, a temperature of 76 ° Fahrenheit, and a salinity of 34.5 parts per thousand.

At these levels you should not have any problems with micro-algae, but to attain these kind of numbers, both your nitrates and phosphate levels must be extremely low,and well within the recommendations given in Part 3.

If you only measure in the tank, close to where the water flows down to the filter, the 390 mv + is the number to look for. If you measure in the sump of the trickle filter, close to the pump intake, the 450 mv number is the one to look for.

However, as indicated, those are the numbers that I personally try to achieve in my tank. You may find that other authors suggest different minima and different maxima.

Remember to check the pH and temperature they took these measurements at, before you compare their numbers with readings taken in your own tank.

Leo Wojcik, a friend of mine, has run his tanks at a constant 550 mv going in, and has not reported any adverse effects. He runs is tanks mostly at about the same numbers as I do however.

Some aquaculturists I know run oyster bed cultures at 750 mv, and do not report any negative results either. That does not mean however that you should try to do the same. Shell and bivalves seem to withstand much higher redox potential levels than fish and invertebrates.

What is important, and can not be repeated too often, is that if your ORP is now low, you cannot raise it to the levels we suggest in a short period of time.

You have to do so over several days or even weeks. Increasing the redox potential around one hundred to on hundred and fifty millivolt per week is safe, as far as we have been able to determine.

23. rH2 Levels - T•factor

Yet another way to express the quality of the water is by its rH2 number. This is generally considered more accurate than the redox potential itself because it takes more factors into consideration.

Water that has a neutral oxidation - reduction activity, has an rH2 of 28. Water that has more oxidative potential has an rH2 over over 28, and when reduction prevails, the rH2 will be lower than 28 (Mir,1979).

No meter measures rH2 directly. It is a number that you have to compute, and it requires that you be able to determine both the pH and the redox potential accurately and then use those numbers in the formula below.

The formula is as follows :

rH2 = Redox potential divided by 29, plus 2 times the pH.

Do not worry about where these numbers came from, they are based on chemicals concepts not within the scope of this book, but true chemical relationships nevertheless.

They are, however, mathematically derived from known chemical constants, the dissociation product of water into hydrogen and oxygen ions, and using decimal logarithmic calculations as opposed to natural logarithmic ones. Those interested are refered to one of the Chemistry books on the matter.

For instance at a redox potential of 390 mv, and a pH of 8.1, the rH2 index would be 29.6, or definitely in the oxidative area, an not in the reductive area.

Numbers over 30 rH2 would indicate water of good quality and purity, with a high capability of dealing with, and neutralizing pollution, especially organic nature type.

Although the rH2 number can give us a more accurate view of the water quality, we felt that the index had to be carried one step further, to include the dissolved oxygen levels, because as Hobbyists we are dealing with an environment where high D.O. levels are most important.

We therefore modified the rH2 index, and created a new comparison number, which we named the "T•factor" : we simply add the desired D.O. in mg per liter, to the rH2 index, to come up with a number that not only reflects a combination of pH and redox potential, but of desirable oxygen concentration at a specific temperature, as well.

To recapitulate :   T•factor = ORP/29 + (2 x pH) + D.O.

Here are some recommended T•factor numbers :

Temp. °F	T•factor
75	38.00
76	38.25
77	38.50
78	38.75
79	38.75
80	39.00
81	39.50
82	39.75

The reason the numbers go back up at higher temperatures, is because at those temperatures, oxygen super-saturation is really a requirement to maintain a well balanced Reef System.

Make the calculations for your tank, and see how you stack up.

Since we also recommend that you keep your temperature low, in the 75-76 Fahrenheit range, the number the aim for is 38.00 to 38.25 or as close as possible to those numbers.

You should never be far off, and if you are, you must determine the cause(s). It may very well be that your system requires additional equipment, probably **in the form of an oxygen reactor**. This assumes that you already use a foam fractionnator and an ozonizer.

Both the rH2 index and the T•factor are new concepts to the hobby. We hope that you will recognize their importance, and start using them when determining your water quality.

They are another tool, and another way to look at how well your tank is doing and are therefore helpful in describing the water quality.

While talking about water chemistry :

At the end of this book we have included a questionnaire. Please fill it out and send it back to us. We will summarize all data and send you a free copy of the results, providing we have your address. This will give you an indication of what others are doing, how their tanks run, at what levels, which we feel will help you in improving your own tank's conditions.

No one likes to fill out questionnaires. This is one is special though. It relates directly to your hobby. Please fill it out and send it in.

Fill in as many answers as you can, and feel free to add comments that you deem necessary to explain tank conditions. You do not even need to fill in your name and address. If you do, the data you give us will be kept confidential, and your name will not be sold as part of a mailing list (a practice that we do not get involved with anyway)

24. Getting detritus off the bottom of the tank

Although we could have classified this in the filtration section, we felt that it would be better to include it in the water chemistry one, because it generally affects the water chemistry negatively, and therefore needs to be dealt with by the Hobbyist.

Detritus needs to be removed as soon as it is noticed to prevent it from starting to decay and alter the water composition, not only by removing dissolved oxygen, but also by adding undesirable intermediate breakdown products to the water.

Often this has to be done manually, but there are ways to chase most of it, at least the smaller parts, into the mechanical fitlration area by directing the jets of the incoming water in such a way, that they strongly move the water mass right above the substrate and push detritus upwards.

This is best achieved by using the techniques described in Part Four of this book, under the section : Water returning to the Aquarium.

Additionally, the third water return behind the corals, the one we described in Part 1, will help move detritus away from that area, and push it forwards and upwards.

This does not mean that some such detritus will not accumulate. It will, but it will be far less than if you did not plan for its movement towards the mechanical filters. Some manual labor will therefore always be necessary

Mulm, which is matter left over after total mineralization has taken place, is inert and does not affect the water quality any longer. You may wish to remove it only because it makes the bottom of the tank look unsightly. It will not affect your dissolved oxygen and redox potential.

25. Airborne Pollution

Airborne pollution is defined as anything that enters the water at the air water interface, or through the air that is injected in the trickle filter's biological column.

We cannot avoid this, because all sorts of fumes, gasses and other matter is mixed in the air. This can be nicotine and tar from smoking, sprays used in the house or appartment, fumes from waxing furniture for instance, kitchen fumes, perfume, emissions from fireplaces, etc...too many to enumerate exhaustively.

Ideally these need to be removed from the air before it is blown into the trickle filter column, where the biological packing material is.

This is best achieved by using a small activated carbon filter. The unit looks similar to an air dryer, but is filled with activated carbon instead of drying compound. Several such units are available on the market.

Do not overlook the effect of airborne pollution, especially if you or someone else smokes regularly in the room where your tank is. It will affect the water chemistry.

26. The tank of the Future

Everything changes so rapidly nowadays that it is not unrealistic to take a "peek" at what the future may bring us.

We envision that in the not too distant future, instruments that are used to monitor aquarium conditions will have milliamp output, or a signal that can be processed by an RS232 port on a computer.

Such an interface already exists, the only part missing is the software.

This will have significant benefits :

• Not only will you be able to record, in a computer file, how your pH, temperature, redox potential, T•factor, dissolved oxygen, etc... behave over the course of the day, and be able to print this information out,

• But you will also be able, through software that is not that difficult to write, to instruct the computer to trigger certain actions, to remedy whatever situation may be out of line.

• You may even be able to access your own computer, via another one and a modem when you are out of town, and instruct the computer to initiate a series of steps.

• It is also conceivable that when "imaging" becomes more within the realm of the average hobbyist, you could even look up a "view" of your tank, from a remote location, via a modem and a video camera.

Do not laugh, the technology to do all this is available today. No one has packaged it yet for the Hobby.

That is sure to follow in the not too distant future. Dupla of Germany will have milliamp output units available in 1989/1990, and my own company Thiel•Aqua•Tech is working on a similar line of instruments.

Granted, you will need to have a PC or a similar computer (Mactintosh, Atari, etc..) but then so many people already do.

With the great steps forward that are being made in "laptops", and their decreasing prices and increased sophistication, this trend will only continue. If you are a doubting Thomas, just look up the size and the features of the new Z88 Cambridge computer.

Keep watching for what happens in this vein of development of the hobby. It should prove most interesting, and certainly not all that futuristic.

One of the products that we are working on, and plan to introduce in 1990 the latest, and that is only one year away for those who bought this book when it first came out, is a master control board for all the instrumentation that you can use on your aquarium.
This board will include a data logger, an instrument that records all the information the meters measure, at regular intervals, and prints them out in numeric and graph form.

That is only one step away from hooking that same board up to a computer.....

The panel will include float switch relay outlets, ozonizer in and ouptut, dual pH and dual redox potential displays, and may other such features that are now done seperately and with different instruments.

More and more accurate controls will be possible, with all be benefits that such control brings about...

Is this overdoing it? We believe not, for once you have the water chemistry under control, you will be able to spend more time enjoying your aquarium. When it comes to keeping successful Reef tanks, everything revolves around water quality, everything.

The latter was in fact recently highlighted by the President of the Marine Aquarium Society of Toronto, Scott Dyer, during one of the many conversations he and I have about Reef Aquariums.

Summit Aquatic Surface Skimmer

Part 4

Setting up the Reef Tank

A Comprehensive Guide to

Installing Filters, Reactors

and

Instrumentation

The Marine Aquarium Reference by Martin Moe Jr.

1. Introduction

So far, in Parts 1 through 3 of this book, we have covered both the aquarium and how to outfit it, and the equipment that can, and in our case will, be used on the Reef Tank that we are setting up.

We have also looked at the instrumentation that we will use to either run the tank, or to monitor the water quality conditions.

We have also taken a good in depth look at that water chemistry, what parameters we are trying to achieve, and what to do if the parameters are not met, meaning if they are out of line.

By now, you should have a pretty good idea of all the sophistication that can go into setting up a modern, advanced Reef Aquarium.

In fact, there is so much, that we hope we have not given you the impression that this is a really complicated and extremely expensive endeavour to get into.

Whether you elect to use all of that equipment is entirely up to you. We have reviewed, and explained, everything we felt would benefit an advanced system. You may elect to only use some of the devices and instruments that we have covered.

There are presently so many ways available to the hobbyist to control conditions in the aquarium, that it may indeed seem like overkill.

Use only what you feel comfortable with, understand, and can fit into your budget. Do not buy for the sake of having the latest ... You must know what it does, how it does it, and whether your aquarium commands that kind of an investment.

If you only have a 55 gallon tank, with few fish and invertebrates, and all are considered to be hardy, you will not need all of the sophistication that we described inthis book.

Many tanks can be run with much less instrumentation and equipment, as long as you are prepared to invest the necessary time to maintain them.

We set out, when we wrote this book, to be as complete as possible. You be the judge and decide what you feel you want to use.

A minimum configuration would include :

• The tank and the stand of course.

• Some form of heating, stick or bayonet heaters are recommended.

• Basic lighting, perhaps the high Kelvin degree fluorescent tubes such as the Color Classer 75 types in regular or high output.

• A trickle filter with an overflow syphon, except if you have had your tank drilled. Size it according to the recommendations we made.

• A good pump and a float switch to protect the pump.

• A columnar skimmer, properly sized, preferably with 2 airstones.

• One more more Poly Filters for chemical filtration.

• X-nitrate for nitrate removal under aerobic conditions . One unit treats 50 gallons. Two treat 100, etc..

• A good fertilizer if you plan to keep macro algae.

• A manual CO_2 system, but only if you keep macro-algae and invertebrates and corals that harbor symbiotic algae (Zooxanthellae).

Since we have now covered the basics, and what devices can be added to the system, we are at the stage where we are actually ready to start installing the aquarium, and give you recommendations how this is best done.

This is a section that some of you may only want to scan through, especially if your tank is already set up. But for those who are starting, or who are contemplating changes, or additions to their systems, this part of the book should prove most useful.

Because it is sometimes difficult to explain in words what one is exactly doing, we recommend that you obtain copies - either buy them, or rent them - of the Videotapes that we produced on setting up Reef Systems.

You should get an even better understanding of how all the pieces fit together, when using both the Book and the tapes.

We cannot conceivably cover every possible situation, as we are sure you can appreciate. There are too many different ways to set up a tank.

We will however cover the items that are most commonly brought up by Hobbyists who call us at Thiel•Aqua•Tech and Dupla Usa.

We would also like to make an observation about the names of the companies that we are using throughout this book : they are not meant to be a commercial endorsement, we have received neither money, nor merchandise.

We just mention manufacturers of products that we feel meet the standards that we like to keep, and that make the type of equipment that is either necessary, or useful, in a Reef Tank set-up.

Because the choice is not very wide, several companies are mentioned many times. Others, such as my own, make products that are so Reef specific that we have to mention them in many parts of the book.

If you are interested in products by specific companies, refer to the index for a listing of where they occur in the book.

If you have questions regarding any of those products, you should call the companies that manufacture them, not Aardvark Press. We thank you.

Photographs were supplied by the manufacturer where indicated. All other photography was done by Steve Ciuccolli, Bridgeport, CT.

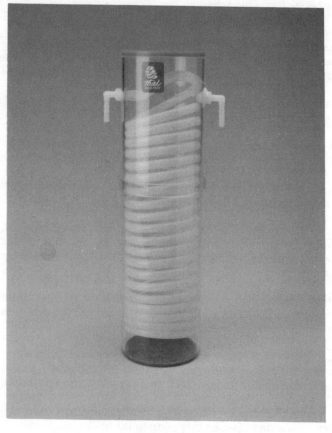

Coil Denitrator

2. The Aquarium

2.1. Preliminaries

Before we begin, we must decide whether we will set the tank up with holes drilled for the water returns and for the water going down to the filter, or whether we will use overflow syphon boxes.

If we use the system that requires holes in the bottom of the tank, we obviously need to drill holes in the tank first. If, on the other hand, the syphon box assembly is used, no holes are required.

This is a major decision, and you should give it the necesary thought, as in our opinion, overflow corner box filters are more practical, skim the surface of the tank properly, and require little or no servicing.

Because of the hole drilling required, it may not be a practical solution for a number of Hobbyists.

Think it over real well, because holes are not that difficult to drill and glass dealers in your area should be able to do so for about fifteen to twenty dollars a hole.

They may want you to take responsibility in case of breakage though. That is something you will have to consider.

Custom tanks can of course be ordered with holes already pre-drilled. A large New York store, World Class Aquarium, has made a specialty out of this, and they manufacutre all shapes and sizes of glass aquariums, out-fitted for use as Reef Tanks.

There are of course others, but World Class is one of the best ones we know. Some of the aquariums they built are just spectacular and, in our opinion, reasonably priced.

2.2. Using an Overflow Syphon Box

After you have unpacked the automatic syphon box assembly, you need to check what the size is of the output fitting. It is in all likelihood located at the bottom of the syphon box. It may be 3/4 inch, or in many cases 1 inch.

At the bottom of the syphon there should be a bulkhead, or some similar fitting. This fitting will have a measurement stamped in the PVC, if not, you need to measure its inside diameter.

It is a good idea to find out what that measurement is when you buy the filter, so you may order, or buy, the acrylic hose and other implements that you will need to set it up, beforehand.

Proceed as follows : hang the unit over the side or the back of the tank, position your trickle filter in place, underneath or next to the tank.

Measure the distance between the output of the syphon and the top of the trickle filter. Connect the two. Use clear acrylic hose of the proper size. Slide the hose over the bulkhead fittings but put clamps over the hose first.

The type of clamps you want to use are referred to as hose clamps. They are made either in metal or in plastic and are available from hardware stores. So is the acrylic hose. Some Pet Stores carry acrylic hose as well.

If you have difficulty getting the hose over the fittings, heat the hose with boiling water or with an air blower. When the hose is on and overlaps the fitting one to one and a half inch, tighten the clamps very firmly..

You must use clamps to ensure that the hose will not slip off the fitting, particularly when pressure starts building up. Such clamps will also prevent salt from creeping between the hose and the fitting. This may seem impossible, but it wil happen.

Your syphon box is now basically ready for use. But we are not ready to do that yet, we still have to install a number of other items first.

The syphon box assembly should have a pre-filter chamber. Most of them come with such a filter anyway. If yours does not, you shoud add filter floss,foam will do the job too, but it must be medium to coarse. If not, it will plug up too quickly and restrict the flow of the water.

Usually the pre-filter, a mechanincal filtration device, is a perforated or slotted piece of pipe surrounded by foam. All the water going down to the trickle filter must go through that foam.

In the process, the foam removes particulate matter and cleans up the water, preventing detritus from entering the trickle filter's biological chamber. If you have to build your own you may want to duplicate that method.

Obtain a piece of pipe that fits the inside of the bulkhead fitting at the bottom of the syphon box. It should be shorter of course than the depth of the box. With a hacksaw, or a similar type of saw, make cuts that are about 0.75 inch apart, and run at a 90 degree angle with the length of the pipe.

You should have such holes on all sides of the pipe. As you make a cut, rotate the pipe somewhat, and keep cutting.

Surround the pipe by foam and your pre-filter is ready to be used. Make sure that the foam can easily be removed when it needs to be cleaned. We suggest you do so at least once a week.

2.3. Drilled Tanks

Drilling holes yourself is an undertaking that you only wish to get involved in if you either already know how , or if you get someone to help you who has the experience.

Failing that, you will have to practice on scrap glass quite a few times. Use glass of the same thickness as the one your tank is made of. That will give you the exact feel of what you will have to do. In our Video-tapes we showed you how to drill such holes and the tools needed.

If you elect to have someone else drill the holes for you, e.g. a glass distributor, make sure that you give them the fittings you will be using as well. That way the holes will definitely be of the right size.

You would normally want 4 holes in the tank. Three are for returning water to the aquarium, and one is to channel water to the trickle filter. You can see, earlier in this book, where these holes are best located.

If you elect not to have 3 water returns, but only 2, then we recommend that you have one in the tank proper, and one behind the coral rock to prevent dead spots in the back and the bottom of the tank.

Dead spots are detrimental to all tank life, as we have already pointed out before, because :

• Low dissolved oxygen areas lead to the presence of facultatively anaerobic - aerobic bacteria,

• May lead to areas that become so low in oxygen that anaerobic activy does start,

• With the ensuing production of hydrogen sufide which is very noxious to corals and invertebrates.

The fourth (or 3rd) hole is for the water going down to the trickle filter. If you run 500 to 600 gph through that filter that hole needs to be at least one inch in diameter. If you run more water than that you must have a one and a quarter inch hole. This is the I.D. size of the fittings, not the exact diameter of the hole itself.

The reason for this rather large size is to prevent this hole from backing up, as that would force you to slow down the flow of water through the tank.

Once you have the tank installed on the stand, you can insert the bulkhead fittings through them, and tighten them from underneath.

If your stand has a "full" top, you will need to make holes through that cover so you can slip the fittings completely through, and tighten them properly.

Again measure carefully, as these fittings may be quite large and require a hole that is far larger than the nominal size of the fitting itself. This means that a one inch bulkhead fitting not only requires a hole of more than one inch through the glass, but an even larger hole through the wood, meaning through the cabinet's top.

Installing the bulkhead properly is done as follows :

• The Neoprene, Buna-N, or rubber ring, is slid over the fitting on the outside of the tank (on the end of the fitting that goes through the glass, but outside of the tank).

• Put a bead of silicone all around the hole inside the tank, and then press the fitting down on that silicone, to make a nice even seal all around the fitting.

• Tighten the ring that turns over the bulkhead firmly by hand. **Do not** use wrenches. If you tighten the fitting too much, stress is created inside the glass, and the tank may crack while you are tightening or at a later time, after all the water and rocks have been added.

This is a most important recommendation. Tighten only by hand, as thight as you can get it. The bulkhead will not leak because of the silicone bead underneath the fitting, inside the tank.

• Once the fitting is.tight, strike out the silicone that now protrudes from around the fitting, evenly all around it. This is done with a wet finger (e.g. saliva) or with a glass of water. If your finger is wet, the silicone will not stick to it, and you will be able to even it out nicely.

Bulkhead fittings are threaded on the underside. That means that you will need to screw another fitting in them. To ensure water tightness, you first have to cover the other fitting with Teflon®, or a similar product. Three turns of Teflon around that fitting should do.

Which fitting you use depends on whether you are hard piping with PVC, or whether you are using acrylic flexible hose.

• If you use hard pipe that fitting will be a "male adapter"
• If you use flexible hose that fitting will be a "barb"

of the size that matches the bulkhead fittings.

We have no personal preference. Both flexible and hard pipe are fine. Flexible is perhaps easier to install. PVC requires primer to prepare the other part, and cement to glue both parts together ; flexible hose requires hose clamps to tighten the hose around the barb to prevent it from sliding off.

If you are unsure about what all these fittings are, refer to the The Marine Fish and Invert Reef Aquarium book. We covered fittings in depth, a whole chapter in fact.

From each of the holes we now need to run pipe or flexible hose to the top of the trickle filter.

Make as few 90 degree turns as you can ; they reduce the flow, cause more friction, and put more back pressure on your pump.

Back pressure on a pump reduces its output and shortens its useful life. It may also make the pump heat up more, and transfer that heat to your water.

Because of the many types of hook-ups that can be made as a result of the versatility of the trikle filter itself, it is not possible to cover all alternatives. You are however welcome to call us to discuss your specific installation with us. We will help you find a solution and explain what parts and fittings you will require. Our phone number can be found in the appendices.

2.4. Un-drilled Tanks

In this type of set up the water returns run from the filter to behind the tank, and up to the top of the tank, then over the top and back down so the returning water jets point towards the bottom of the tank.

Angle the water returns in such a way that the pipe or hose points to the middle of the aquarium.

Here is what you do :

• connect the pump to the trickle filter by means of either hard pipe, or flexible hose. If you use flexible hose do not forget the clamps.

Between the pump and the filter you must put a check valve to prevent water from syphoning back from the aquarium to the filter. This is a most important step.

Check valves can be obtained from plumbing supply places. They must be all plastic. No metals are allowed because salt water will corrode the metal, and leach heavy metals in the water. This can lead to the loss of invertebrates and fish.

Back-syphoning may occur when the pumps stop. Although this is not supposed to happen, it will every time that you experience a power failure, and it will also occur whenever your pump fails.

If your water returns are submersed, back-syphoning could theoretically empty your whole tank. To prevent that from happening you need a check valve . If they are not submersed, or only slightly you may not need a check valve.

Since you will be installing a water return behind the corals, at least one of the water returns "will" be submersed, and since it is positionned at the bottom of the tank, it can back-syphon the whole aquarium.

Some hobbyists drill little holes in the water return pipes, about half an inch underneath the water level. This will break the syphon as soon as half an inch of tank water has back-syphoned.

This is fine, providing you remember to check regularly whether the hole is in fact still open. These holes plug easily, and if they do, you are back to square one, meaning your tank could empty itself. It is much safer to install the check valve and not have to worry.

We cannot tell you which fittings you will need to hook the pump up because it will depend on its brand. Some manufacturers make pumps with half inch fittings, sometimes male, sometimes female, others use 3/4 inch, or even 1 inch, as in the modified Iwaki pumps that we use.

You will have to look at your own pump and decide which parts you must buy to complete the installation.

We now need to run the connections from the output side of the pump to the water returns.

Since we are piping to more than one return, we will obviously need to divide the water return line up. Either in two or in three lines, depending on how many water returns you are using.

We will use three returns. But because we are using more than one pump, our case is slightly different that yours may be. For the sake of being complete, we are describing both methods.

Our case :

• We are using three Iwaki model 55 pumps. We run hard pipe from each pump to each of the water returns. The reason we use three pumps will become clearer later, and has to do with alternating the side from which the water re-enters the tank, using a special device such as, for instance, a T•A•T Ocean Motion or a Route 4 Wavemaker.

• Between the pump and the actual water return we place a true union ball valve to allow us to control the pump's output. All piping from the pump to the tank is done with Schedule 40 PVC (one can also buy Schedule 80, but it is more expensive and no needed in aquarium installations. It is made for applications with higher temperatures and pressures).

From the trickle filter to the pump we have used Eheim flexible hose, to allow us to easily disconnect the hose and the pump if for some reason we needed to do so.

• To prevent back-syphoning we have placed a check valve in each line between the pump and the water intake of the trickling filter. The check valves, by Hayward Industrial Plastics, are threaded, and we inserted barbs of the proper size, tightened them, after putting a few length of Teflon around them.

We then hooked Eheim hose to them on both sides, and clamped the hose down with 316SS clamps.

• We will be installing more fittings and filters in these water return lines, but will explain what we are doing later in this section, when we get further into the installation process.

The fittings are for pH and redox potential measurement, and the filters are Poly Filter discs, inside that company's cannisters.

Your case :

Let us assume, for this explanation, that you are using 3 water returns, and one pump. This is the more difficult one to do, so we thought that would be the better one to explain.

Run a short length of pipe or flexible hose from the pump. Attach a "cross fitting". This is a fitting that has 4 openings. Three are for the output to the 3 water returns, and one is for the input from the pump, which gets its water from the sump of the trickle (trickling) filter.

Run PVC or flexible hose from each hole in the tank. One line goes to the back, and then to the right side of the tank, the other one goes to the back, behind the tank and then to the left side of the tank. The third one goes to the back, and then to the opposite side of where your corner overflow, or syphon is.

All three water returns then go up to the top of the tank, and then over, so that when water comes out of the returns, it ends up in your aquarium and jets downwards and sideways.

To go over the top you will need fittings, either one or more 90 degree Ell fittings (for an explanation of all the fittings, refer to The Marine Fish and Invert Aquarium Book if you are not familiar with them).

Once you are over the top you can then direct the water return towards the bottom of the tank, at a 45 degree angle : for more details see the illustration.

Of course, the one return which runs behind the rocks needs to be handled differently. After you go over the top, you need to run the pipe or hose back down to the bottom of the tank, and then sideways.

CO2 reactor with venturi

That pipe then extends the whole length of the tank, and has holes per-forated in it, about one inch apart, facing alternatively down, and backwards. Use a regular hand drill to make the holes. Quarter inch is large enough.

This will result in a water flow that will move water behind the rocks continuously, and prevent dead spots, but it will also move detritus away from behind those rocks, forward, to areas where it can be removed much easier since it will now be in the front, where you can get to it with a hose or a pair of tongs.

On the illustration that shows both types of set-ups, you can see exactly where we have located the holes for our 3 water returns, and also where you should bring the water back in, if you do not drill holes.

Once these connections are completed, and the filter is installed, you can theoretically fill the tank, add the salt, and start up the pumps. If however you are planning on installing other equipment you should obviously not do so yet.

All this may be rather difficult to visualize, but is very clear if you watch Tape 1 of our videotapes.

It is not easy to explain how you run pipe or hose, and if what you have just read is not clear enough, we suggest that you re-read it once more.

If, after that, you still need more explanations, feel free to call us and we will help you solve your installation problem.

2.5. Installing additional Filtration : Poly Filters

As indicated already, we will be installing Poly Filter Discs, in cannisters, in each water return line. To this effect we cut the pipe in an appropriate location, where we have space to install these cannisters, and pipe them in line with the main water returns.

Make sure that you follow the manufacturer's instructions carefully with regard to the water "in" opening, and the water "out" opening, as in Poly Filter cannisters the sequence is reversed.

Since we will have to exert some force on the cannister to un-twist the housing when we want to open it, the cannisters must be placed in such a way that they are supported by brackets. Such brackets are available in many hardware stores, or from plumbing supply places.

Because the cannisters are installed in line with pipe or hose through which water flows, we need to be able to open them without all that water coming out when we service them. This is achieved by placing a shut off, or ball valve, on each side of the cannister.

When servicing is necessary, proceed as follows: first shut off the pump, then close the valves, remove the cannister housings, change the discs, reassemble the cannister, and finally re-open the valves.

To do all this you must remember of course first shut off the pumps. Do not forget to re-open the valves before switching the pumps back on ! Over-pressure inside the pipes or hose may cause fittings to come lose, which will result in water running everywhere.

If, as it is likely, you install the cannister(s) underneath the tank, inside the cabinet, you can usually mount it against the underside of the cabinet's top. Plastic and other brackets are then screwed into that wooden top and hold the cannister firmly in place.

It is a good idea to review the lay-out of the various devices that you are installing underneath the tank to ensure that you have enough space. It is important too that you can get to all of them easily to service them once they are installed.

This is the planning that we referred to earlier in the book. There is nothing worse than having all the right equipment, but installing it in such a way that servicing becomes a chore. The latter will only result in the servicing being put off.

Besides the molecular absorption disc filters you can also install micron, or sub-micronic filter systems manufactured by the same company. You may elect to use other brands, as there are several on the market.

These filters can be obtained in various mesh sizes, so fine in fact that you can filter out to as low as 0.2 micron (2 tenths of a micron). This even filters out free floating parasites. In fact the 0.65 micron mesh filters will remove free floating parasites as well, and put less stress on your pump(s).

We have such units installed in our own set up. They are piped in right after the PMA (the Poly Filter discs) cannisters. For optimum efficiency we have installed one such cannister in each line.

If you pipe such a unit in right after your main pump and before the

Tee-fittings, you will only need one, even though you have two or three water returns.

Micronic or sub-micronic filtration is optional, but for high water clarity and some parasite control we strongly recommend them. You must however use strong pumps, lest the water flow through your tank will diminish more and more as a result of the clogging of the mesh bags in these filters.

2.6. Where do we stand ?

So far we have installed the filter, the overflow and/or syphon box, and we have hooked up the filter and the water returns. We have also piped the molecular absorption and the sub-micronic filters in line.

This brings us to the stage where we need to make provisions for how, and where, we are going to measure the pH and the redox potential, as this is the appropriate time to do the necessary cutting and cementing and putting the necessary fittings in place.

If you have decided to place your electrodes in the tank, or in the sump of the the trickle filter, then section 2.7 does not apply to you.

You may however want to consider the alternative ways of hooking some of the instrumentation up described in that section, and then what follows will be germaine.

They involve a greater expense, because we will be using 2 each of the electrodes, Thiel•Aqua•Tech 2 probe switchers, and a special fitting to install the electrodes directly in line with the water flow.

You can of course install the electrode you use in line, even if you use only one of each. Using two is not a requirement. It is just another option that is available to you.

2.7. In-line Electrodes

To install an electrode in line, you will need either a special fitting or an in-line electrode. The fitting is in reality a modified Tee-fitting. A regular Tee is piped into the water return line, and on the open side of the Tee a special compression fitting through which the electrode is pushed in, and then tightened, is placed.

These fitings will run you around 17.00 to 20.00 dollars, depending on who you buy them from. Push the electrode in just far enough, for the tip to be about one quarter inch inside the Tee-fitting. This will make all the water that goes through the pipe, or hose, run over the tip of the electrode continuously.

In-line electrodes are already epoxied into a piece of rigid pipe with a threaded end, and can be screwed in to a Tee-fitting directly without the need for the compression nut. Figure on spending about $ 160.00 for such an electrode.

Although the reading you get with electrodes piped in-line is more accurate, the drawback is that your electrode may need more frequent cleaning. This is not the case if the water that returns to the aquarium through the pipe is first pre-filtered. Many trickle filters are equipped with such pre-filters, and this may therefore be a moot point.

What we have done in our 150 gallon demonstration Reef tank is install 4 such fittings :

• 2 in one of the water lines going back to the tank,
• 2 in the water line coming down from the tank to the trickle filter.

This gives us 2 readings for the pH, and 2 readings for the redox

Pressure gauges for carbon dioxide

potential. We thus know what the pH and the ORP of the water leaving
the trickle filter is ; this is the water going back to the tank. And we also
know the pH and the ORP of the water coming down from the tank,
back to the trickle filter.

This is not something you may want to do, but it gives us more control
over the actual conditions. Since we experiment a lot, for articles in
Marine Reef our Newsletter, mainly, we need to have that kind of
control, as we try to bring you information that is as accurate as
possible.

Although we run 4 electrodes, we only use 2 meters. Each meter is
equipped with one of our own electrode switching devices. This device
takes 2 electrodes on one side, and connects to the meter on the other.

An internal switching relay lets us see the pH in both locations, on an
alternating basis. A push button system lets us switch manually from
one probe to the other one, if we wish.

Knowing both numbers, and in the case of the ORP a third one, the
redox potential of the water coming out of the skimmer, is an advantage, but may only be necessary if you are researching, or testing
products or methods.

Measuring both pH and ORP in the tank, close to where the water flows
down to the trickling filter, is probably the best spot for the Hobbyist.

Measuring in the trickle filter itself is fine too, but you must be careful
as the numbers you obtain may be somewhat distorted for the following reasons :

• CO_2 will affect the reading, and the real pH will be higher,

• water from the skimmer, mixing with the water in the sump, will
make the reading higher than the true redox potential in the tank.

3. Installing Reactors

At the time we went to print there were only two companies that marketed reactors for use on Reef Aquariums : MTC (1) and Thiel• Aqua•Tech (2). Following is what they offer for sale :

- Dissolved Oxygen Reactor : 1·, 2
- Carbon Reactor : 2
- X-nitrate Reactor : 2
- Carbonate hardness Reactor : 1, 2
- Ozone Reactor : 2
- Carbon dioxide reactor : 2
- Self-leveling Oxygen and Ozone reactor : 2

* Number refers to Company : (1) MTC and (2) T•A•T

In addition, Coralife, Poisson and the two companies already mentioned, market carbon dioxide Reactors.

Reactors are nothing more than specially equipped cylindrical acrylic tubes, that allow you to do a number of things "outside" of the tank and "outside" of the trickle filter, and in a much simpler fashion, especially if your trickle (trickling) filter is small, and little space is available inside to place compounds, pumps, etc...

We have dealt with the reasons for using these reactors in the section on equipment. We will concern ourselves here only with their installation.

There are two broad categories of reactors :

• some reactors work under a small overpressure, e.g. the D.O. reactor

• some are filled with a compound and water is just being pushed through the reactor and the compound, e.g. the X-nitrate reactor.

Their installation is very similar, but for ease of classification we will seperate them.

3.1. Reactors without Over pressure

This includes : X-nitrate reactors, activated carbon reactors, Poly Filter reactors, reactors with resins such as de-ionizers, reactors filled with special compound, for instance zeolites or magnesite to remove silicates, and others.

The hook-up of such reactors is similar to how you would install a cannister filter. Attach hose to the input side, connect that to a pump, and connect the pump to the sump of the trickle filter.

You will need to install a ball valve to be able to adjust the output. On smaller pumps this may not be required, but generally you will need to do so to allow you to adjust the flow inside the reactor.

Often a strong power head such as the Aquaclear 800 can be used to run these filter-reactors. If you are looking for high flows however, a regular outside pump will be required.

The latter requires a pump hook-up to the trickle filter, which in turn requires a hole in the sump so you can make the connection. Again this is something you have to decide upon before completing the set up of the filter.

You will also want to put a union ball valve between the pump and the sump of the filter, to allow you to shut off the water in case you need to service the pump. You can use both half union, and true union type valves.

From the output side, run a length of hose back to the sump, or directly to the aquarium, and the hook up of this type of reactor is complete. Do not forget to place clamps around the hose to barb connections, and tighten them firmly.

When maintenance time comes around, stop the pump, remove the clamps and hoses, and empty the reactor. Most of them have some sort of compression nut that you can unscrew and remove to be able to remove whatever is inside the reactor, and replace it with new compound or resin.

Reactors are made of acrylic tube and are fragile. Be careful when you handle them.Watch out for Pets, as they may knock them over and break them, as happended to me recently when changing a large X-nitrate Reactor.

Place the reactor near the trickle filter ; this will put less stress on the pump, and you will get a better flow. Most reactors are from 2 to 2.5 feet tall, some fit underneath the cabinet, and some do not.

If the reactor contains filter floss, change that too. If you got the reactor with floss in it, it was obviously there for a reason. When changing the com-pound make sure you place floss in the reactor as well. It is usually there to prevent the compound from getting out of the reactor.

3.2. Reactors that work under Over-pressure

This includes the Dissolved Oxygen reactor, the Ozone reactor, and the Carbon dioxide reactor. The over -pressure is only slight, usually around 0.1 bar, or ± 1.5 psi.

You can however run higher over-pressures providing you have a strong enough air pump. 1.5 to 2.5 psi should however be plenty for your reactor to work efficiently.

These reactors have an inlet for either air, or ozone, or CO2, in addition to the water in and outlets.

The latter two get hooked up the same way as we described in section 2.8.1, and usually need to be run with an outside pump

Although the reactors described in the previous section can be run with good strong power heads, the reactors in this section usually cannot, because of the over-pressure, which power heads may have a hard time dealing with.

The Aquaclear 800 power heads however are really strong, and may do the job if you are not pushing too much head (meaning distance upwards, which puts back pressure on the motor).

3.2.1. Dissolved Oxygen Reactors (Pressurized)

This is perhaps the most frequently advertised of all the reactors.It is probably also the one you will need most.

D.O. reactors can increase the amount of oxygen in the water quickly and easily. All you need is the reactor and a good air pump, for instance the Whispers 1000 or 900, Schego, Wisa 300, and Rena 301 air pumps.

Run a length of airline tubing from the air pump to the air inlet of the reactor, and plug both the air pump and the water pump in. Water and air now enter the reactor.

You must now adjust both to maintain a constant water level in the reactor. That constant level is really low, just enough to keep the overpressure exerted by the air continuous.

This means that no air, or air mixed with oxygen , may escape the reactor, through the water outflow tube. You will notice it very quickly should it happen, because of the noise involved when it occurs.

Adjusting your Reactor is done as follows :

• the air pump is running at full output,
• the water pump is running at full output,
• watch what happens to the water level,
• it is more than likely rising inside the cylinder,
• turn the output of the water pump down somewhat,
• if the water level still rises, turn the pump down further,
• do this until you stabilize the water level at about 2 inches of water height in the cylinder,
• watch what happens for a while longer, and if the level stays where you adjusted it to, you now have a properly running Reactor.

The real height of the water in the bottom of the cylinder is in fact determined by how high away from the bottom the water output tube is.

Keeping the water level about one inch higher than that level, will prevent the air, or air-oxygen mix, from escaping from the tube and dropping the overpressure to zero.

The following problems can occur :

• the water level never comes up :

You are pushing too much air in the reactor for the strength of the pump that you are using.

Solution : use a stronger water pump or reduce the air input by putting a clamp over the airline tubing. This will reduce the backpressure on the water pump, and the water level should rise, as this way less air goes in the cylinder.

This is however not the best way to solve this problem, because as you push less and less air, you are defeating the purpose of the exercise. The best solution is to use a stronger water pump.

• to maintain the desired level in the reactor, you must turn the output of your pump down considerably :

This is due to either using too strong a pump, or not a strong enough air pump. Or a combination of both. Mind you, you may want to change the diaphragms on the air pump and see if that helps. When these diaphragms wear out, and they obviously do, the air pump can no longer take backpressure, and the air output is greatly reduced.

Regulating the oxygen reactor correctly will take a little time. Indeed small changes in either air input, water input, or both, may take 5 to 10 minutes before one can see what the new level actually is.

This is very much like making small changes on a protein skimmer, where such changes also may take quite a while - 15 minutes or so is not unusual - before you actually see what happens.

Modifications to the basic Reactor :

• One modification is to use a mixture of air and oxygen, instead of just air. To this effect you will need a supply of oxygen, special fittings and gauges, an oxygen resistant check valve - two would be better - and some Tygon tubing.

To be able to see how much oxygen you are adding to the air stream, you must also use a "bubble counter" (e.g.Thiel•Aqua•Tech).

The bubble counter gets filled with water, Tygon or similar chemical resistant tubing (not airline hose), is attached from the bottom of the bubble counter, and goes to the O_2 valves and gauges.

More hose is then run from the top of the bubble counter, to a small plastic Tee fitting in the hose carrying the air to the reactor. See the diagram, especially where to place the check valves.

When using oxygen you must use Tygon or a similar type chemical resistant hose for all connections, and you must also place a check valve between the air pump and the reactor (see diagram). It is better to use 2 check valves rather than one. This provides extra protection for your valves.

You should clean out the check valves from time to time, as dirt will get into them and prevent them from funtionning properly, defeating the purpose. Get check valves that you can open and clean.

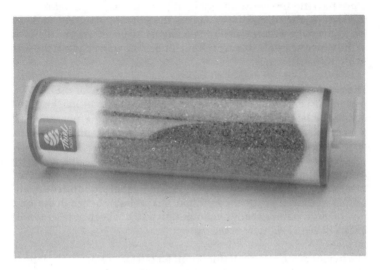

Single deionizer

There are several types of small check valves on the market. Ball checks are the more reliable ones but are the more expensive one too.

• Yet another modification is to make the reactor self leveling. This is done by using a small solenoid that controls the air pump, a pressure transducer, and a pressure sensing device inside the reactor.

Such reactors are not on the market yet, but Thiel•Aqua•Tech will be introducing such a reactor in March or April of 1989. All you will have to do is install the air and water hook-up, and your reactor will be running and maintaining its own level.

Because of the additional labor and the additional devices necessary, this reactor will obviously be more expensive than the basic model.

For most Hobbyists the latter should however do the job, and once you understand the principles behind these reactors, you will not have too many problems adjusting them correctly, and quickly.

• You do not necessarily need to use Bioballs in the reactor, there are other packing materials available. It just turns out that, because of their shape, they distribute and break the water up so nicely, making it a much more efficient medium for oxygen to penetrate and dissolve in the water. They also prevent chanelling of the water against the side walls of the reactor.

The two models now on the market both use Bioballs, for the obvious reasons just explained.The more the water breaks up inside the cylinder, the better the transfer of oxygen can take place, the more efficient your dissolved oxygen reactor will be, and the larger its impact on your dissolved oxygen level will be.

Although it may appear that you can build such a reactor yourself rather easily, beware. Proportions, height, and size of pipe and so on, are all factors that enter into the equation. It is probably better, in the long run, to buy a commercially available unit that has been tested and will work efficiently right from the start.

The height of the column is important for obvious reasons. The longer the water trickles down inside under over-pressure the more that same over-pressure can force oxygen into the water. I personally consider two feet a minimum.

3.2.2. Ozone Reactor

The general principles underlying the operation and construction of oxygen reactors, apply to ozone reactors as well.

The Reactor itself is the same as the O₂ one, except for the inlet nipple for the ozone, which in this case must be made out of ozone resistant material, lest it will disintegrate within weeks.

The tubing used should be Norprene and not Tygon. Although Tygon will resist ozone for quite some time, Norprene is totally safe and is sold as an ozone resistant material. This is not commonly available in Pet Stores but can be bought from scientific supply places, or from my own company.

The set up of the equipment is now slightly different of course, as it includes more components :

• an airpump,
• an ozonizer,
• an air dryer,

- 2 ozone resistant check valves,
- the reactor itself,
- plus of course the water pump in and output assembly,
- a residual ozone test,
- and an activated carbon chamber, through which the water that comes from the reactor is flowed.

This is a most important part of the set up, lest you want to run the risk of having residual ozone in the tank and lose both fish and invertebrates.

Because ozone is pushed under pressure in the water, the redox potential of that water will rise.

As that water mixes with the water in the sump, it will raise the overall redox potential, and T•factor of the tank's water.

In the process of raising the redox potential, ozone will oxidize some of the matter that is in the water - in fact if it did'nt, your ORP would not go up - and some hobbyists therefore flow the water through a fine filter first, and then through the activated carbon, to remove detritus that come out of the ozone reactor.

Such a filter is nothing more than a cylinder, divided in two parts, an upper and a lower part, the upper part is filled with a material that filters mechanically, and the lower chamber is filled with the activated carbon. The upper compartment will need to be cleaned regularly of course, to prevent water from backflowing over the top, and also to remove the trapped material before it manages to break down further.

If you do not use such a double filtering method, the fine filter in the sump of the trickle filter will remove the broken down matter too, and will of course need regular cleaning as well.

What output do you set the Ozonizer for ?

There is no real answer here either. The principles that we explained in the various sections on ozone, elsewhere in this book (see index), apply here as well.

The quantity you will need depends on various factores :

• how high a redox potential are you looking for,
• how much pollution is being created in the tank by the bio-load,
• how much pollution is already present in your tank,
• the latter determining how much ozone it will take to neutralize it.

The air dryer, and the check valves are important components of this set up, as they ensure that :

• no water can get into your ozonizer,
• your ozonizer produces the amount it is rated for.

We also use a small air filter because the production of ozone falls when dust particles enter the inside of the tube where the ozone is electrically generated.

Cleaning these types of reactors is usually not necessary, but you should watch that no large amounts of detritus get into it. They cannot easily be removed, since pressurized reactors are sealed.

To run these reactors, we use Eheim pumps, the submersible Hobby model, which has a fine filter built into the front chamber, right in front of the impeller.

If you run your ozone reactor in conjunction with a redox potential controller, the latter unit will of course turn your ozonizer on and off, depending on what level you set it for.

The Thiel•Aqua•Tech Redox Controller has additional settings, i.e. high and low settings, and can therefore be used to monitor whether or not your Redox potential level goes over a certain number, or stays lower than what you wanted.

Ozone reactors are not a commonly used piece of equipment and you will therefore find very little, if any, references to this reactor in Hobby magazines. They work extremely well, and can be used in addition to skimmers, if water quality needs still further improvement.

Using Ozone reactors reinforces the need to determine whether or not you are using too much ozone, and can always easily be checked by running a residual ozone test.

This is really a test that you cannot do without if you are working with ozone. We keep repeating this because it is important indeed.

There comes a point, of course, where adding more ozone to already very high quality water will raise the redox potential to levels beyond what the animal life in the tank can tolerate.

The only way to determine whether you are getting too close to that level are is through the use of a redox potential meter or controller which can stop your ozone input at any number that you have decided to set the controller for.

3.2.3. Carbon Dioxide Reactor

CO_2 reactors are usually much smaller than the ones we have reviewed so far. Their only function is to ensure a proper mix of the water and the carbon dioxide that is being added to the tank.

Fill the reactor with Bioballs, or a similar material, or with any other non-calcareous material. Plastic, ceramic, any type of rock will do, as long as it does not contain carbonates or bicarbonates. Inject water in the reactor and also some CO_2, either manually or by using one of the automated systems now on the market.

Our own T•A•T Tech•Reactors are narrow and about 12 inches long. They have a water inlet and a water outlet, and a nipple where we inject the Carbon dioxide, in-line with the water flow to ensure a proper mix.

Water and carbon dioxide mix thoroughly inside the reactor, the mixture comes out from the bottom, and re-enters the sump of the trickle filter. That is where the water came from to begin with. In the process the amount of dissolved carbon dioxide has increased, and we have achieved what we set out to do.

How much CO_2 you should inject and how to regulate the system, is explained elsewhere in this book, and was dealt with in even more detail in The Marine Fish and Invert Reef Aquarium. Carbon dioxide can be added through a fully automated system, or through a so-called "manual" system as well.

There is however a great difference in price and, as already pointed out, the manual set-up will do just fine for more Hobbyists. A good auto-mated system, even a US made one such as the ones sold by Poisson, Route 4, MTC and my own company, will run you close to $ 900.00.

The most important thing to remember when using carbon dioxide is that you must check your KH (carbonate hardness) regularly. If your KH drops below 9, carbon dioxide will have a greater impact on your pH, and the latter may fall to below 8.0, and do so rapidly. This must be avoided as it stresses tank life.

Carbon dioxide and water form carbonic acid which will make the pH drop quickly, unless the water is properly buffered.

Maintain KH levels of 12 to 18, with 15 being what we maintain our own tanks at and have had very good success with over the years.

You can bank several of these reactors to obtain a better mix. This will use less carbon dioxide, and dissolve it more thoroughly in the water. Simply place two or more such reactors in series, and the desired result will be achieved. Strong pumps are required to push the water all the way through 2 or more successive reactors.

Remember too that in fish-only tanks the addition of carbon dioxide is not required. If you keep macro-algae and invertebrates with sym-biotic algae, then adding carbon dioxide is a definite improvement over older methods where CO_2 is not used.

Do not fill your reactor with calcareous matter, as if you do, you have in fact installed a carbonate hardness reactor. This reactor is discussed in the next section.

Only PVC or silicone tubing should be used on all the carbon dioxide line connections. You must use check valves in both the air and in the carbon dioxide lines (see the oxygen reactor diagram).

The check valves should not have rubber check disks inside, as the rubber will distingrate. Buna-N, Neoprene, Tygon, and other such specialty tubing will however do. Silicone and PVC tubing are the best. Viton will also resist CO_2 without giving you any problems, but costs much more.

Finding such specialty tubing is not always easy, but if all else fails, try Cole Parmer in Chicago, or Markson's in Phoenix. They carry such specialty products, and even offer technical assistance if you need it.

3.2.4. Carbonate hardness Reactor

Carbonate hardness reactors are similar to carbon dioxide reactors, except that they are larger, and are filled with calcareous material, e.g. broken pieces of coral, or coral rock, oyster shell, or any other calcareous material that you can find.

They are run with a slight overpressure, on the same principle as the ozone and oxygen reactors. Regulating the water level is done in the same way as we explained in the oxygen reactor section as well.

Again, only PVC or silicone tubing should be used for the carbon dioxide connections. Acrylic airline tubing will become brittle in a short period of time, and crack, making you lose CO_2 and internal pressure in the reactor.

Silicone and PVC hose must be obtained from specialized places, e.g. scientific instruments companies, or from my own company Thiel• Aqua• Tech. It is not something that the average pet store carries, as we already indicated.

As the carbon dioxide enters the cylinder, the pH of the water will be lowered somewhat. This water then comes in contact with the coral pieces, or whatever calcareous material you used. The effect of this contact, and the carbon dioxide within the cylinder, dissolves some of the carbonates and bicarbonates, and these obviously go into solution.

Chemically speaking, carbon dioxide turns some of the carbonates into bicarbonates. The latter dissolve easily in water and increase the dKH of the water.

The latter will help you maintain a more stable carbonate hardness, which is exactly what we were trying to achieve to begin with by using these reactors.

This alternative method to keeping higher KH levels is perhaps somewhat more involved than just adding KH tablets, or a KH generating liquid to the water, but in the long run it will prove beneficial because of the stability of the method.

The amount of CO_2 that is added is of course important. The same principles as were explained for the use of CO_2 apply. In essence, although you are adding carbon dioxide to the tank, your pH should not be affected by more than a maximum of 0.1 to 0.15 pH.

If it is, your carbonate hardness is not high enough to begin with, or you are adding too much CO_2 and you must adjust the settings. Turn the supply of carbon dioxide down somewhat, and adjust the dKH manually before installing a KH reactor.

Recommendation for using KH Reactors :

• Flow only small amounts of water through the reactor. 20 gallon per hour will do for small tanks, and 50 to 60 GPH should be sufficient for larger tanks, e.g. 150 gallons.

• Do not install a KH reactor unless your dKH is at least 10.

• If it is not, adjust the KH hardness first. Bring it up slowly by using a liquid buffer. Tech•Reef•KH buffer is excellent for this purpose and is inexpensive. Half a gallon costs around twenty dollars. Use 5 ml in the morning and 5 ml in the evening until your KH is up to around 12.

Test your kH about 2 to 3 hours after you have added KH generating products, do not test within minutes because the effect of most additives will not be testable yet.

• Monitor your pH to ensure that its level does not drop below 8.0; test regularly.

3.3. How many Reactors ?

Many hobbyists want to know whether they can use just one reactor, and inject both ozone and carbon dioxide, as well as air. This is a very justified and understandeable question of course.

The answer is unfortunately a definitive no. It cannot be done. Gasses with different solubilities in water cannot be mixed in one and the same reactor.

Each additive serves a different purpose and each needs to be added through a seperate reactor. This is obviously more expensive, but there is really no other way of doing it.

We have now reviewed both pressurized and non-pressurized reactors. The guiding principle is the following :

• if you are trying to force a gas into the water use the pressurized version of the reactor,

• if you are trying to flow large amounts of water "through" a compound, for example X-nitrate or activated carbon, use the non pressurized version.

You can also install a reactor filled with Poly Filter pads or discs, but since special in line cannisters already exist for this purpose, we see no need to use special reactors.

Even if you do not buy the special cannisters that are made to house the Poly Filter "discs", you could always make your own by cutting up several Poly pads, and placing them inside a regular aquarium cannister filter that you may already have.

3.4. When should you install Reactors ?

Everything depends on the water quality of your tank. If your tank is only doing moderately well, start by testing the water, write down the results, and in light of those, decide on a course of action.

Following tests, and or meters-controllers are recommended :

• Dissolved oxygen levels,
• Biological oxygen demand : similar to the D.O. test, but done on tank water that has been stored in the dark, in an airtight container, for 24 hours or sometimes for 48 hours,
• Redox potential (if you have meter, or controller)
• pH
• T•factor
• KH, carbonate hardness
• NO_3
• PO_4
• Residual Ozone

If your T•factor is lower than 38 you defintely need some of the additional water chemistry treatments that we have described (Reactors).

Look at your dissolved oxygen level. If it is not at saturation, and if you cannot make it rise to that level, even after you clean all filters, etc... you will need an oxygen reactor, providing you want to improve the conditions in your tank of course.

If your dKH is real low, and you do not want to add tablets, or liquid, to increase it, a carbonate hardness reactor will make the difference.

If you keep macro-algae and corals with symbiotic algae, and you want to create a better environment for them, a CO_2 system will improve conditions a great deal.

If your skimmer just does not seem to do it, you may want to consider adding an ozone reactor.

You are the judge, we have explained what the various Reactors can do for you, and you must now decide which ones, if any, you will add to your Reef Tank.

They all improve tank conditions, but it is all a matter of involvement, and of course finances that you want to dedicate to your aquarium.

Keep in mind too that all these reactors take up space, may require extra pumps, and that you may need to look at all your options carefully.

Indeed, making changes to your filter may be less costly, easier to accomplish, and may solve your problem too.

As you may have surmised by now, nothing is simple when it comes to water chemistry. We have still to find a "cure all" type solution. It just does not exist.

Problems with Reef tanks can be solved. You must first determine what the problem is however. Once you have identified the problem(s), you can then start working at solving them, keeping in mind that each problem may require a seperate piece of equipment.

Mechanical Float Switch Low

4. The Carbon Dioxide Diffusion System

We have explained, in great detail we think, the merits of having a carbon dioxide set up installed on your tank.

On the system that we set up, and used during the Videotaping, we have installed such an automated system, using equipment made by Dupla Gmbh, supplemented by equipment from other companies.

Since we already pointed out that many of you can, more than likely, use a "manual" system, and get excellent results nevertheless, we will go through both types of set ups to give you a better understanding of the work involved and the equipment needed.

Keep in mind too that not every Hobbyist needs to add carbon dioxide. It depends on the type of tank that you keep.

For technical explanations on quantity and reasons for carbon dioxide, we refer you back to the sections on CO_2 (see index) in this book, and also in The Marine Fish and Invert Reef Aquarium book.

Using carbon dioxide is much safer than you think. The literature that talks about fish-kills, because of excesses of carbon dioxide and its purported dangers, fails to take the carbonate hardness of the water into account, and looks only at part of the equation and equilibrium that involves pH, carbon dioxide and carbonate hardness.

All three are "linked" so to speak, and one can therefore use carbon dioxide safely, providing one controls the other two. This is exactly what we do, or should do, when we use carbon dioxide on our Reef Tanks.

Our only general observation is that CO_2 comes in pressurized cannisters, and that these cannisters must be treated with the same kind of "respect" as you would treat the propane bottles that you buy for your outdoor grill.

You must always open the cannisters slowly, never point the output at anyone, and you must hold the cannister firmly when opening it. Do not refill your cannister yourself, but go to an authorized place, e.g. a welding supply shop, or a carbon dioxide distribution place.

As indicated, open the bottle or cannister slowly to prevent the bottle from falling out of your hands because of the high back pressure exerted when the gas escapes.

All cannisters have pressure relief fittings that will prevent the cannister from bursting. If the bottle is overfilled, that fitting will crack, and the bottle will empty itself safely.

Do not place the bottle of carbon dioxide directly on the ground, rather, place it on a piece of wood, or styrofoam, so that its base will never be in water. This will prevent pitting of the base.

Pitted bottles may not be re-used. You must discard any you may have, and never buy a pitted one.

4.1. The Manual CO_2 System

We know of only one company in the United States that sells a manual CO_2 package that includes all the pieces that you may need. Coralife however sells most of the pieces individually, and so does Thiel• Aqua• Tech.

In Canada you can obtain a similar package from Poisson Filters and Accessories. Tetra used to sell such a set up as well, but we have not seen it on the market recently. You may want to check with one of their distributors however.

To run a manual system, you will need to install the following basic pieces of equipment :

• A cannister with the carbon dioxide,
• A regulator valve, allowing you to adjust the cannister's output,
• CO_2 resistant hose. It is best to use either silicone or PVC hose,
• One or two small check valve,
• A diffuser to add the carbon dioxide efficiently to the tank.

In addition to that You will need :

• a high pH testing kit,
• a carbonate hardness testing kit,
• carbonate hardness liquid, or if you prefer, tablets

Optional but helpful :

• A pressure reducer that works in conjunction with the regulator. This will bring the pressure at which the CO_2 comes out of the bottle down to a more manageable level.

• A "Bubble Counter", a small device, filled with water, that allows us to count how much carbon dioxide is being added by monitoring the number of bubbles that go through the device.

 It also visually shows us what the result of changes made to the regulator on the the carbon dioxide bottle do to the quantity of carbon dioxide being dispensed. As you change the regulating knob, you can see how many more or how many less bubbles are being dispensed.

• A carbon dioxide reactor rather than a diffuser, to mix the CO_2 and the water more efficiently. They are available in many sizes. Larger ones have a tendency to be more efficient, especially if the carbon dioxide inlet is done by means of a small venturi.

• Gauges on the regulator and pressure reducer to tell us what the pressure in the bottle is (this will give you a better idea when your bottle is nearly empty), and what the outcoming pressure is as well.

• A bracket to hold the CO_2 bottle upright. Because of the high pressure inside the cannister, the CO_2 inside is in liquid form. We want to draw off the gas, not the liquid, and that can only be done when the bottle is upright. One should never lay a carbon dioxide bottle on its side, or use it upside down. This will ruin your valves and gauges in no time at all and require either major reconstruction, or their replacement.

• A carbon dioxide testing kit. Some of the scientific instrument companies sell such tests. So does Dupla. Since 3 to 4 mg per liter is the desired amount in the water, this test will tell you whether your manual system is in fact keeping that level where you want it to be.

Preliminaries :

Perform a pH and a KH test. Write down both results. Your dKH must be at least 10, and preferably higher. Anywhere from 12 to 18 is much better and much safer too. As already pointed out, we maintain ours at a dKH of 15 (dKH = German degrees of hardness, which corresponds to ppm divided by ± 18.5).

If it is lower, you will need to adjust it first. Do not add carbon dioxide if your dKH is lower than 10. The effect on your pH will be too drastic. Use either tablets, or better, liquid buffers, that are made for use in salt water aquariums.

If you are using a protein skimmer, check to determine whether the buffer that you are using contains anything that may make your skimmer foam excessively. If that is the case, you will have to adjust the level in your foam fractionnator. T•A•T liquid Reef buffer does not contain such colloidial materials and can safely be used without need to change the skimmer settings.

Sodium carbonate, Baking soda, Calcium carbonate, Calcium Hydroxide, and other such products should not be used, unless you understand the exact chemistry behind them.

Some raise your pH much too quickly, others upset the mineral chemistry of the water, others are insoluble, etc...It is therefore best to stay away from them, unless your really know what they do to the water and how to use them safely.

The reason you need to know the pH, will become clear as we guide you through the quantity adjustment procedure.

Installation of the Basic Manual System :

(Note : we use KH and dKH interchangeay and in both cases it refers to the carbonate hardness as expressed in German degrees of calcium carbonate hardness equivalents.)

• Test both the pH and the carbonate hardness of the water. Do not add carbon dioxide if the KH is lower than 10.

If the latter is the case first adjust the KH. Use a liquid buffer (best) or tablets (second best).

• Double check to ensure that your bottle of CO_2 is closed and filled.

• Connect the regulator to the bottle of CO_2. Ensure that the regulator output knob is closed.

• Do not open the bottle of carbon dioxide yet.

• Soak the carbon dioxide diffuser in water and suck water through it, until it is filled. This is, by the way, easier written than done. It will take you a while to get it full, but it is a necessary step with the Dupla diffuser. If you are using a different brand of diffuser, follow the instructions that came with it.

• Install the diffuser in the aquarium, or in the sump of the trickle filter. The deeper in the water the diffuser is, the better off you are, as that will increase the contact time between water and carbon dioxide, and a better diffusion will result. You will also use less CO_2 because you are using it more efficiently, with less waste.

• Connect the diffuser to the regulator using silicone or PVC hose; place the check valve in line, in a convenient space. Make sure you install the check valve in the right direction, as otherwise it will prevent carbon dioxide from getting through. Read the instructions, as some check valves need to be installed perfectly vertically.

• Make sure the regulator valve is closed.

• Open the valve on top of the carbon dioxide cannister completely.

• Open the regulator valve ever so slightly, and keep doing so until you actually see a little CO_2 come out of the diffuser, and mix with the water.

• Let the small amount of CO_2 mix with the tank water for about 10 minutes.

• Re-test the pH of the water. Compare with the original number.

• If your pH has gone down by more than 0.1 you are adding too much carbon dioxide and you must reduce the amount slightly.

• If the pH was the same, increase the amount of carbon dioxide slightly. If you are using a bubble counter, you will see the bubbles of carbon dioxide inside the bubble counter. If not you can monitor how much CO_2 is coming out of the diffuser.

• Wait 10 minutes, meaning let carbon dioxide enter the tank's water for 120 minutes, then check your pH again.

You must keep doing this until your pH has dropped by 0.1 pH, but no more. If you have a CO_2 test, you now perform the test, and determine how much CO_2 is actually in the water.

Because carbonic acid will, over time, lower your carbonate hardness, you must test it regularly, and re-adjust its level whenever necessary. This is a very important maintenance point to remember.

Both the size of the carbon dioxide container, and the size of your tank determine how often you will need to refill the bottle at an authorized location.

Since the difference in price between small and e.g. 5 pound bottles is not really all that large, you would be well advised to get such a larger size. It will save you many trips.

When testing the dKH of your water, make sure that the product you are using tests for carbonates. Several such tests exist on the market. You are testing the carbonate hardness, not the alkalinity, not the general harness, not total hardness. Just the carbonate hardness.

Make sure too that the expiration date has not passed, and that your test is still chemically active. To check your test all you need to do is add some baking soda to 10 ml of water. Then add drops of your test. If the color change that you are looking for does not occur after 10 drops, your test is still active.

Once you have regulated the output, and determined that it is the quantity that you need, meaning it does not alter your pH by more than 0.1 pH, your job is now over, and you are adding CO_2 to your tank in a safe manner.

Since at night, when the lights are out, photosynthesis is not taking place, adding carbon dioxide does not make sense.

You should therefore close the bottle at night, and re-open it in the morning. Not the regulator knob, only the knob on top of the carbon dioxide cannister itself. If you change the position of the regulator knob, you will have to go through the entire adjustment phase that we just described, all over again. So beware. The output adjustment procedure takes time, and is not the most pleasant task I can think of.

Make sure too, that others who may help you with your tank maintenance, if any such people do, know that they should never change that setting.

4.2. Installation of the Automated System

You will need the following instruments and equipment :

• A pH controller, with a general purpose electrode, suitable for continuous immersion in a liquid that is high in salt content and organics. This means that you need a relatively good quality electrode. Something in the 150.00 to 250.00 dollar range more than likely.

Although the quality of the controller is important, it is the quality of the electrode that determines how accurate your reading will be, and for how long. Buy a good electrode, and take care of it. Clean it regularly, and then re-calibrate it.

• A solenoid, also called magnetic valve, that is CO_2 resistant. Several such valves exist. It should be relatively small, and able to handle the pressures that you will be working at (usually around 800 PSI).

• A set of CO_2 pressure gauges, indicating both the pressure inside the bottle, and after the carbon dioxide has gone through the built in pressure reducer.

Combination gauge-regulator sets allow you to regulate that outcoming pressure. They are available from CO_2 supply shops and from Coralife, Poisson, MTC and T•A•T.

Set that pressure to around 2 to 3 bar. Higher if required, but normally that pressure should be sufficient. 2 bar equals about 29 psi.

• A bubble counter to allow you to visually determine how much CO_2 is going into the water.

• A CO_2 reactor to properly and efficiently mix the carbon dioxide with the water. This unit should be filled with non-calcareous material, for reasons explained earlier.

• Enough CO_2 resistant hose to do your hook-ups. The exact length will depend on where you place the cannister and other devices.

• A cannister of carbon dioxide, preferably the larger sizes, e.g. 5 lbs or 10 lbs.

• Two check valves. They will protect your equipment and it is therefore worth investing in the second one. Thiel•Aqua•Tech sells such check valves for around eleven dollars.

• Enough electrical outlets to plug in the equipment.

• Connections and fittings to bring water to the carbon dioxide reactor, and then guide the outcoming water back to the tank or preferably the sump of the trickle filter.

Usually, the water going to the carbon dioxide reactor is T-eed off the main water line, using an extra fitting to reduce the Tee to match the size of the reactor water inlet.

The actual installation proceeds as follows :

• Install and calibrate your pH Controller. Follow the instructions that came with the Controller. Place the electrode in a spot that is not directly in the flow of water coming out of the reactor, if you have decided to locate it in the sump of the trickle filter.

Alternatively, place the electrode close to the syphon or corner overflow in the tank. Or place it in-line, as explained earlier. The latter is the prefered installation and gives the most accurate readings.

• Check to ensure that the CO_2 cannister is full, and closed.

• Attach the gauges to the CO_2 cannister, and place it in a convenient location, preferably slightly off the ground.

• Mount the bubble counter in a spot nearby, after you have filled it with water. Place it in a conspicuous spot, to allow you to easily see how many bubbles are going through the water inside. Make sure it is air and water tight. If not add more Teflon to the threaded barbs.

You may want to use liquid Teflon, as its liquid form is easier to apply to small surfaces than the tape variety.

• Connect the output of the gauges to the solenoid with **"pressure tubing" only** ! Do not use plain flexible tubing, as, whenever the solenoid is closed, that tubing will blow up like a balloon, and burst because of the pressure from the gas coming out of the CO_2 cannister.

This will empty your cannister in no time, and you will have to have it re-filled for a reason that you could have avoided easily.

That section is pressurized, and only pressure resistant hose can be used.

• From the solenoid run silicone or PVC flexible tubing to the bottom of the bubble counter.

• Run similar hose, from the top of the bubble counter to the CO_2 input on the reactor. Tighten the hose with plastic ties to ensure that they will not slide off as a result of the internal pressure in the reactor. Between the bubble counter and the reactor you should place a check valve.

• Make the water input connection to the Reactor. This can be done by using a dedicated small power head, or by piping a Tee fitting into the main water return line, then stepping that Tee down, inserting a barb that matches the input side of the CO_2 reactor , and connecting the two with appropriately sized flexible hose. Here again we prefer silicone or PVC flexible hose.

• a small clamp, or ball valve, should be placed in line, to allow you to control the amount of water going through the reactor. If too much water goes through, CO_2 bubbles mixed with water will shoot out of the reactor, which is an indication that you must turn the water input somewhat down.

When bubbles come out the reactor from time to time, your reactor is set for the proper flow rate.

• If your CO_2 reactor is outside the sump of the filter, connect the output of the reactor to the sump with silicone or PVC hose.

• Wherever hose was used, tighten the hose down with clamps or plastic ties. This will ensure that they do not come off, because of either CO_2 or water pressure.

• Now set the pH controller for the lowest pH that you will live with while CO_2 is being added. This is the trigger point, so to speak, where the controller will shut off the CO_2 supply by closing the solenoid.

This can be anywhere between 7.9 and 8.2. More than likely you will want to set it for around 8.0 to 8.10 because it turns out to be both safe and efficient.

Most Hobbyists who use CO_2 will select a number between 8.0 and 8.1

anyway, as that is a pH level that is common in Reef tanks and will make the addition of CO_2 not only smooth, but also regular.

Indeed, the controller senses the pH, and only switches the solenoid on when the pH is higher than the setting you selected.

If you select e.g. 8.3, and the pH in your tank never reaches that number, exceeds it I should say, your CO_2 will never be switched on.

If, on the other hand, you select 7.9, your CO_2 will probably be running most of the time, and you will constantly be adjusting your carbonate hardness.

Neither of these two situations are desirable, and setting the Controller for a pH of 8.0 to 8.1 is therefore the recommended level.

Settings between a pH of 8.1 and 8.2 will work fine too. The carbon dioxide will not come on as frequently. This setting is to be desired in tanks that do not have a great deal of macro-algae and corals with symbiotic algae.

• Open the CO_2 bottle completely. This is the knob on the bottle itself, not the one on the regulator. After you have done so, the high pressure gauge will more than likely show a pressure of around 650 to 800 psi. That is normal, and also indicates that your bottle is full.

• Now start opening the regulator knob slowly. How this is done, depends on whose regulator you are using.

Dupla's regulator is preset for 28 psi. With the black knob on the side, you adjust how much CO_2 is actually coming out of the bottle. You can see that quantity in the bubble counter.

At a low setting you will be able to count the bubbles. At a high setting, it will go so fast that all you will hear is a gurgling sound. The correct setting is about 60 bubbles per minute, or one every second.

Other regulators may not be preset, and you determine the pressure yourself by turning a knob, or similar implement. Turn that device until, again, about 60 bubbles per minute go through the bubble counter. Usually you will find that the output pressure will be around the same 28-30 psi.

The exact number depends on the pressure that the pump exerts in the line. This is the pressure that the carbon dioxide has to overcome before it can actually get into the reactor. (If your reactor is equipped with a small venturi valve, the pressure required to operate the carbon dioxide system will be minimal, because instead of exerting back pressure, CO2 will be drawn in).

As a result, stronger pumps, especially in larger systems, will require higher CO_2 output pressure.

• Your installation is now complete. As you add CO_2, the pH will go down. The electrode senses this, transmits the signal to the controller, which shuts the solenoid when the pH reaches the number you set the controller for. This is what we referred to earlier as the lowest pH that you will accept in your tank.

This stops the CO_2 input until the pH rises again and goes over the number that you set the controller for. This re-opens the solenoid, and the process starts all over again.

Suppose you forgot to check the carbonate hardness,

and it lowers itself to the point where the pH stops going up and over the setting you selected on the Controller. The only thing that happens is that you will have a pH equal to that setting, or maybe just below, and your CO_2 system will not come on anymore, because the pH never exceeds the setpoint.

As such, the automated system is fool proof. But of course you are no longer adding carbon dioxide either.

It is therefore important to regularly check the dKH , and add KH Generating liquid to adjust the number back to the desired level of between 12 and 18.

The CO_2 you added benefits the macro-algae, the corals and invertebrates that harbor symbiotic algae. Both need it for photosynthesis, during which they remove CO_2 from the water. As a result, the more such lifeforms you have, the less the CO_2 will affect your buffer (dKH).

Conversely, the more such lifeforms you have, the more oxygen will be released in the water as a by-product of photosynthesis. This will translate in higher dissolved oxygen levels.

This also means that your system will add CO_2 to the water for longer periods of time, as the pH will be less affected. This translates into more CO_2 being used. Which is of course normal as, the more macro-algae and other corals and such you keep, the more CO_2 is necessary for proper photosynthesis.

During the night, when the lights are off, when photosynthesis does not take place, and algae etc... release CO_2 in the water as opposed to taking it out, your pH will not rise as much, and your automatic CO_2 system will not switch on as often, if at all, especially in tanks with lots of macro-algae.

As you can see, carbon dioxide can be used very safely, and can be provided to those animals that need it, and to macro-algae, without having to fear for your tank.

Automated systems are fool proof and are not difficult to install, but they are expensive. Manual systems require more monitoring, will suffice for most Hobbyists, and are inexpensive; about the same price as a good cannister filter.

You are the judge and based on what type of tank you run, you should seriously consider acquiring such a carbon dioxide system.

5. Installing the Heating System

This is, in our opinion, not an area where Hobbyists have many problems, or experience difficulty. We will therefore only cover this very briefly. We have moreover already discussed heating earlier in the book.

5.1. Using the Bayonet type heaters :

Submersible bayonet or stick heater units can be installed in the sump of the trickle filter. They are to be prefered. Use more than one unit. E.g. if you need a total of 200 watts of heating power, use either four 50 watt heaters, or one 100 watt and two 50 watts.

This has several advantages :

• If one unit fails to work, the other heaters will at least still heat the water and your tank will not drop to too low a temperature.

• If one of the heaters sticks, meaning continues to heat even though it should not, the others will switch off, and the chances of your "cooking" the fish and invertebrates are much smaller, particularly if you use low wattage heaters.

It is indeed highly unlikely that all heaters will fail, or stick, at the same time, and it is unlikely too that all of them will fail to heat your tank at the same time.

Units that are covered with plastic or some other material, are to be preferred as, in the event of breakage, the parts do not end up in the sump.

We have used both Ebo-Jaeger and Aquastabil heaters, and they are both quite reliable. The temperature adjustment is easy and "precise" which is of course very important.

Newer heaters are always introduced, and by the time you read this, there may even be units on the market that are better. If not better, they may allow more precise control which is really all that matters.

5.2. Cable heating

This is perhaps the best type of heating as it spreads the heat very evenly, and, because it operates at low voltages, it poses no danger to Hobbyists and tank life alike.

The Dupla heating system, probably the most advanced one on the market, consists of a silicone cable, a step-down transformer, and a control unit or thermostat.

Unfortunately this type of heating is still very expensive and can only be considered by a limited number of Hobbyists.

Many size cables are available, covering most size tanks. So-called "S" cables, for supplemental heating can be obtained as well.

If you are concerned about how well distributed your heat is, and want to ensure that no anaerobic activity takes place in your substrate, then this type of heating is what you want to install.

At the time of this writing, the complete heating system was selling for around $750.00, not within everyones budget of course.

Rena, the air pump people, also have a cable heating system, but its cables are much shorter, and the wattage was rather low.

In many cases Marine Reef tanks do not need to be heated because one should try to keep the tank's temperature down to around 75 to 76 °F.

The best way to go, we feel, is still the perhaps not so modern bayonet type heating, placed in the sump of the trickle filter.

Get the better quality ones, and, as suggested , use several of them to make up the total wattage that you feel you will need.

In our Videotape tank, we have used the Dupla set up, with a 250 watt low voltage transformer and 2 S-cables, for a total of 200 watts of heating, mainly to demonstrate how this heating is installed, and how the pieces fit together.

5.3. Quartz heating

Quartz heaters are a variety of bayonet heaters and are usually only available in very high wattage versions, e.g. 500 watt and up.

There are some models around rated at 200 watt as well, and since they are really small they can be put to use in trickle filters. At some point Sea Klear Reefs Inc. was selling such units. You may want to check with them whether they still do.

These heaters often come without the control unit, and a seperate thermostat needs to be added to the cost of the basic heater. This puts them cost-wise in the same category as the Dupla heating system, especially if you decide you want a digital meter-controller.

We have not reviewed the availability of these heaters in depth, and there may be units available that are both reliable and affordable.

Research the matter more thorougly if you are interested in this type of heating.

Several manufacturers offer titanium bayonet heaters, making them suitable for use in marine tanks. Scientific supply houses advertise both types in their catalogues.

Liquid Gold, the most complete reef additive

6. Installing Redox Potential Equipment

6.1. Introduction

The Redox Potential equipment set-up that we are using is a little more elaborate than in a normal tank set up, but we have installed this equipment to be able to monitor conditons more accurately, more thoroughly, and with more measurement repeatability.

The main reason for this more intricate installation, is that we do a lot of testing and experimentation on that tank, and want to be able to determine the exact effect of additives and equipment, on the water quality. It also assists in another thesis we are preparing.

The benefits of knowing the redox potential should be quite evident to you by now. We have covered the subject in great detail, both in this book, and in The Marine Fish and Invert Reef Aquarium.

Oxydation Reduction Potential and the T•factor are really the only two very reliable indicators of water quality that we have. You should therefore make it a point to try and install such a meter, or better, a controller, on your own aquarium.

Thiel•Aqua•Tech's Redox Potential Controller, built in the USA, retails for around $ 370.00, including a Platinum-silver-silver chloride electrode. That is substantially lower than other controllers on the market, especially because of the quality of the electrode.

It is also one of the meters that we are using on a our demonstration tank, in addition to a German unit made by ATK, and another one made by Jenco. The latter unit features two relays, each with their own set point.

This feature can be used to control two electric devices. In our case, the first relay controls an ozonizer installed to run on our protein skimmer, and the second relay controls a second ozonizer which is hooked up to an ozone reactor, and only activates should the redox potential go below 350 mv.

When no ozone is produced, which is most of the time because of the quality of our filtration system, the reactor performs as an oxygen reactor because we are injecting air on a continuous basis.

Because we measure the redox potential in various locations we use two electrodes and the Tech•Probe•Switcher already mentioned earlier in the book. We also use more than one controller.

6.2. Installing the Redox Potential Controllers

For reasons already explained, we are using three redox potential controllers. On a typical tank however, you will only need one of course, not three.

We have installed these units in the following manner :

1. In the water line coming down to the trickle filter, we piped in a Tee-fitting that can hold an electrode, and we measure the ORP of the water that is coming down from the tank to the filter.

This tells us what has happened to the water while it was in the tank. It has obviously gone down, and we are interested in knowing how much.

2. In the water line that pumps the water back up to the aquarium, we also installed a Tee-fitting that holds an electrode, and we measure the ORP of the water going back up to the tank. That tells us what the quality of the water entering the tank is.

3. In the activated carbon chamber, where the water from the protein skimmer runs into, we measure the ORP of the skimmer's water. This electrode is not in-line, but is positioned inside the chamber, on a suction cup with a probe holder. This tells us, for instance, when it is time to change, or better, regenerate our air dryers.

Once the drying compound has exhausted its drying capacity, the redox potential of the water coming out of the skimmer will indeed start dropping. The more moisture in the drying compound the less ozone will be generated, and the lower the ORP will be.

There is of course nothing particular about mounting these units. They are all held in place with brackets, and are just plugged in to a regular house current outlet.

The ozonizer is then plugged into the controller, in the spot provided for it. Depending on which unit you use, this spot will vary, and the way you make the hook up will differ. Some even require adapter plugs.

If you do not install the redox potential electrode "in-line", we suggest that the best location is in the tank, close to the syphon, or close to the overflow corner box (you can also place the electrode inside the syphon overflow box itself).

In both those spots the water movement is strong and representative of the water quality of the aquarium.

Do not immerse the electrode completely. The top endcap, with the wire leading to the meter/controller, must be out of the water, unless you have a special "submersible" type electrode.

They exist, are more expensive, and need a special adapter assembly. You can obtain them from scientific instrument companies, or from my own company.

You must clean your electrode on a regular basis. Slime, algae, and other forms of pollution will adhere to the semi-permeable membrane, and to the electrode tip, and must be removed.

Cleaning solutions can be bought, and should be prefered over home made solutions and techniques. Electrodes are expensive and you do not want to damage yours by improper cleaning.

Not cleaning the electrode results in erroneous readings. Slime on the tip and semi-permeable membrane will result in lower than true readings, since the sensing ability of the electrode is inhibited.

Algae, on the other hand, will result in higher than true treadings, especially during the day when the lights are on, and those algae give off small amounts of oxygen which increase the strength of the signal sensed, and result in a higher millivolt number being displayed.

7. Installing Conductivity Meters

7.1. Purpose

Conductivity can be used as a means of determining the salinity of the tank's water, as we explained earlier in the book.

Such meters are not commonly used, as most hobbyists still rely on either specific gravity testing or salinity testing.

We have explained that specific gravity is both dependent on the temperature of the water itself, and also on what temperature the hydrometer that you are using was calibrated at. This is often 59° F which is not the temperature of the aquarium. This results in erroneous readings.

Conversion charts are published in various books; you should use them if you are trying to get an accurate reading of your specific gravity.

Alternatively, a conductivity meter is a simpler but more expensive way to monitor salinity.

Since these meters can be bought with built-in relays, these units can be used to adjust the salinity automatically by triggering the release of either brine, or freshwater, depending on how the salinity is behaving in your particular system.

Using the combination of the controller (a meter, with one or more relays built in) and the brine and the freshwater vat, allows for a more stable and much more precise salinity control in the aquarium.

We realize that many Hobbyists may not want to carry the stability this far in view of the increased expense, but we have outlined the techniques for those who "are" interested, and looking for yet another way to control water conditions more completely, more accurately, and in an easier fashion.

7.2. Installation

You will need the following items :

• 2 small vats that can hold a few gallons of water each. One holds the brine, the other one holds the fresh water. Use de-ionized or good quality distilled water.

• 2 small solenoids. The types that come as replacement parts for lawn mowers and other such equipment. Both ASCO and Richdel make such units.

• A conductivity controller : check the scientific instrument company's catalogues, or call Thiel•Aqua•Tech. We sell such controllers.You will of course also need the conductivity cell. The latter are usually sold seperately and can be fairly expensive, depending on its quality. T•A•T controllers sell for 370.00 dollars including the electrode.

The read out on the meter can be :

- in Microsiemens, in which case you will need a meter that reads between 40 000 and 60 000.

- in Millisiemens, in which case the meter must read between 40 and 60. For instance, 49.4 would correspond to 49400 microsiemens.

The controller must have 2 relays as you will want to control not one, but two solenoid valves. Keep in mind that such units are more expensive that single relay units, and that you have to add the cost of the solenoids to the price of the controller.

• Flexible hose and a few fittings to make the connections.

• Hose clamps to tighten all connections.

Installation procedure :

• Mount the conductivity controller in a convenient location, and hook up the conductivity cell. Position it in the sump of the trickle filter, but not directly where the brine, or freshwater, will come in.

Since these cells are installed with suction cups and clips, you can always move it to another location later, if you had reasons to. One such reason for moving the conductivity cell may be that the reading is affected too much, and too quickly, by the brine or fresh water that is added to the sump.

• Install the two vats; preferably higher than the sump. In this fashion you will not need pumps to move the liquids, as they will move down by gravity. Since the vats you are using only need to contain a gallon or two, you can place them on top of the sump, or next to the sump, on a raised platform.

They do not have to be right above the sump either. Any location underneath the tank, or even on the side of the tank will be fine.

• Drill small holes to accommodate the input side of the solenoids, and screw them in with some Teflon tape. Most solenoids come with threaded ends.

• Make the two solenoid and Conductivity controller hook ups, using the instructions that come with both these devices. This may involve straight wiring. If it does, the manual that came with your controller should be referred to, and instructions followed accurately.

• From the output side of the solenoid run some acrylic airline tubing, or a size slightly larger, to fit the solenoid, to just above the water level in the sump of the filter, about one inch away is fine too. The exact height does not really matter that much.

• Adjust the conductivity set points on the controller. One is set for high, and will trigger the freshwater vat solenoid to open, letting some pure water go into the sump. This will lower the conductivity that is being measured, which will re-close the solenoid. Use R.O. or D.I. water.

Both reverse osmosis and de-ionized water have very high resistivities, meaning their conductivity is very low, usually in the 10 to 20 microsiemens range.

• Fill one vat with freshwater using preferably distilled or de-ionized water.

• Fill the other vat with strong brine. Again, use D.I. or distilled water and add aquarium salt to it. About 5 times the amount of salt you would normally use. If needed, to improve solubility, warm the water up somewhat.

The low setting on the conductivity controller will trigger the opening of the solenoid on the freshwater vat ; the high setting will trigger the opening of the solenoid on the brine vat.

As the conductivity increases or decreases the controller will open the required supply and maintain a very stable salinity .

The total cost of such a set-up is estimated at around $500.00-550.00.

Remember this is an optional addition to your system, not a requirement. If you opt for the manual control, test a least once a week.

Checking salinity should be part of your regular husbandry schedule.

In the Marine Fish and Invert Reef Aquarium book, on pages 203 to 205, we listed a suggested maintenance schedule, against which you may wish to check your own techniques.

8. Installing Alternating Pumps

8.1. Reasons

It has always been a challenge to better the water circulation in the Marine Aquarium. This is especially so in Reef Tanks, where so much rock and coral placed in the tank, usually towards the back, can easily and greatly impede the even flow of water throughout the aquarium.

If water does not flow evenly, so-called "dead spots" occur. These areas then hold water with less, or significantly less, oxygen, depending on how stagnant the area actually is.

Additionally, irregular water circulation does not provide the kind of water movement that invertebrates and corals are accustomed to on the Reef, where wave action on the surface, and the action of irregularly shaped portions of the reef, constantly alter the direction and to some extent the force of the water passing over the corals and other lifeforms.

In an effort to duplicate this action, hobbyists have come up with various methods of returning the water, and also with devices that change the flow every few minutes.

Two such methods have been used on the Reef tank that we have been describing all along in this book.

One consists of having three water returns, through the bottom of the tank, and alternating how the water is returned in two of them.

Another method consists of using alternating power heads in the aquarium itself, and switching their operation at regular intervals.

We have used both, and the two methods are described in this section.

8.2. Alternating Power Heads

You will need the following items :

• Two, four, or six power heads. The number depends on the size of the tank. On a 150 gallon tank, you could, for instance, use 6 Aquaclear 400, or 2 AquaClear 800 models.

• A device to alternate the current that powers these pumps. Route 4 Marine Technology, and my own company Thiel•Aqua•Tech make such units. The units plug into a wall outlet, and the power heads are plugged into the back of the devices.

The unit T•A•T makes has an additional feature, it allows you to stop all power heads for 5 seconds to 10 minutes, and the pumps will then restart automatically. You decide how long.

This is useful when feeding to prevent the food from ending up in the filters. Both units can handle up to 10 amps of pump capacity.

Installation :

• Place an identical number of power heads over each side of the tank. Position the power heads in such a way that they shoot the water straight accross the length of the tank. Make sure that the air intake hole is under water, and that the air intake tube has been removed.

• Plug the power heads into the back of the alternating device, and plug the device into a wall outlet, or power strip.

• Set the desired switching time. Our units allow up to 2 minutes maximum in each direction. Route 4's units allow slightly less. Anywhere from one to two minutes is fine, as it will create the necessary water current.

• If you decide on using the timed "off" switch on the Thiel•Aqua•Tech model, set the desired time that you want both sides to be off for.

That is really all there is to it. The power heads will now shoot water in each direction for the amount of time that you have set them for, and then reverse the direction, creating a totally different current.

If the amount of turbulence created is too strong, turn the output of the power heads down somewhat. Then watch the anemones, and other lifeforms sway from the right side to the left side, each time the current is changed. Just like we show you in the beginning of our Videotapes.

8.3. Alternating Pumps

This method is similar to the one just described, but instead of two or more power heads, you will require 2 regular outside pumps, or one pump, and some electrically actuated ball valves, or solenoids.

8.3.1. Using 2 Pumps

This type of installation requires that two water out-takes from the sump of the trickle filter be installed, or one outlet, that leads to 2 pumps, by means of a Tee fitting.

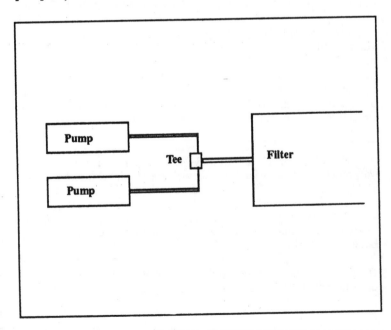

In most cases, the latter method, is probably what most of you who install alternating pumps will use.

The diagram shows the installation of the pump, and the Tee-fitting, leading to the water intake from the sump.

Run a water hose, or hard PVC, line to each water return in the bottom of the tank. Or if you are using the other method we described, going behind the tank, and then over the top, attach one pump to each side.

Plug the pumps into the alternating device. Set the desired switching time, and your alternating water returns are ready to start working for you.

This is the simplest method, as it involves relatively little piping.

You can also attempt to set this system up using only one pump, but there are some drawbacks. Not in terms of efficiency, but in terms of labor and parts.

We had described one of the methods in The Marine Fish and Invert Reef Aquarium book, and have since improved on that method.

8.3.2. Using 1 Pump, and Electrically Actuated Ball Valves

This method requires one pump, and two electrically actuated ball valves, of the same dimension as the water pipe or hose coming off your pump.

From the pump, run two water lines, by means of a Tee-fitting, and pipe an electrically actuated ball valve in each line, then connect to the water inlets either underneath, or behind and over the top of the tank.

The ball valve must be of the normally closed type. When current reaches such a valve, it opens and lets water through. Since current only reaches one of the valves, water will only enter the tank from one side.

Wire the electrically actuated ball valves to the alternating device, one to each outlet, and set the desired switching time. Two minute is probably about right.

The pump will now push water through whichever line is open at the time, and the latter is regulated by the switching device.

Because the valves do not open and close at exactly the same split second, internal pressure will build up for a brief moment, inside the water line between the pump and the valves. You must therefore make absolutely sure that those fittings are tightly cemented (in the case of PVC), or that hose clamps are real tight (in the case of flexible hose).

We recommend that if you are hard piping the water return lines, that you definitely use PVC primer before cementing.

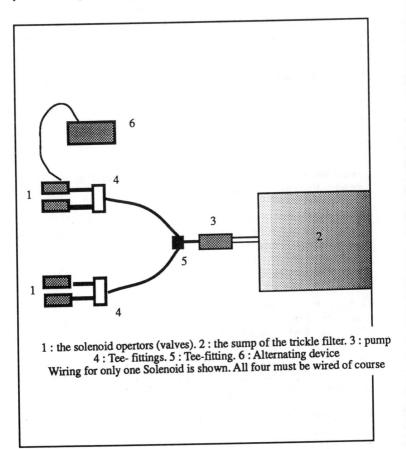

1 : the solenoid opertors (valves). 2 : the sump of the trickle filter. 3 : pump
4 : Tee- fittings. 5 : Tee-fitting. 6 : Alternating device
Wiring for only one Solenoid is shown. All four must be wired of course

Although this is a workable solution, the cost of 2 electrically actuated ball valves will exceed the price of an extra pump. It will be more economical therefore to use the metod described under 8.3.1.

8.3.3. Using one Pump, and Solenoid valves

This is the more problematic of all the methods because the solenoids that we have to use only have 1/2 inch internal diameters. Remember all parts must be of plastic or totally salt water resistant materials.

The largest such solenoids we could find are made by Hayward Industrial Plastics, and have a 1/2 inch I.D. (internal diameter).

This means that most of you will need 4 solenoids, 2 in parallel in each line. This makes it a very expensive way to go, as these solenoids list for around $ 185.00 a piece.

It is however another way of achieving the same alternating result.

The hook up is identical to the actuated ball valve method, except that you will be wiring solenoids.

Diagramatically the set up looks as follows :

The 2 solenoids in each line are re-connected with another Tee-fitting, and each line then goes to one of the water returns.

Should you be able to find solenoids that are larger than 1/2 inch I.D., you will need one for each line. This may still prove more expensive than installing two pumps.

8.3.4. Conclusion

Cost, and ease of installation, seem to both indicate that the best and least expensive route to go is the use of 2 pumps, and the water current alternating device (Ocean Motion maker from T•A•T for instance).

If you decide to use this more advanced water return method, meaning alternating the incoming water current, we recommend you set up your own system using an laternating device.

It is a definite improvement over the older methods, and ensures a much more thorough and continuous mix of the water.

8.3.5. Addendum

As we were about to go to press with this book, news reached us from Hayward Industrial Plastics that solenoids in larger versions are now available as well. Besides quarter and half inch, they now manufacture three quarter and one inch sizes as well. All such solemoids are made of CPVC, and all parts that are in contact with the water are salt water safe and resistant.

This negates the need to use 2 solenoids in parallel in each line, and requires only one solenoid in each water return line, for a total of 2 rather than 4 solenoids.

Large solenoids are however more expensive, and the cost of two such solenoids may well be over five hundred dollars depending on who you buy them from.

More interesting news arrived at the same time.

Actuated ball valves are also manufacutred in 3-way types.

To divert the current from one water line to the other, we would only need one such 3-way electrically actuated ball valve. This reduces the cost of this method by about two hundred dollars, but is not yet the total solution - the expense is still steep.

We still feel that wórking with two motors and one alternating device is the most economical way of setting up this type of water circulation.

Venturi Skimmer

9. Setting up Your Protein Skimmer

9.1 Introduction

Whether you should use a Protein Skimmer or not has been discussed elsewhere in this book, and we made it quite clear that we feel that such protein skimming is a must if you keep a Reef Tank.

There are various types of skimmers, better called foam fractionnators. The main ones that we are concerned with in this book are the columnar reverse flow, and the Venturi "power" models.

Although many in-tank models are sold, even Venturi models, we strongly feel that these units are too small for Reef tanks, and were really developped many years ago, for fish-only tanks.

Unless you have a really small aquarium, a 15 or 20 gallon model, such skimmers do not fit the requirements needed to improve the water quality of your aquarium significantly. Do not let someone convince you that such skimmers will handle your 100 gallon tank. **They will not !**

They have the additional drawback of not enabling you to use ozone.

Indeed the water coming out of such skimmers enters the main water body immediately, and so would any ozone that may still be present in that water. As already explained, that is both dangerous and nefarious.

Dollar for dollar they are not a real good deal either. Small skimmers cost a lot, and you get very little.

Columnar models are your "best buy". If space is a consideration you may wish to acquire one of the Venturi types, e.g. Tunze or T•A•T. They are small and very efficient.

Keep in mind that the Tunze model is an in-tank, or an in-sump model, and that the manufacturer recommends against the use of ozone. Since such recommendations may change, check with them before you buy such a unit if you plan to use ozone.

9. 2. The Columnar Foam Fractionnator

We will be using a Thiel•Aqua•Tech 3 foot skimming column, running with 2 large limewood airstones. Including the scum collection cup the unit is 44 inches tall, and with the Ozone Cap its total height is 50 inches.

The unit runs on its own pump, attached to the sump of the trickle filter. We are using one of the newer 3 speed Aqua-Pumps, and running on the first speed, which delivers in the vicinity of 300 gallons per hour, or on the second speed when more skimming is required, e.g. after the introduction of new livestock.

We sometimes run the pump at its second speed setting when we test new products, e.g. foods.

A Tech •Ozonizer, a dryer and a air filter from the same company are used as well. The air pump is a Wisa 300.

There is no real magic to installing such a skimmer, the procedure is really simple :

• The Aqua-pump is pushing water from the sump of our trickle filter into the skimmer and is piped with acrylic flexible hose and clamps. The skimmer's water inlet is at the top of the column. Hose is run to the inlet and held in place with a 316SS hose clamp.

• From the water outlet, at the bottom of the skimmer, we run a length of PVC hose to the sump of the trickle filter. We use PVC to prevent deterioration due to the ozone that is present in the water.

• Right underneath the area where that water re-enters the sump, an activated carbon chamber is placed.

• All the water must flow through the carbon before it can mix with the water in the sump. We have explained the reasons for this already.

• In that same chamber we have a redox potential electrode, to measure the redox potential of the skimmer's outflowing water.

• At the end of that return hose, we have installed an "angle" valve. Such valves allow fine adjustments of the outflow, much finer than with typical ball valves. This in turn allows us to easily control the exact level of the water inside the skimmer.

For those not familiar with a skimmer's operation, here is how it works :

• As water is pushed into the skimmer it first rises in the column and then it starts flowing out at the bottom, and gets back into the trickle filter's sump.

• Depending on how fast the water runs out, or how little water you are pushing into the skimmer, the water level inside the skimmer may not be high enough.

• To artificially raise that level, all you need to do is restrict the outflow, alternatively you can increase the amount of water you are pushing into the skimmer.

• Since how much water you need to run through your skimmer is really determined by the size of your tank, it is better to first get the right amount to flow through the skimmer, then reduce the outflow somewhat and maintain the desired level.

Angle valves allow fine adjustments, and are just what we need to stabilize the skimmer wherever we want it to be, with precision.

Where is that desired level ?

It varies from skimmer to skimmer and is usually explained in the instructions that came with your unit.

In our case, it is 0.5 inch below the top plate, right where the narrower neck, which leads to the scum collection cup, starts.

Many columnar skimmer models are available from companies such as Sander, MTC, Coralife, Summit, Route 4 and my own company. The choice is yours.

Position the base of the protein skimmer at the same level as the base of the filter. This makes connections easy and short.

Additionally you will not have to try to figure out what the impact of the different levels will do to the way the skimmer runs.

Things to watch out for :

• Since you cannot put a check valve in the protein skimmer outflow line, you must keep in mind that, if the power fails and the pumps stop, most of the water in your skimmer will keep flowing into the sump.

The sump should therefore be large enough to hold that extra amount of water. If not, it will overflow. Calculate the quantity the skimmer holds, and test whether that actually fits in the sump.

You can however prevent this, by installing an electrically actuated ball valve in line with the outflow. This valve runs on the same power line as the skimmer's pump.

If that power goes, the ball valve shuts, and no water flows out. These valves may cost around $150.00-250.00 but they are certainly worth the investment.

When the power comes back on, the valve re-opens, and things are back to normal. Hayward Industrial Plastics makes such valves.

• Anytime you add something to the water, e.g. Vitamins, dKH builder tablets or liquid, and many other additives for that matter, you must watch what the impact of that additive is on the skimmer's performance.

Often the water will foam more, and you run the risk that the skimmer will overflow from the top cup. This is due to the surface tension breaking ability of many of these additives. Tech•Reef•KH does not make your skimmer foam more than it does normally and is a very strong buffer with a dKH of over 1000 degrees.

Watch what happens, and re-adjust the skimmer, or add very little at a time, so that the impact on the foaming is negligeable.

Those of you who are using dosing, or better still metering pumps, will more than likely not experience these problems. But check anyway.

• Valves, e.g. the ball or angle valve that you are using to regulate the output, respectively the level inside the skimmer, trap dirt.

This does not happen overnight, but dirt gets trapped inside. This will affect the level in your skimmer. It is therefore a good idea to clean the valves from time to time.

• Airstones trap dirt too. As a result the size of the bubbles they produce will change. They become larger. Larger bubbles do not skim as efficiently as small bubbles. They rise faster, resulting in less contact time with the water. Contact time is the one important factor that determines the efficiency of your skimming.

Change the airstones regularly. Every 2 weeks is probably safer, and better, than every month. Make it a habit to change them whether you think they may still do the job for another week or not. Large limewood airstones are the better kind.

Oak airstones are around too. They make small bubbles as well, but require very powerful airpumps.

Lately, ceramic re-usable airstones have appeared on the market. At the time we wrote this we had not had the opportunity to try them out. We will keep readers of Marine Reef, our newsletter, aware of what we find. One such airstone is made by Rena.

• Since your skimmer removes "organics", small free floating algae and particulate matter, that so-called "scum" collects in the cup that sits on top of your skimmer.

You must remember to empty it regularly, or it will overflow, or fall back into the main column. Both are to be avoided. Whatever your skimmer removes is very messy, and stains.

If you have a drain nearby, you can hook the output of the scum cup to the drain by means of flexible hose. Make sure that the hose does not clog, use a large enough size. 3/8 to 1/2 inch is probably best.

You could also use a larger container in which you can let the scum collect. You will have to empty that container from time to time.

• All hose that comes in contact with ozone must be ozone resistant; use Tygon, or better even Norprene.

The reason is two-fold :

- ozone will make non-ozone resistant hose disintegrate,
- and in the process of doing so, that portion of the total ozone output that is attacking your hose, is no longer active and is not cleaning up your water. What we mean is that interaction between hose and ozone greatly reduces the amount that will actually get into the water inside the skimmer.

Columnar skimmer with reverse flow (the water comes in from the top, and the air from the bottom) work extremely efficiently and can remove up to 80 percent of all organics in the water.

You must however remember to monitor their performance, and make adjustments when neccessary. This includes changing airstones and regulating the level as required.

9.3. Venturi skimmers

Several companies market a skimmer that is referred to as "Power" skimmer, or Venturi skimmer, or a combination of both.

These skimmers are as efficient as columnar skimmers, and can skim that efficiently even though they are much smaller. The latter is the main reason for their popularity. You can easily fit a unit that will handle a large tank underneath the cabinet.

Unfortunately they are usually quite expensive, mainly because a lot of manual labor is involved. Two models deserve mention : the Tunze skimmer from Germany, and the Thiel•Aqua•Tech Venturi skimmer, made in the USA (as all other T•A•T products are).

Venturi skimmers do not require an airpump. The Venturi valve draws in the air using the force and the pressure differential created by the water flowing through the pipe.

The Venturi principle itself has been around for many many years but has only been applied to the hobby for a few, and only T•A•T manufactures a U.S. made model.

The Tunze Skimmer is a really efficient unit that is installed in the tank, or in the sump. As far as we know, no ozone can be used with it, but this may change. Check Tunze's recommendations in this respect. If you decide to use ozone with these skimmers, you will have to find a way to remove the ozone from the outflowing water.

The T•A•T model is an outside the tank unit, and can safely be used with ozone.

Venturi valves are very efficient if they are correctly built, especially if they include a Pitot tube. Our own model does. Such a Pitot tube, Venturi assembly is shown in the diagram.

It looks fairly simple, but is really quite difficult to make, because of the relative size of the inner tube to the outer tube, the length of part 2 in the diagram, the size of the restriction, and how far past the hole the Pitot tube enters the main water pipe.

Additionally the location of the hole is important too. Molded venturi valve assemblies can be bought from specialized companies. They are often so application specific that they can unfortunately not be used in the hobby. This is unfortunate indeed because, if they were, more such skimmers would be available.

Hooking up a Venturi skimmer is similar to hooking up a columnar unit. The main difference is that you will not require an air pump.

Venturi valve (molded)

Follow the instructions that came with the skimmer carefully, and adjust the water level as recommended.

If you have to restrict the water output side to maintain the right level in your skimmer, use an angle valve (best), or a ball valve (second best).

Our own model can be used with Ozone. The installation of the ozonizer is as follows :

• From the Venturi valve assembly run a length of ozone resistant tubing (Norprene) to the output side of your ozonizer.

• From the input of your ozonizer run a length of tubing to output of the air dryer.

• Leave the intake of the air dryer as is.

• Hook the ozonizer into your redox potential controller, or if you are not using such a unit, plug it into a wall outlet.

• Remember to perform residual ozone tests to ensure that no ozone is present in the water.

Skimmers do not need to be underneath the tank, or right next to it. They can be placed anywhere where it is convenient. You may need a stronger pump, and you will need more hose to make the connections but that is all there is to it.

For those Hobbyists who use ozone :

Always flow the output of the skimmer over activated carbon.

10. Installing Denitrification Filters

Although I have always felt that these units are very complicated to operate by the average, and certainly by the beginning, Hobbyist, there has never been any doubt in my mind that these units work and are a definite benefit to the Reef tank..

They work extremely well in fact, and will remove most nitrates and some phosphate from the water as well. In fact if you run them properly you can make them remove most of the phosphates, not just some.

The problem is, and has always been, the continuous adjustments that they require of both the water and nutrient input side on one hand, and the clogging of the output side on the other.

10.1. Input side problems :

• Because we need to "trickle" water into the denitrification filter, drop by drop, airline tubing and a clamp to restrict the flow are generally used. At the point of restriction, detritus will plug up the very small opening that is left, and the water will drip, first slower, then not at all.

This results in your filter turning completely anaerobic, unless you catch the problem rather quickly, and re-adjust the drip rate.

• Similarly, the nutrient supply must be carefully administered, and spread evenly over the period of a whole day. This is best done by using a metering or dosing pump, or by using a solenoid and a timer, as in the Coralife model, only recently introduced, and sold with all the necessary implements.

• Salt encrustations may appear on the input nipple, which will result in the inflow of water slowing down, or stopping altogether.

10.2. Problems on the output side :

• As the filter starts running, a number of bacterial processes start, one of which produces a stringy slimy mass that has a tendency to plug the output holes in a matter of 7 to 10 days. This backs up the water in the denitrifying filter, which may overflow, unless you catch the problem in time.

• As the holes between the various compartments get clogged by the slimy mass inside the filter, the water does not transfer properly, and again, the potential exists that the unit may overflow.

10.3. Problems with the operation :

• If the water runs through the denitrator too quickly, nitrate is not removed at all, or not completely, and nitrite is produced as a by-product. In fact your filter is operating as a semi-biological filter, because too much oxygen is present, which is not conducive to the controlled anaerobic activity that we are looking for.

• If water runs through too slowly, or not at all, the bacteria inside attack the sulfate in the water - after they run out of nitrate - and your filter will produce Hydrogen Sulfide. That is of course totally undesirable and dangerous for all animal life.

• If the water runs at the correct rate, but you do not add enough nutrient, you will again find some hydrogen sulfide in the output, and nitrate will not be removed completely.

We certainly do not want to discourage you from using these filters. They really work and clean up the water better than you even imagine. But it should be clear from the problems that we have outlined, that this is not the easiest filter to operate.

You must get both the drip rate adjusted correctly, and maintain that level continuously, and also add the right amount of the right nutrient.

Since the right amount of nutrient is dependent on the amount of nitrate in your system, that amount will vary, and depend on the water quality.

As time goes by, and as less and less nitrate is present, more nutrient is required, but within limitations of course. This is not a process that runs ad infinitum. Alternatively, you could speed up the drip rate, as that would bring in more nitrate.

Do not under-estimate the importance of using the right nutrient mix! I have refined the formula that I use now over the course of nearly one year, contantly changing its mix and the type of ingredients, while monitoring results and making copious notes (Lab books 9-11-17 THIEL).

This research led to the nutrient mix that I now add, which ensures that this difficult to operate filter gets a better chance at operating the way it should, even if you do not always pay careful attention to it.

At least you will be adding the right kind of nutrient mix (Tech• Denitrification•Nutrient in 4,8 and 32 oz bottles).

Setting denitrification filters up correctly is a real game of trial and error, especially in the beginning. Each change you make will take some time to bring about a new type of output water chemistry.

Each time you make an adjustment you will have to wait a few hours before re-testing to determine whether the desired change has happened.

You must therefore be prepared, and willing, to give this type of filtration quite a bit of attention, or your efforts will be frustrated.

The ideal result is water exiting your filter that contains n either nitrate nor nitrite, and that has at least a slightly lower phosphate content than the water in the tank.

Cycling a denitrification filter will take 5 to 6 weeks. This is longer than most Hobbyists imagine.

While that happens your filter will put out both nitrite and nitrate. This is normal and no reason for concern. The amounts are small and should not be detectable in the main water body, although they will be quite high in the water that comes out of the denitrator. It should not put out hydrogen sulfide. That you have to monitor.

10.4. Adjusting the Denitrator :

• Once the nitrate in the water from the denitrator is lower than the nitrate in the tank water, you must start adjusting the drip rate, until no more nitrite is present in the water coming out of the denitrator.

• Make small changes only. If you slow the filter down too much, you will find, and smell, Hydrogen sulfide in the water. If that happens you must speed the drip rate up some what again.

• When you first start up the filter on a tank that has a lot of nitrates, the nutrient quantity is not all that important, but as the nitrate level is reduced day after day, monitoring the amount you add becomes a must.

• Since different filters use different nutrients, you must follow the manufacturers instructions carefully. There is no universal dosage that applies to all filters. Unfortunately so.

For those Minireef· users out there, we add that, yes, your filter uses a different type of nutrient, one that needs to be replenished about every 30 days, and is not added daily as in most other denitrification filters.

We find however that our nutrients work better, and are more reliable. Both Leo Wojcik, Scott Jerome, George Bepko and myself were able to demonstrate that empyrically.

If you are not able to maintain your denitrator daily, you can always resort to using X-nitrate from Thiel•Aqua•Tech, either in your trickle filter, or in a cannister or reactor. You will get excellent results as well, and without the work involved in running a denitrator.

10.5. Installating and starting up your denitrification filter:

• You must create a by-pass on the main water return to the tank that can be sized down to airline tubing size. That is indeed the input size of most denitrators.

This can be done by piping a Tee-fitting in line, and then using reducing bushings (fittings) to bring the size down to airline tubing.

• All you need to do subsequently is attach a length of tubing from that reduced Tee, to the input of the denitrator.

• Next, hook up tubing from the output of the denitrating filter back to the sump of your trickle filter. Use 3/8 or 1/2 inch tubing to prevent clogging up of the outflow line.

• Alternatively, you can place a length of airline tubing in the tank, start a syphon, and clamp the airline tubing down with a Keck clamp or some other clamp that allows you to restrict the flow.

• Attach the airline tubing in the tank by means of a good suction cup. Attach the other end of the tubing to the input of your denitrator.

• Tighten the clamp over the tubing to reduce the output to just a slow drip rate. Use the manufacturer's recommendations.

• Install the nutrient feeding device if you are using one. This could be a solenoid and a timer, as in the Coralife system; or it could be a drip method or a metering pump (best) as in our own system.

• Return the output to the sump of the trickle filter, and your unit is up and running.

10.6. Running the filter : Procedures

• Fill the denitrification unit with water.

• Let stand for 36 hours to remove most of the oxygen that is in the water now in the filter.

• If using our nutrients, add 40 drops.

• After 36 hours start up the filter at a drip rate of 30 drops per minute and maintain this drip rate for at least 4 weeks, or until the output water does no longer contain nitrites and nitrates.

• If at any time hydrogen sulfide develops (you will be able to smell it) speed the drip rate up by 15 drops per minute.

• During the cycling period add nutrients as recommended by the manufacturer of your filter.

• Monitor the output every day starting day 10.

• Once the filter has cycled, adjust the inflow of water for as long as needed, until no more nitrite and nitrate can be found (you must test) in the outflowing water. This will take some time for you to determine. It also requires either speeding up the flow, or reducing it.

• Never speed the inflow up by more than 10 to 15 drops per minute at a time. Then re-test about 2 hours later.

• Never slow down by more than 10 drops per minute at a time. Then re-test the outflowing water and make further adjustments if necessary.

• Once the filter is operating properly (meaning no nitrate can be found in the effluent), keep testing it every other day by taking off the lid and smelling to determine the presence of Hydrogen sulfide.

• Monitor the effluent water on a regular basis. Nitrates should be zero ppm. Nitrites should be zero ppm as well. Phosphates should be lower than their level in the tank.

• Remember to replenish the nutrient supply regularly. We have seen recommendations on how to make a home made nutrient. As far as we are concerned, the ones we saw in the hobby magazines are far from containing all the nutrient required. We recommend that you stay away from them. Buy a commercial product. You will be better off in the long run.

11 . Installing Reactors and Equipment

11.1. Cooling Units

Cooling units, described in the Equipment and Instrumentation section, can be installed in the main water return line, or, as we have done, in the third water return line; the one that brings the water back behind the coral rock formations.

Water is taken from the sump by means of an outside pump, and runs through the cooling unit, set for 75.5 degrees Fahrenheit. That water return line then runs through a Poly Filter cannister, and ends up entering the aquarium, through a hole in the bottom of the tank, behind the coral.

The hook-up of a cooling unit is very simple. There is an input and an output to which barbs can be attached if you are piping with flexible hose, or PVC fittings if you are running hard pipe.

To operate efficiently, a certain amount of water needs to be flowed through the cooling unit. You must check the instruction sheet and ensure that you meet that minimum, otherwise your water will not cool enough, or only very slowly.

If the unit you have fails to cool the water sufficiently, you probably are using too small a unit. The strength is usually expressed by giving the rating of the compressor, e.g. 1/4 or 1/5 HP, etc..Quarter horsepower units will do fine on 150 gallon tanks, and in most cases one fifth HP will do the job too.

The type of unit you need does not really depend on the size of the tank alone, but on how many degrees the water needs to be lowered, and that is determined by the magnitude of the heat transfer from the equipment that you are using.

Aquariums with overhead metal halide lighting, that use powerful pumps, and several of them, may find that they need quarter HP units, whereas the same aquarium run with different lights, and different and less pumps, may only need a fifth of a HP.

Cooling units for reef tanks should have titanium coil cooling elements. They are totally safe. Units that have Teflon coated copper tubing will do fine for possibly a long time, but the Teflon may wear or get cracket by pieces of sand, or coral that enter the water stream. If that happens, copper will enter your tank, and we all know what problems will ensue.

Our recommendation is therefore that you pre-filter the water going through the cooling unit to prevent the Teflon coated inner tubing from being damaged.

Most Hobbyists think that cooling units are both expensive and noisy. That may have been the case a few years ago, but the price has come down considerably and the noise level is nowadays much lower than you think.

If you are in the market for a cooler we suggest that you try Aquarium Sales and Services, and discuss your needs with them. Many hobbyists have reported excellent service from this company.

11.2. Poly Filter cannisters

We already described this installation in the equipment section. We wish to point out again that the filter(s) must be installed "upright", otherwise you will not be able to service them without spilling water.

Additionally you must place shut-off valves on at least the aquarium side of the filter. This will allow you to close the water line coming from the tank, and again service the unit without spilling water. It is better still to put shut off valves on both sides.

We have made one addition to the basic set up : we have installed a pressure gauge before the Poly filter cannister. This allows us to determine when the time has come to replace the filter discs, based on the PSI indicated by the gauge.

Since gauges usually have brass ends, we also use the Hayward Industrial Plastics "gauge guard" assembly, a fitting that transmits the pressure of the water, via a Viton™ seal, to glycerine, and then to the gauge. This way, no salt water comes in contact with the brass. The cost of the gauge, and the gauge guard, was around 35.00 dollars.

Both the gauge and the gauge guard must be bought seperately. The filling of the gauge guard and the calibration of the gauge is best performed at a plumbing supply shop. This will ensure accurate pressure readings and leakage around the gauge guard.

Depending on the strength of the pump you use, you can probably run the cannister with discs until the PSI reaches 13. That would however require a rather strong pump, and it is likely that you will have to change the discs sooner.

We use modified Iwaki 55 pumps and run the disks until the pressure reaches 13, then we wash them out with tap water, and if they are not brown we place them back in the cannister for another cycle. If they are brown we replace the disks (the method was first brought to our attention by Leo Wojcik).

Washing removes dirt from the discs and lets the water easily through again. The pressure drop after cleaning the discs is typically around 2 to 3 PSI.

If you do not clean the disks, and if you do not use a strong pump, you will have a strongly reduced water output, because the pump you use cannot handle the back pressure and as a result it moves less water through the cannisters.

For those interested, to go from maximum head rating on the pump to pounds per square inch (PSI), multiply the maximum head rating by 0.44.

A pump with a maximum head rating of 16 feet will handle a maximum of 7 PSI , 25 feet corresponds to 11 PSI, and so on.

11.3. X-Nitrate Reactor

Install the reactor close to the sump of the trickle filter, or on the side of the aquarium.

Take water from either the tank by means of a power head pumping the water down to the reactor, and then back from the reactor to the sump; or use a dedicated outside or submersible pump, taking the water out of the sump, and returning it back to that same sump.

Special size reactors can of course be made, or ordered, to fit just about any situation.

The important factor to keep in mind with these reactors, is that you must flow a lot of water through the compound. That will ensure that it removes the nitrates as well as some of the phospahtes properly and efficiently.

Our reactors, and Route 4 Marine Technology's, both take male threaded half inch barbs to which you can attach flexible hose with clamps, or you can screw in a half inch male adapter, and then hard pipe the unit.

A ball valve should be placed on the output side, to allow you to adjust the output, if required.

The water coming from the reactor could be used to feed into another reactor, before returing it to the sump of the filter. If you opt for this type of a set up, you will need to make sure that the pump that you are using can handle the flow and backpressures that will develop over the water line.

It can be done, and will save you the cost of an additional pump, but the pump that you use must be strong. Power heads will not allow you to run the reactors in this fashion; they cannot deal with the back pressure.

Adjusting multiple reactors can be frustrating, but is not difficult. It just takes more time and patience.

X-nitrate is a very efficient compound, but it cannot be regenerated. You will need to monitor your Nitrate levels from time to time, as long as they stay stable or go down, X-nitrate is still actively working, when they start rising again, change the X-nitrate.

11.4. Oxygen - Carbonate Hardness - CO2 Reactors

We already discussed in great detail how to set these reactors up in Part Two.

Our only additonal comment is that, to ensure that the over-pressure inside the cylinder is maintained, you must watch the level on pressurized reactors regularly.

If it is not maintained, you are not increasing the dissolved oxygen level, or not using the ozone efficiently, and your reactor is not performing its function.

Self-leveling units will be available in the near future. In fact by the time you read this, they may already be on the market. This new feature will make the operation of all reactors much easier, and also much more efficient of course.

We already have working models at Marine Reef, and only manufacturing arrangements have to be set up to get them to the market. These should hopefully be completed shortly.

11.5. Dosing Pumps - Metering Pumps

Both these pumps are meant to dispense fluids on an even basis over a given period of time.

Dosing pumps deliver a fixed amount, at pre-set intervals. Metering pumps run continuously, and dispense pre-set quantities.

This is not the same. Let us illustrate this a little more :

• a dosing pump can be used to dispense, for instance, 5 drops every 2 hours, or 23 drops every six hours, or any such combination. They are used to dispense small quantities of a liquid, evenly over a 24 hour period at pre-set intervals.

These liquids could be fertilizers, vitamins, trace elements, dKH builder, etc...All these compounds may be mixed in the right proportion, diluted somewhat, and then dispensed evenly.

How to prepare your mixture based on the particular additives that you use is discussed in The Marine Fish and Invert Reef Aquarium book, as well as elsewhere in this book (see index).

• Metering pumps are used to increase the evenness of the distribution even further. Metering pumps run continuously. You can again dispense all the additives that you normally use, but now you will have to mix them in such a way, that their proportion is adjusted for the amount that the metering pump adds to the tank in 24 hours.

Example : we use a metering pump that delivers (is set to deliver is more accurate) 1 gallon of a mixture per 24 hours.

That one gallon contains all the additives that we use. Why ? Because we have prepared the mixture in the vat from which the pump draws the fluid that it pumps, that way.

The vat holds 25 gallons, but only 20 are in the vat. That represents, at one gallon per day, a 20 day's supply. We have multiplied the daily dosage of all our additives by 20, and added that amount of each to that vat. An air pump, with airstone, keeps the mixture stirred, and all elements in the water properly mixed.

Because metering pumps continuously add fluid, and dosing pumps only intermittently, we prefer using the metering pump.

You can of course use smaller vats, the only difference will be that you will have to prepare your mixture, and fill the vat, more often.

A Tech•Doser metering pump will run you around $275.00, which is quite a bit less than what you pay for dosing pumps, and for much better results. At least that is our opinion after having tried both for quite some time, and having been able to determine fertilizer and other additive levels at various times of the day under both set-ups.

11. 6. Installation of the Water changer

Our installation may be different from your particular need, but the general principles still apply. You may have to adapt the method somewhat, to cope with the situation that you are dealing with.

We will be using the following items :

• A 25 gallon reserve vat,
• 2 mercury float switches,
• A submersible March pump,
• A Micronta Radio Shack Timer,
• Flexible hose and clamps
• An overflow outlet from the sump of the trickle filter to a drain.

The vat contains the reserve salt water. We add one and a half gallon of new water per day. This is done by activating the submersible pump for two minutes every day.

The output of that pump has been adjusted by placing a clamp over the hose coming from the pump, and closing it more and more, until the output in two minutes was exactly one and a half gallon, as measured with a graduated plastic container.

As the water rises in the sump, it reaches the drain level. Water keeps being pushed in on the opposite side, and the drain hole/pipe now starts running off the excess water to the floor drain.

After two minutes the pump shuts off, the drain runs for a little while longer, and then the levels are re-adjusted.

In the 2 minutes that water is being added, and excess water drained, we have changed one and a half gallon of water, but because the incoming water was running into the same vat as where the drain is located, dilution has to be accounted for. We have calculated that to be a loss of about 33 percent. This means that in reality we have added about one gallon of new water.

A float switch is positionned in the trickle filter sump and is set to stop the March pump in the reserve vat, if the level in the sump rises too much. This is a protection against the sump overflowing should, for some reason, the drain pipe become clogged.

The second float switch is used to prevent the reserve vat from running dry, should we forget to refill it. 25 gallons is enough for slightly more than 3 weeks of water changes, and I usually prepare new salt water on the morning of the 19th day. The water can then aerate for 24 hours, before it is pumped into the tank.

If no drain is available, you can let the water drain into another vat, and you will have to empty that vat from time to time (see The Marine Fish and Invert Reef Aquarium for more details).

Of course space may still be a constraint. No one says, however, that this second vat needs to be underneath the tank. It could be hidden in a closet, and connected to the sump by means of acrylic hose.

Ideally, and if you have that option, you can install all the equipment in your cellar. This usually resolves both space problems and aesthetic look requirements of some of the equipment used.

You must think the process through, and see how you can utilize the available technology to suit your specific needs and work around the constraints that you have to deal with.

Usually the two main one are : look and space.

Cabinet extensions can be bought or can be built, equipment that does not fit underneath the tank can be installed in these cabinet extensions.

You may not want to go that route, but you should consider it. Outfitting your tank and restricting what equipment you are using because "it would not look good" or "I don't have any space for it" are not very professional approaches.

You cannot expect such tanks to perform at their optimum as you will have made to many trade-offs and unprofessional additions to your tank and filtration system.

Any reader having problems with his or her set up is welcome to call us, and we will gladly try to help find a way. We have already offered to do this several times in this book. We mean it. If you are up against a problem that seems to have no solution, call us, we may have run into something similar in the past and know of a way around it.

12. Miscellaneous

12.1. Installing Check Valves

You will need check valves in any water line that can back-syphon water from the aquarium, or bring water back by gravity to your filter.

This includes all water hose and pipe that returns water back to the tank, even if you have no holes drilled in the bottom of the aquarium. The gravity of water in a hose, or in a pipe, will draw more water from the tank if it can, and as long as no air enters the hose or pipe, it can do so.

Any tube, pipe, or hose that is placed in the tank, under the water level, can potentially back-syphon.

It is important that you look at your set up carefully, and visualize what could happen. Run through the worst case scenario, and if you think you need to make modifications, you probably do, and should.

Check valves must also be installed in all air, oxygen, and carbon dioxide lines, and also in the ozone line running to an ozone reactor. This will prevent water from damaging your equipment.

The latter are much smaller check valves, and because of their special-ized applications, can be relatively exzpensive

Use the right check valve for the job. Check valves with rubber flaps inside, do not work in salt water for very long. You must use ball check valves, or better even so-called Y-check valves. Ball checks sometimes rattle, a very unpleasant noise to hear all the time I can assure you.

Y-checks do not have this problem. Hayward Industrial Plastics makes an all PVC spring Y-check valve, including a PVC spring.

The rattling of ball check valves can usually be prevented by applying the following guideline :

• place the check valve between the pump and the trickle filter, or
• place the check valve as far away from the pump output as you can,
• or, best, use an oversized ball check valve and use bushings to reduce it to the size of the pipe or hose that you are working with.

12.2. Water Top-off System

You can use an inexpensive and simple principle to effect your top-off function.

It is based on the same principle used in drinking water bottles and dispensers - the kind you see in offices. The ones that have the big plas-tic bottle on their top, in upside down position, and that work on nega-tive inside pressure.

Within the dispenser is a small reservoir that fills up when you turn the bottle upside down. But although the bottle is open, it does not empty itself. The reason is that as the bottle empties itself a little, and the level in the small reservoir underneath rises, that reserve, and the opening of the bottle touch.

Since suddenly no air can enter the bottle, because its opening touches the water, no more water flows out; it is held in the bottle by the vacu-um that was created when some water flowed out at first, and some bubbles went up.

This same principle can be put to work for us. Place an airtight contai-ner on top of the sump, install a ball valve, or a simple shut-off valve, run a small length of hose to the surface of the water in the sump.

Make the length such that it just touches the water in the sump, providing the level in the vat is the one you want all the time. If not, adjust the level first, and then cut the hose. Open the ball valve. It is best to use rather rigid hose so it will not bend and curl.

When evaporation now reduces the amount of water in the sump, and its level, the end of the hose will be out of the water. This will cause some water to flow down from the container, until the tip of the hose touches the water again.

This process continues all the time, and compensates for evaporation. Remember to refill the container when necessary.

The top of the container must be air tight of course, otherwise this system will not work. Since you must be able to refill the container without removing it, you should be able to remove its top and then re-seal it. We used a plastic container with a 2 inch hole in which we placed a compression nut. Tight fitting plastic one or two gallon containers will do the job as well. They must be relatively strong, lest the vacuum will collapse the container on itself.

You could use a totally different system altogether. We already mentioned the Tech•Doser pump (metering pump) used to dispense additives.

Proceed as follows :

• Determine as accurately as you can how much evaporation occurs every day. If you cannot determine it in one day, wait two or three days, then determine the amount and divide the number by 2 or by 3.

• Set the Tech•Doser to dispense that amount of water every day into the sump of your trickle filter. Add all your additives to that quantity.

• If you use a larger vat, say one that can hold a 10 day supply of water, mix 10 times the amount of all your daily additives , in that amount of water. If you do not have space for 10 gallon vat, use a smaller one, and adjust the amount of additives accordingly.

You now have an automatic top-off system. We recommend that you use distilled or, better, de-ionized water for this purpose.

This is a much more reliable and a much more even way of topping off the tank ; it entails the use of a metering pump and the costs associated with buying such a device.

12.3. Protein Skimmer Scum Collector

To reduce the number of times you need to empty the cup on top of the skimmer, run a length of hose from the top scum collector to a container with a tight lid standing on the floor.

Make a hole in the lid that can hold hose of same diameter as the output nipple of the skimmer cup.

Push the hose through the hole in the lid. When scum now enters the cup, it will flow down to the larger container underneath. Depending on the size container you have used, you may only have to empty it every week, or every 10 to 12 days. Remember to empty it though.

If you wish, add some deodorizer to that vat. Do not use an airtight container for this purpose. Make one or two pinholes so air can escape. If it doesn't, internal pressure builds up and the scum will not come down.

You may also be able to guide the outflowing scum directly to a drain. This is a good idea, but if it is a floor drain you must maintain some deodorizer in that drain, to prevent unpleasant odors.

12.4. Ozone Cap for Skimmers

Those Hobbyists using ozone sometimes find that ozone escapes from the top of the skimmer, mixes with the ambient air, and makes the whole room smell .

This can easily be remedied. All you need is an ozone cap. This is a cup, of the same diameter as your skimmer's scum cup, which is filled with activated carbon, placed on top of some floss.

The bottom of the cup has a few holes. All the air coming out of the skimmer must now escape through those holes, and go through the activated carbon, which adsorbs the ozone.

If the fit is not tight enough, and some ozone can still be smelled, use some tape around the edges where the two cups connect, or even kitchen plastic cling wrap.

If you do not want to buy such a cap, place a bag with carbon over the top of the scum cup, and your problem will be greatly alleviated though not resolved.

12.5. Making Extra Test Cylinders

As long as you have one test cylinder, or graduated beaker, you can make as many as you want.

Fill the one you have to e.g. 10 ml, or some other number. Transfer that water to another non-graduated container, bottle, vial, of any type.

Make a mark with a suitable pen, or use the top of a gummed label as a reference point.

If you need more than one content mark, proceed as above, and make additonal marks where appropriate.

If you want to buy commercial measuring cups and cylinders, scientific supply houses and pharmacies are both a good source.

If you perform a battery of tests on a regular basis, as you should, it is important to have clean and adequately market test cylinders or beakers available. This enhances the accuracy of your testing.

On average, a hobbyist who monitors his or her tank regularly, should have from 3 to 5 such test cylinders, vials or beakers.

12.6. Starting Overflow Syphons

Overflow surface skimming syphon assemblies, usually with one box-like part inside the tank and another usually larger one outside, come in many shapes.

We cannot give you a universal way of starting them. There are however two main types :

12.6.1. Syphons with a bent acrylic Tube :

Prime the syphon tube in the same fashion as you did in the old days, on box filters that you used, the ones hanging over the side of the tank.

Alternatively draw the air out of the syphon tube either from the top, by means of a piece of airline tubing, or if no hole for airline tubing is provided on the top, stick a piece of tubing into the tube, through the opening on the shorter side, and draw out the air.

As you draw out air, the prime is created and the syphon will start flowing. These type of syphons will not re-start automatically. If you lose the prime, you will have to re-start them manually by performing what we just described each time it is necessary.

The syphons obviously work, but are much harder to maintain than the ones described in the next section.

12.6.2. Overflow Assemblies that are closed

Four manufacturers offer such syphons : Summit Aquatics, Route 4 Marine Technology, MTC and T•A•T.

These type of overflow boxes are provided with a nipple on the top of the unit. You simply attach airline tubing to that nipple, suck the air out, and your syphon is primed.

After you have done so, the syphon will start running. To get the maximum flow rate you must remove all the air from the inside of the assembly.

Check whatever syphon arrangement you are using regularly for air, and remove it as necessary. This will keep your system running properly, and at a good flow.

All the syphons mentioned will re-start automatically as, when the pumps stop, you do not lose prime. This is due to the way in which they are built.

12.6.3. Credits

Mike Helton and David Nikodym perfected this model which we originally saw in Germany. They should get all the credit and we gladly extend it to them here.

Unfortunately, in this wonderful hobby of ours, unscrupulous people often try to take credit for systems, modifications, and improvements introduced by others. This is really very unfortunate, and we are glad to set the record straight, at least with regard to syphons.

12.7. Drip Systems

Drip systems can be used to dispense many types of additives and are a less expensive way to do so than using metering and dosing pumps.

We have covered various types of drip methods earlier (see index), here is yet another one :

• Use a medical or similar I.V. drip type bottle. Medical supply shops sell them over the counter. You can often find them in scientific supply house mail order catalogues as well.

• Fill it with water. Clamp the output hose down somewhat.

• Let water flow out of the bottle into a graduated cylinder. Determine the quantity that came out in e.g. 15 minutes.

• Multiply that by 4 and then by 24. This will give you the output per 24 hours of your drip system.

• Determine how many times the bottle can hold that quantity. I.V. bottles are small and may not hold more than half a gallon to one gallon maximum.

• Figure out how many days of supply that is.If your system needs 12 ounces per day, and the bottle holds 1 gallon, you have about 12 days of supply.

• Multiply the daily quantity of additives that you normally add to your tank by that same number.

• Add that quantity to the bottle.

• Start the drip system. You now have an automated drip system that will dispense the right quantity of all additives very evenly mixed.

We used such a system for several months, to dispense Tech•Reef•KH fluid, diluted, to maintain our dkH at a steady 15 dKH degrees all the time and had no difficulty what so ever with the system.

We first determined of course how much carbonate hardness our tank was losing every day, and we then diluted Tech•Reef•KH fluid to dispense that needed quantity.

You can use this method to dispense any fluid that you want to add to the tank, including using it as yet another top-off system.

There are some problems associated with these drip systems that we need to mention :

• it is difficult to maintain a steady drip rate unless the fluid being dispensed is extremely pure and does not contain particulate matter.

If it does, the drip rate will have a tendency to slow down, and eventually stop.

• This will require monitoring and frequent adjusting of the drip rate, probably on a daily basis.

• If fluids that do not mix perfectly are used in such systems, they will seperate unless the liquid in the container is stirred all the time.

The heavier ones will sink, and will be dripped into the water to the detriment of the others. Non-water soluble vitamins will do this, so will non-water soluble elements sold in pet stores.

• You can avoid this by either using inserting a small airstone in the container and running air through the fluid. You will also need to vent the container from the top to prevent pressure build-up. All that is required is a pinhole at the top of the container or drip bottle.

Part 5

Cycling The

Reef Aquarium

Platinum Filter without accessories

1. Procedures

We have now completed the installation of the filters, mounted all the instruments, added the equipment, adjusted the salinty and the pH, and we are now ready to add life to the aquarium.

But first we must discuss how the tank needs to be cycled. Those readers unfamiliar with this procedure are referred to one of the many books available in the hobby that deal with installing and starting up a tank, as well as The Marine Fish and Invert Reef Aquarium, and our own Videotape number 1.

There are presently four main theories that you can follow :

• Cycle the tank inorganically by using ammonium chloride or ammonium hydroxide.

• Cycle the tank using only small hardy fish.

• Cycle the tank using only a mixture of rock, sediment rock and so-called live rock.

• Cycle the tank using a combination of fish, live rock and invertebrates.

Each method seems to have merits and all seem to have, at least, some drawbacks.

Additionally each of the above methods can be ran "naturally", or with the addition of "enzymes".

The latter do not alter the cycling procedures very much, except for the fact that it may speed the cycling up by several days, up to a week perhaps, and that adding enzymes seems to make the process less stressful on whatever animal life you place in the aquarium.

Since this is now a tested method, and since several brands of such enzymes are now offered for sale, we recommend that you do use them if you are starting up a new aquarium.

They are safe, and will make the whole process more manageable, with less loss of lifeforms. You may even want to use enzymes later, after the tank is cycled, when adding several new fish and/or invertebrates to reduce overall stress and accelerate the biological cycle .

In an effort to be as complete as we can, we will review all the above methods, albeit not in great detail. Many books and articles have been written on the subject, and you have, no doubt, read some of them.

One excellent book is the Marine Tropical Aquarium Guide, by Frank deGraaf, published by TFH Publications (reference PL 2017)

2. Cycling with Live Rock Only, Using Enzymes

This happens to be my favorite method, the one that has always worked best for me, and it is the reason why I would like to start with it.

It builds up an extremely potent biological filter that is able to adjust rapidly to increased fish populations, once you are ready to add some to your tank.

• Use 1 pound of Live Rock per "real" gallon of water in your tank. By live rock we mean rock that has some live forms on it. This may be algae, coralline algae, small zoanthids and para-zoanthids, rock anemones, tube worms, sponge, encrusting sponge, and so on.

• When the rock comes in, or after bringing it home from the Pet Store, check it carefully for stone crabs -small ones hide in the rock's crevasses and also for bristle worms - again they hide in the crevasses.

You must check really carefully, small crabs and small worms match the color of the rock so well, that they are hard to spot.

Small crabs and small worms grow quickly and damage fish and ane-mones. Once the are in your tank they are very difficult to remove.

We have experienced this ourselves many times, and have had to take tanks down, meaning remove all the rock, just to catch the crabs and the worms.

Watch out too for small bottom dwelling toad fish, they grow very quickly, and are "all mouth", swallowing small fish very easily.

• Rinse the rocks in a bucket of water taken from the aquarium in which you will shortly place them.

• Do not add the sediment that comes with the rock. You may think that it contains all sorts of lifeforms, and that it is a good idea to add it nevertheless. It usually is not. Don't take chances therefore.

• After the rock is rinsed, place it in the tank. Try to shape the "look" of the tank somewhat, but do not pay too much attention to it. You will have ample opportunity to change everything around afterwards.

This is especially so since you will be adding more rock at a later date anyway. The one pound per gallon we suggested earlier, will more than likely not fill up the tank in the fahion you wish.

• Add enzymes, the quantity is as recommended by the manufacturer. We personally used Biozyme, the marine variety, with great success in the 150 gallon tank that was set up for the Videotapes we made.

You may find that adding enzymes will bring about some unpleasant smells for a day or two. Either you added too many enzymes, or your filter is really cycling well. In either case patience is the only solution. After a few days the smell goes away.

• In this method no fish whatsoever are added, until the tank has cycled completely.

• Observe the tank, and start your tank diary. This is the best time to do so. You will have information right from the start.

• After all your live rock is in the tank, wait about twelve hours and perform the following tests :

- Dissolved oxygen.
- Ammonia : its level will in all likelihood be zero, but check anyway.
- Nitrite : same remark as for ammonia.
- Carbonate hardness : will more than likely be around 9 dKH.
- pH : will be between 8.0 and 8.2
- Nitrates : very low or zero. It depends on the salt you used.
- Phosphates : very low but it depends on the salt you have used.
- Redox potential (if you have a meter or a controller).
- T•Factor.

Write all the results down, and use a diary that looks like this :

Date	Time	F°	pH	NO2	NO3	PO4	D.O.	KH	Mv	Fe	CO2	Cu	Comments

It is important that you keep records. This will allow you to compare what is happening to your water chemistry, and will give you historical data that you can refer to.

In addition to the above chart, which you could consider the left side of a two page lay-out, you will use the whole right side to make any comments that may be appropriate.

The first few days that may not be of real interest, but after a week or more, as you make changes and add or remove water, or add chemicals, it becomes real important.

You will be able to gauge the impact of those changes, based on the result they produce, which you then record.

Most of the work is now done, and you can leave the tank alone, perhaps until the next day, or if you did the work in the evening, until 24 hours later.

In all likelihood the water may still be cloudy from adding the rock. This will however clear up. Perhaps in as little as a few hours, to as much as a day or two. There is no need to use diatomaceous earth filters or water clarifiers.

It is likely that after the tank has cleared up, a whitish haze will appear after 24 to 48 hours. That is normal. It is part of the new tank syndrome and will go away by itself. You do not need to do anything about it. In fact the less you do to your tank in the first few days of its operation, the better off you probably will be in the long run.

After a few days, tiny moving white animalcules will more than likely be seen on the glass, and in areas where there is a lot of light.

That is normal too, and they will go away by themselves. You should not worry, they are not parasites. And even if they were, since there are no fish in the tank, they would not be able to do any damage anyway.

After about 5 days, you should perform all the tests again, and write the results down. Add any comments that seem appropriate. E.g. tank cloudy, feather dusters (the small ones on the rocks) open or not open, rock anemones open or not open, etc...

It is unlikely that a lot of ammonia and nitrite are present at this stage, although depending on where your rock came from, there may be some.

If you determine that there are, write the amounts down. Check the KH and the pH too, and write those numbers down as well.

The pH may have started to go down somewhat due to the beginning of biological activity. That is normal. Do not do anything about it.

It should still be in the area of at least 8.0 or perhaps still higher. It will go down however, perhaps as low as 7.6.

For the next couple of days, perform all your tests and write the results down. If your carbonate hardness goes lower than 8 dKH, you must adjust it, and add either liquid buffer (e.g. Tech•Reef•KH), or tablets, to bring it back up to around 12.

Do this slowly. Do not alter it by more than one degree per 8 hour period. Dripping KH building fluid in the vat of the filter, or directly in the tank, is the best and safest way to adjust your KH. This should re-stabilize your pH somewhat, although it is not necessarily so.

Ammonia should start rising by now, and will soon peak, usually around day 10-11 or 12, and nitrites will start appearing if they haven't already.

Nitrite will rise, and will keep rising. The enzymes you added should however keep things pretty well in check.

Make sure that you follow the directions that came with the enzymes. A second treatment is usually recommended, and you must, we repeat must, add more enzymes.

Check the dKH every day, and adjust as required. Do not pay too much attention to the pH, as you have not much control over what happens during the cycling time.

Do not change water ! If you do so, you will only delay the whole process, and your cycling time will be longer. Perhaps 6 to 7 weeks, instead of the normal 3 to 4 when using enzymes.

Do not run your protein skimmer and your ozonizer either. This is done only once the tank has completely cycled.

As you keep testing, every day from day 10 onwards, ammonia will disappear, nitrite will rise, and then suddenly overnight, nitrite will be down to zero as well.

This may happen sooner, depending on how much life there was on the rocks you got, and on how well the enzymes worked for you.

About the only thing you should have adjusted up to this point, if you followed our instructions, is the carbonate hardness, and added enzymes for a second time.

You will eventually get to the point where ammonia and nitrite are both zero. This is the time to add more rock. No fish yet. Just more rock.

You can now add the balance of what you had in mind to place in the tank to begin with. Perhaps another 1 pound per real gallon of water in the aquarium.

Proceed as outlined before. Add enzymes, but only about 1/2 the amount that you used the first time.

Since the filter is now partially cycled, the bacteria will multiply very rapidly, and catch up with the additional animal load that you have added to the tank.

Remember, you must check the KH and adjust it when necessary. The pH should now be back to the normal ranges of between 8.0 and 8.3, which is fine, and which is what we are looking for.

The second cycle, the one brought about by the addition of extra live rock, will take about 10 to 14 days maximum, perhaps less, again depending on how much life there actually is on the live rock that you have added.

Each type of rock is different. There are no "standards" for live rock. We cannot, therefore, give you absolute numbers regarding cycling time and levels of ammonia and nitrite during the cycle.

If you were monitoring the millivolt, redox potential, you will probably have found that it started off around 230/240 mv, before you added rock, that it went down rapidly after you did, to perhaps as low as 90 or 100 mv, and that, as the cycle progressed it started climbing again.

After the first cycle was completed, it should have been around 200-250 mv, but then went down again, after you added the extra rock.

As this part of the cycle progresses the redox potential will start going up again, and should reach somewhere in the middle 200's after about 2 weeks.

So far the cycle has taken a maximum of about 6 weeks, and a minimum of possibly 4.

Before adding any more lifeforms to the tank, you must wait until all ammonia and all nitrite is gone. Both readings should be zero.

Nitrate will have started to rise, as, when the cycle progresses, nitrate is produced from the nitrite that was present in the water. This is normal, and no reason for concern. Whatever level you may detect is in all likelyhood very low anyway.

This is providing of course, that you have used water that did not contain nitrates to fill your tank, and that the salt you used did not have excessive amounts of it either.

During the cycling, some of the lifeforms on the rocks may have died. You may notice this by a white toothpaste-like matter forming on the rocks, or you may just have observed that rock anemones or mushrooms, or other forms of live just decomposed.

There is unfortunately not much that you can do about this. You can observe it, perhaps remove some of it, if you can get to it, but it is part of the cycling syndrome, something you have to live with.

A great amount of life should have survived the cycle however, and should look in good shape now that the main, and secondary, cycles are passed.

You must keep testing for KH to ensure that it is in the right range, and adjust it whenever necessary. At this stage, keep it at 12 if you can.

After you have added the second batch of rock, and after the second cycle which resulted from this addition is passed, you may start adding invertebrates. Do not add more than 2 of them at a time, and wait at least 4 days before adding any more.

The type of invertebrates that we are refering to here, include soft and hard corals, leather corals, anemones, feather dusters, disc anemones, goniopora corals, bubble coral and the like.

We still do not want to put any fish in the tank. One of the benefits of cycling this way, is that by the time we are ready to add fish, any free floating parasites, and any tomonts containing parasites, will have died off for lack of a host.

Two weeks after you add the last invertebrates, you can buy fish that are compatible with a Reef tank.

In Advanced Reef Keeping Part II, we will deal with fish and invertebrates, as well as macro-algae in great detail. That book is slated to be ready in September of 1989. It was about half completed at the time this book went to press.

Cycling your tank in this manner should not give you any trouble, and should result in a really potent biological filter.

Since no fish have been in the tank for at least 6 to perhaps 10 weeks, it is unlikely that you will have problems when you introduce fish.

You must however "drip" fish that you buy, to acclimate them to the tank conditions. This is most important. It is not a pleasant task, but it is one that will save you from may parasitic infestations. Many books describe how dripping the fish is performed. Refer to one of them if you are not familiar with this simple technique.

How to deal with parasitic outbreaks will be covered in detail in Advanced Reef Keeping II.

3. Cycling with Fish Only and Enzymes

The process outlined under heading 2 applies here as well. The only difference is that you will now be using fish. Hardy fish, such as demoiselles and perhaps wrasse.

• After starting up the filtration and the pumps, add 1 small fish per 7.5 gallons of water in your tank.

• Add enzymes following the instructions that came with the brand that you bought.

• By small fish we mean fish that are 1.5 to 2 inches long (excluding the tail) and 1/2 to 3/4 inch from top to bottom.

• Refer to section 2 for the kind of tests that you need to perform.

• After you have gone through the first cycle, add 1 fish per 15 gallons as long as you stay with the same size. If you select larger fish, reduce their number accordingly.

• For instance, adding a medium yellow tank of about 3 inches by 2.5 inches, would be the same as adding 3 of the smalller types.

• Follow these guidelines and you will not run into massive die-offs.

• When additional fish are added, the filter will catch up rather quickly, and you will not find ammonia and nitrite after perhaps as little as 3 days.

• This is a sign that you can add more fish if you like.

• The whole cycling process will also take about 4 to 5 weeks. The use of enzymes may shorten this by perhaps a week.

• The real key is to closely monitor your H_4 and NO_2 levels each time you add fish to the tank, and not add any others until those readings are back down to zero ppm. In that fashion no excessive stress is placed on the fish. (Note : depending on which test you are using, you may be measuring ammonium or ammonia).

• Additionally, each time you increase the load, your filter is able to absorb the additional pollution slowly, and build up to a real potent level quickly.

• Once the tank has been cycled, and you have added several other fish, and let ammonia and nitrite levels go down to zero again, you can start adding corals and anemones.

• Go slowly and watch those ammonia and nitrite levels. This will save you from parasitic infestations, and also from losses of fish and inverts.

• How many fish and invertebrates a tank can handle is dependent on so many factors that we cannot explain it in a short few paragraphs. We will get into it more in detail in Advanced Reef Keeping II.

In short though, adding more fish, and-or more invertebrates should only be done for as long as your water quality does not suffer. If it goes down, and does not come back to its original level in a matter of 3 days, you have overloaded the tank.

The key to success, with this and other methods of cycling is simple : go very slowly. Check your water chemistry, and do not add more life-forms unless all ammonia and nitrite is gone.

You must of course follow the same recommendations that we already made under section 2 with regard to the carbonate hardness.

It is important that you check the dKH regularly, and maintain it at levels higher than 8, but preferably at levels of around 12.

As indicated, make all changes slowly, and if you can, use a metering pump to dispense the carbonate hardness fluid.

If fish die during the cycling period , you must of course remove them. To know whether any have died, you must know what you put in the tank to begin with.

We recommend that you write down whatever you add to your tank on the test record sheet, and that you test all parameters before adding any lifeforms. Remember you must go slowly.

Impatience is not a characteristic of the serious Reef Hobbyist.

Twenty four hours after adding livestock, test again and you will be able to gauge what the addition of these lifeforms has done to your water chemistry. Test again the following day, and see whether con-ditions have improved.

If your tank is not overloaded, they will, perhaps not in 24 hours, but they should come back to what you tested originally, within 72 to 96 hours.

Follow these recommendations and you will minimize losses and problems with your tank. Most Hobbyists want to go too fast, and wnat to add new fish and new invertebrates too soon. To be successful, you must learn to be patient.

4. Cycling with Fish and Inverts

Although you can of course cycle the aquarium with both fish and invertebrates right from the start, we strongly recommend against it.

One of the main reasons is that fish and invertebrates react differently to the stresses generated by the cycling chemistry, and that keeping control over conditions is therefore that much more difficult.

Additionally, if you cycle with fish only, and some disease starts, you can easily catch the fish and remove them, as there are no rocks behind which the fish can hide.

When cycling with live rock only, disease is not a factor and problems seldom occur.

When mixing the two, a host of new problems are introduced that will only complicate your life. Granted, the tank may look a little better right from the start, but the problems that you can run into are not worth taking that risk, especially since, if you cannot get the matter under control, you may have to take the tank down and start all over again.Not a pleasant prospect.

And after all, we are only talking about a few weeks waiting time before you will be able to keep both fish and invertebrates anyway.

Although this may be the method that you had in mind, or that you used when you set up your existing tank, stay away from it, and cycle with live rock only and enzymes.

We assure you that you will find that your tank will cycle with far less problems, and with far less live losses.

Once the cycle is over you can then add fish without fear that you will lose them to the cycle, or that they will become diseased after only a few days in the tank.

5. Cycling inorganically

This method which uses ammonium chloride for a number of days to build up the biological filter is of course totally safe, as no fish or invertebrates are in the tank while the cyling process occurs.

It is also relatively simple and the kits that are sold in pet stores come with all necessary instructions.

Moreover, it has been described in so many books that we feel that you can find exhaustive material enough.

Personally we do not like that method because it does not condition the filters for the type of lifeforms that will eventually be kept in the tank. It conditions the filters for inorganic sources of nitrogen but not for the organic sources that will eventually end up in the aquarium.

Many of my friends have tried it, and their opinions vary as well. Some persist and eventually find that their tanks recycle when fish are added, although they went through a complete inorganic cycle.

In my opinion, they have achieved only one thing : the cycle took much longer, and the end result was that they had to re-cycle organically anyway.

6. Conclusion

About 3 to 5 weeks after you started cycling your tank, you should be ready to add more invertebrates and fish.

You are now a true Reef Hobbyist, with all the responsibilities that such entails.

Keep in mind that fish and invertebrates are living beings and that they deserve your attention, care and dedication.

The mere fact that you bought them and paid good money for them, does not give you the right to neglect them. You should do all possible to provide them will a living environment that will give them a chance to survive.

The more you follow our recommendations the better that goal will be achieved and the more pleasure you will derive from your tank.

We sincerely hope that you have enjoyed this book and that you have learned more about all the techniques that can be employed to better the conditions of your Reef.

We hope that you can appreciate how difficult it is to write this type of a book. On one hand it needs to be understandable by beginners, and on the other it needs to be at the level of the advanced Hobbyist as well. Blending the two poses quite a few problems in terms of what vocabulary to use and how far to carry the technical explanations.

We hope you have enjoyed reading it as much as I enjoyed writing it.

We welcome your comments and critique.

Addendum

Reef Aquarium Invertebrates, Corals and Fish

The real reason we keep Reef Aquariums is that we enjoy the sight of both fish and invertebrates in the same aquarium. Moreover, such a combination makes the tank look truer to nature and therefore much more realistic and appealing.

There is, of course, the "challenge" of being successful at it too. Since these aquariums are so problematic, or at least can be, we somehow want to prove to ourselves that we can do it, that we can keep the fish and invertebrates alive and looking well for extended periods of time.

That is perhaps one of the main reasons for the present success of the Reef Tank. Indeed, because the equipment and the instrumentation is now available and is starting to be understood, more hobbyists are willing to take up that challenge.

We have taken you through both the theoretical and the practical aspects of setting up these aquariums with the two books we published :

• The Marine Fish and Invert Reef Aquarium, Aardvark Press, now in its 6th printing

• Advanced Reef Keeping I, Aardvark Press, which you are reading.

Advanced Reef Keeping II will deal with the Invertebrates and the Fish that you can safely place in the Reef Aquarium.

It will do so in detail, and will include a description of the specimen and how to care for them. The introduction to the book will set the tone by discussing the water quality parameters required, and the acceptable limits that you can safely work with.

Advanced Reef Keeping II will also include a section on Macro-Algae, and should be available around September 1989.

That book is being written and produced with the assistance of Leo Wojcik, my good friend, who has dedicated many many hours to researching and testing new methods and techniques, both for, and with me.

Marine Reef, the technical newsletter that we produce is going strong, so strong in fact that we have recently lowered the subscription price. If you want to learn, and **keep learning** about Reef Tanks, you should subscribe. From the comments we recieve from subscribers, we know we are on the right track.

A subscription form is included in this book, together with a discount offer.

Advanced Reef Keeping I has brought you the options that are available to you. There are many as we have seen. Most of them are costly and may require careful evaluation.

We cannot repeat the recommendation that you need to plan your tank enough. You must know where you are going, and decide how you will acquire all the pieces.

As time goes on, some filtration methods may be simplified, e.g. system tanks may be introduced that include the filtration equitpment and reduce the space required to set up a Reef Tank.

Nothing can however replace the instrumentation. It can be made less expensive by combining it with other items required for the tank, but the nature of precise intruments is that they are costly.

You will never be able to buy an all inclusive system, with all meters and controllers for a few hundred dollars. It is just not possible, especially if the equipment is of quality.

Keep up-to-date on all these developments by subscribing to

MARINE REEF. You will not regret it.

Advanced Reef Keeping II

Later this year, 1989, we will bring you Advanced Reef Keeping II, the continuation of this book.

It deals with the fish, the invertebrates and corals that you can keep in your aquarium.

It describes the species and gives recommendations on how to care for them. The book has been in the works for nearly a year now, and is about half completed.

It is the logical sequel to Advanced Reef Keeping I.

You may order the book by sending in the coupon below. Do not send any money yet. We will contact you as soon as we have set a pre-publication price.

Send original or photocopy.

To : Albert J. Thiel, 120 Wendy Rd, Trumbull, Connecticut 06611

Please enter my name and address in the Advanced Reef Keeping II database.

Name : ....

Address : ....

....

....

Date...Signature...

....
....
....

Videotape Discount Coupon

Yes, please send me Tapes 1, 2, 3, and 4 of the Series The Marine Fish and Invert Reef Aquarium for the special price of $ 129.99 instead of the normal price of $ 159.99. A $ 30.00 savings !

Name :...

Address :..

....

City...Zip :.................................

Payment enclosed : Check or money order please. No cash. No COD's
Mail to AARDVARK PRESS, 575 Broad Street, Bridgeport CT 06604

Marine Reef Newsletter

I would like to subscribe to Marine Reef, the technical newsletter dealing with Reef Aquariums published by Albert J. Thiel and issued every 3 weeks.

Please enter my subscription at the listed special prices for :

- 17 issues (one year) for the special price of $ 35.00

- 8 issues (six months) for the special price of $ 20.00

(select one)

Name ....

Address ....

....
....
City.......................................St.................Zip...................

I enclose payment. No billing, no COD's. Mail to Aardvark Press.
575 Broad Street, Bridgeport CT 06604

Advanced Products for the Reef Aquarium

Check the list of Thiel•Aqua•Tech products on the facing

page. If you have any questions feel free to call us at

~~203-368 2111~~

We will gladly discuss your concerns and problems

with you.

505-526-4000

A short list of T•A•T Advanced Products for the Reef Aquarium

We do not re-label. We manufacture our own products or have them manufactured nearby so we can control the quality at all times.

Tech•Macro•Algae : a specially formulated fertilizer for marine macro-algae. Sold in 4, 8 and 32 oz containers. Contains all elements known to benefit your green macro-algae. Dispensed daily either by hand or by using a metering pump. Contains EDTA chelated iron and manganese compounds. No phosphate based chelators are used in this superior product. A freshwater version of this fertilizer is available as well.

Tech•Doser : a chemical metering pump that allows the even addition of all fluids that are added to the tank, including KH generating liquid, as well as topping off the aquarium at the same time. If you are looking for stability in water chemistry, this is it.

Tech•Reef•Elements : Chelated form of trace elements for the discriminating Marine Reef Hobbyist. Stable and long lasting. Sold in 4, 8 and 32 oz containers.

Tech•Coral•Nutrient : "The" food for your corals. Sold in 4 oz containers only. Each container is stamped with a series number, a lot number, and the expiration date. Contains amongst others extracts of what corals feed on around the real Reef. Use in combination with other foods.

Tech•KH buffer : a fluid with a carbonate hardness of over 1100 degrees that is added to the tank to maintain it at the correct KH level. Sold in quart, half gallon and one gallon size. Does not make your skimmer foam more than it does now. Stronger than KH tablets. Can be added manually or with a metering pump. Proven to work on our own tanks (as all our products).

Tech•Reef•Salt : a superior salt for the Reef. No phosphates. All trace lements known to be necessary. Clean and non-contaminated. Expensive, but we think it is the best salt you can buy. Comes in 25 ,50 and 100 gallon sizes.

Tests : we manufacture and sell a series oftest for the reef, including KH and Fe as well as phosphates and hydrogen sulfide.

Vita•Trace•Complex : our own vitamin mix. Stabilized and water soluble. Add to the food or to the water. Sold in 4, 8 and 32 oz containers. We have used it with success for several years. Contains extra B-12 and Biotin.

Ocean•Motion : our water current alternating device. See details in book.

Tech•Probe•Switcher : use 2 electrodes with one meter or controller. Can be used with pH and redox potential equipment. Measure in two location, or measure two tanks with only one instrument.

Tech•Ozonizer : our powerful yet safe ozonizer. Can produce up to 325 mg of ozone if you require that quantity for short periods of time.

Residual Ozone Test : Check for residual ozone rapidly with a one part test. Check its potency by using tap water. Each test will give you at least one hundred and fifty or more testing sessions. A must if you now use ozone, or are planning to. 4 oz bottle only.

Air Dryers : 19 inches tall and 3 inches in diameter. Indicating compound. Nearly 4 pounds. Can be regenerated in conventional oven and in microwave.

Air Filter : small and long lasting air filters for in-line use with ozonizers.

Columnar Skimmers : we manufacture 3 models. All run with 2 limewood airstones. Total height including the cup is : 30 inches (up to 100 gallons), 44 inches (up to 250 gallons), 84 inches (up to 1000 gallons). All skimmers have a 6 inch diameter tube, can be operated safely with ozone and are out of the tank models.

Venturi Skimmer : one model, up to 500 gallons. 6 inches in diameter and 22.5 inches tall. No airstones, no airpumt needed of course. Can be run safely with ozone.

Tech•Denitrator : 24 inches long, 4 inches wide, 11 inches tall. Large compartments. 1/4 inch in and 1/2 inch out fittings.Greatly improved version of more traditional models. Much easier to operate.

Denitrating Fluid : our own multi-element mix, guaranteed to give you satisfaction. Not just a generic product. Researched and tested.

Tech•KH•test : a two part highly accurate carbonate hardness test. Comes in 2 excellent qualty Nalgene dropper bottles.

Oxygen Reactor - Ozone reactor : 26 inches tall. 6 inches in diameter. Filled with Bioballs, 1/2 inch in and out female threaded fittings.

Carbonate hardness Reactor : 26 inches tall, 6 inches in diameter, 1/2 inch in and out fittings. Easy to install.

X-Nitrate Reactors : same size as reactors above. Comes filled with our own X-nitrate compound. Removable compression nut allows replacement of the compound when necessary.

Carbon Reactor : same as the above reactor but is filled with high quality activated carbon.

This is just a partial list. We carry and manufacture many other products. **Call or send the coupon in for a catalogue and prices.**

Catalogue Request :

Please send me one of your new catalogues and retail pricing :

Name ....

Address ....

....

....
City...ST...........Zip...........................

For stores only :

Please include a copy of your business licence and we will send you a store price list.

Check our Marine Reef

Special Price Subscription

offer on pages 399 and 407

X-Nitrate by TAT

SUGGESTED READING AND BIBLIOGRAPHY

Seawater Aquariums, A Captive Environment
Stephen Spotte, 1979
John Wiley & Sons
Wiley InterScience

Marine Aquarium Keeping
Stephen SPotte, 1973
John Wiley & Sons
Wiley InterScience

Chemistry of Water and Microbiology
N.F. Voznaya
Mir Publishers

Advanced Chemistry
P.R.S. Murray, 1987
Pan Study Aids

Sigma
Sigma Chemical Company
Company Catalogue 1987

Comprehensive Chemistry
John Hicks, 1963
Macmillan Publishers

Grzimek's Animal Life Encyclopedia
Volumes 1, 2, 3, 4
Dr. B. Grzimek, 1984
Van Nostrand Reinhold

Aquatic Chemistry
W. Stumm and James Morgan, 1981
John Wiley & Sons
Wiley Interscience

Lange's Handbook of Chemistry
John A. Dean, 1985
McGraw Hill

The Advanced Aquarist
Pet Library Series

L'Aquarium Marin Tropical
Frank deGraaf
Bordas Publishers

The Aquarist's Encyclopedia
Blandford 1985

Fresh and Marine Aquarium Magazines
Various issues on Reef Tanks
Don Dewey, Publisher
R/C Modeler Corporation

Niedere Tiere I
Peter Wilkens
Engelbert Pfriem Verlag

Niedere Tiere II
Peter Wilkens, Johannes Birkholz
Engelbert Pfriem Verlag

Today's Aquarium Magazine
Aquadocumenta Verlag
Bielefeld, West Germany

Das Perfekte Aquarium
Kaspar Horst, Horst Kipper
Aquadocumenta Verlag
Bielefeld, West Germany

Productivity in Aquatic Environments
Charles Goodman

Coral Reefs
Pederson Field Guides
Eugene E. Kaplan

Fishes of Hawaii
Spencer Wilkie Tinker 1978, 1982
Hawaiian Service Inc.

Photosynthesis Energy Transduction
A practical Approach
M.F. Hopkins, N.R. Baker, 1986
IRL Press Oxford

Light and photosynthesis in Aquatic Ecosystems
John T.O. Kirk
Cambridge Press

The Marine Fish and Invert Reef Aquarium
Albert J. Thiel, 1988
Aardvark Press

Marine Reef - Issues 1-11
Newsletter
Aardvark Press

Living Invertebrates
Pearce and Buchsbaum, 1987
Boxwood Press

Niedere Tieren im Tropischen Seewasseraquarium I
Peter Wilkens
Engelbert Pfriem Verlag

Niedere Tieren im Tropischen Seewasseraquarium II
Peter Wilkens
Engelbert Pfriem Verlag

Dr. Axelrod's Atlas (Marine)
First and second Editions
TFH Publications

Today's Aquarium Magazine
Various issues
Aquadocumenta Verlag
Bielefeld, West Germany

A Texbook on Algae
Kumar and Singh, 1971
Macmillan

Various Articles by
John Burleson
Horst E. Kipper
Frank Grecco
Dr. Gerd Kassebeer
Dr. Sharon Sasha
Dr. Scott Siddall
Dr. Peter Lewis
George Smit
Don Dewey
Albert J. Thiel

Marine Invertebrates
Dr. Patrick L. Colin
TFH Publications H-971

Marine Reef Newsletter

A technical newsletter dedicated to furthering the keeping of fish and invertebrate aquariums.

Edited by Albert J. Thiel, author of this book and of The Marine Fish and Invert Reef Aquarium.

No advertising. Just plain information and helpful advice to assist you in keeping a better Reef Aquarium.

Published since March 1988. Copies of all back issues are available.

Subscribe now. Learn more about your tank and become a better Hobbyist. Understand what happens to your tank and be able to deal with it. By experts for discriminating Hobbyists.

Published every 3 weeks. 17 times a year. Not once a month. Mailed to you first class U.S. Mail.

One year subscription $ 43.00 (special price for readers of this book, with coupon, is $ 35.00)

Or better even, fill in our questionnaire and pay only 20.00 dollars for a full year's subscription. A $ 23.00 value. We will also send you a copy of the questionnaire's tally and an interpretation of the results.

Articles on all the facets of keeping Reef Tanks, both technical and life forms that you may wish to keep.

Not for everyone, but if you are serious about your aquarium you should subscribe.

Sample copies are available. Send $ 3.00 with your name and address to :

Aardvark Press, 575 Broad Street, Bridgeport Connecticut 06604.

All back issues are available too. We reward contributionsthat are published. Send us your findings and if they fit the quality we are publishing, we will.

Useful Addresses

FAMA
Fresh and Marine Aquarium Magazine
144 West Sierra Madre Boulevard
Sierra Madre, Ca 91024

Route 4 Marine Technology
143 Broadway
Elmwood Park, NJ 07407

Ocean Clear Filters
1350 2E. Vista Way
Vista, Ca 92084

Poly-Bio-Marine Inc.
PO Box 426
South Orange, NJ 07079

Eheim
c/o Hawalin Marine Imports
PO Box 218687
Houston, Tx 77218

Sea Kleer Reefs Inc.
7484 Old Alexander Ferry Rd
Clinton, Md 20735

Lewis Books
PO Box 41137
Cincinnati, Oh 45241

Hayward Industrial Plastics
sells only through distributors

Savko Plastic Pipe and Valves
683 E Lincoln Avenue
Columbus, Oh 43229

Aquanetics
1177 Knoxville Street
San Diego, Ca 92110

Aardvark Press
575 Broad Street
Bridgeport, CT 06604

World Class Aquarium
2015 Flatbush Avenue
Brooklyn, NY 11234

Aquarium Products
180 L Penrod Court
Glen Burnie, Md 21061

Rainbow Plastics
PO Box 4127
El Monte, Ca 91734

Trop-quarium
Chuck Burge
1873 Piedmont NE
Atlanta, Ga 30324

Florida Bay Brand Live Rock
5800 Overseas H'way
Suite 35-121
Marathon, Fl 33050

Execufish
5557 S. Ouray
Aurora, Co 80015

Reef Displays Live Rock
10959 Overseas H'way
Marathon, Fl 33050

Thiel•Aqua•Tech
Dupla USA
Marine Reef
Tech Products Intl.
575 Broad Street
Bridgeport, CT 06604

Duro-Test Lights
only via Distributors

Energy Savers
CoraLife
22138 S Vermont Ave
Building C
Torrance, Ca 90502

Poisson Filters
96 Annette Street
Toronto, Canada M6P 1N6

Tetra Sales USA
201 Tabor Rd
Morris Plains, NJ 07950

Aquarium Sales and Services
4410-B W Victory Blvd
Burbank, Ca 91505

Aquaclear- Hagen USA
Mansfield, Md 02048

Daleco Master Breeder
4611 Weatherside Run
Fort Wayne, IN 46804

Tropical Fish Hobbyist
211 W Sylvannia Avenue
Neptune, NJ 07753

REEF TANK QUESTIONNAIRE

Fill out this questionnaire and receive a one year subscription to

Marine Reef for only $ 20.00 (a $ 23.00 saving)

Name (optional..

Address (optional)

....

....

Please include full address and Zip if you decide to give it to us. It will be kept confidential. We do not sell names to mailing list houses. If you want a copy of the survey and a discount on Marine Reef we need your address.

1. Description of your Tank

Size.........................Type.........................Glass...........Acrylic...............Other.............

How long have you had this tank up and running ....

If Reef Type, give us a short description if you wish. Use extra paper if necessary.

....
....
....
....
....

2. Filtration

Type...

Size of filter...

Packing material used ....
How long has it been set up ....

What other types of filtration do you use
....
....
....
....

Describe the various types in brief (e.g. chemical, separate mechanical, etc..)

....
....
....
....
....
....
....
....
....
....
....
....
....
....
....

If you use Chemical filtration, what type ?

....
....
....

Do you use Resins e.g. Poly Filters or Hypersorb etc..Please describe

....
....
....
....
....

Do you change carbon and other chemical filter matter regularly. Describe procedure.

....
....
....
....
....

Do you still use an undergravel (reverse, normal, other etc...) Describe briefly

....
....
....
....
....
....
....

3. Water

What type of water did you fill the aquarium with ?

....
....

....

Do you use reverse osmosis and how large is the unit ?
....

Do you use de-ionizers. If so what type ?
....
....
....
....
....

How much of a water change is done on the tank, and how often ?
....
....
....
....
....
....

What type of water is used for water changes ?
....
....
....

What type of water is used for top-offs ?
....
....
....

What kind of salt do you use ?
....
....

Do you adjust the water temperature before adding it to the tank ? Be honest. This is just a survey.
....
....
....

Do you check the salinity before adding water to the tank and make sure both are the same ?
....
....

4. Tests

Please check off the tests that you perform and fill in how often. This is only a survey, please be as honest as you can.

Dissolved oxygen..

Biological oxygen demand (BOD)..

Carbon dioxide..

Nitrate ....

Nitrite ....

Ammonia ....

Copper...

Phosphate ....

Carbonate Hardness...

Iron ....

Hydrogen Sulfide ....

Phenol ....

pH...

Redox Potential ....

T•Factor ....

Salinity..

Temperature ....

Do you keep records? ....

Give us a description of your testing methods and the brand of tests you use (the latter is optional)

....
....
....
....
....
....
....
....

After testing do you take action to correct problems. What do you do for instance ?

....
....
....
....
....
....

....
....
....
....

Who do you go to for help if and when it is needed ?
....
....
....
....
....

What books do you refer to ?
....
....
....
....
....

What tests would you like to see offered ?
....
....

What is your opinion on the quality and price of the tests now offered ?
....
....
....
....

Is testing useful to you ? What does it do for you ?
....
....
....
....

5. Tank Parameters

Fill what the values are for the tests you perform. Either test now or give us
the results of your last testing session.

pH..........	Salinity............	Temp..........	N03.........	NO2..........
Cu........	PO4.........	D.O.............	BOD......	CO2........
Mv............	T•Factor........	Fe............	NH3......	KH.......

List any other you want us to know about :
....
....
....

6. Equipment and Instruments :

List all the instruments and the equipment you now use

....
....
....
....
....
....
....
....
....
....
....
....
....
....
....
....
....
....
....
....
....

What equipment are you still planning to add ?

....
....
....

What do you think (a good estimate) your present tank cost, not incl.
livestock ?

....
....

What is the value of the livestock ?

....

How much more do you think you spent since you had your tank ?

....

How many hours a day do you spend working on your tank ?

....
....

Do you work on it during the week-end ? How many hours ?

....
....

Do you consider the work you do "coping with problems" or "regular
husbandry"

....

....

Are you the only one who takes care of the tank ?...

If not, how many others do ? ....

Do they do other work besides just feeding the fish and inverts ? ....

If so, what ? ....
....
....
....
....

6. Maintenance Techniques

Give a short honest description of what you do to your tank and to the
equiment, and how often.

....
....
....
....
....
....
....
....
....
....
....
....

7. Miscellaneous

Do you use a denitrator, which brand ?..

What is your feeling about them ?
....
....
....
....
....
....
....
....
....

Do you add nutrients and which brand ?...

How long has it been running ....

How many hours do you spend regulating it ? ....

What do you feed your fish and invertebrates?

....
....
....
....

Do you use an   Oxygen Reactor.....................................
                     Ozone Reactor......................................
                     Carbonate Hardness reactor................
                     Ozonizer ....Size.............
                     Air dryer...........................How many ....
                     Water flow Alternator ....
                     Power Heads.................... How many ....
                     How many pumps are on the system...................
                     Protein Skimmer.......... Columnar .... Venturi..........
                     Conductivity Meter-controller..........
                     pH meter - controller ....
                     Carbon dioxide diffusion ....
                     Oxygen injection with pure O_2 ....
                     Cooling Unit................HP strength.............
                     KH buffers..........liquid...........or Tablets..........
                     Macro-Algae Fertilizer........... Brand.............
                                  Nr. of drops per gallon per day..............
                     Dosing Pump ....
                     Metering Pump ....
                     Float switches .... Type.................How many ....
                     Water flow meters................
                     Air flow meters......................

---

8. Lighting

Tell us the strength in watt, type, and how many bulbs you us. Give us your honest feelings about the light you are now using

....
....
....
....
....
....
....
....
....

If you were to change your light, what type would you buy ? Give reasons if you can.

....
....
....
....
....

....
....
....
....
....
....
....
....

9. Heating : Wattage and type of heating please

....
....

10. Any other comments you may want to give us

....
....
....
....
....
....
....
....
....
....
....
....

11. What equipment would you like to see offered in the hobby ?

....
....

....

....

....

....

....

....

....

....

....

....

....

We thank you for taking the time to fill out this questionnaire.
Call us if you have any questions

Index to Major Topics and Companies

Silicic acid 105, 111, 261
Silicic acid and Calcined magnesia 261
Silicic acid and cation exchange 262
Silicic acid and Dolomite 261
Silicic acid and Hydrochloric acid 261
Silicic acid and Sodium aluminate 261
Silicic acid and Sulfuric acid 261
Silicone 160
Silver chloride 248
Silver in filters 73
Skimmer : bubbles 182
Skimmer cautions 350
Skimmer connections 352
Skimmer contact time 182
Skimmer dimensions 185
Skimmer hose 352
Skimmer level 349
Skimmer operation 349
Skimmers and ammonia 236
Skimmers and dyes 236
Skimmers and medicine 236
Skimmers and ozone 352
Skimmers and phenol 244
Skimmers columnar 348
Skimmers organics 236
Skimmers scum cup 351
Skimmers venturi 181
Skimmers venturi 352
Skimming surface 46
Smit George 11, 12
Sodium aluminate 261
Sodium carbonate 164
Sodium vapor 119
Sodium vapor lights 124
Solenoid valves 68
Solenoid valves 187
Solenoids 35, 37, 39
Solenoids installation 344
Solid state switches 62
SPDT timers 213
Specific gravity 86
Spectrum and fluorescent 131
Spectrum light 124
Spectrum longevity 130
Sponges in filter 159
Spotte S. 84
Spotte S. 94
Spotte S. 108
Spray pipe 36
Spreadsheet using 142
Sprung J. 107
Staggering lights 122

Stainless (316), 41
Stainless steel 41
Stand 49
Standpipe 30, 34
Starch paper 260
Starting overflows 373
Storing electrodes 247
Stress and heat 114
Sub micron filters 208
Submersible pumps 44
Substrate 107
Substrate and KH 109
Substrate and pH 108
Substrate non calcareous 110
Substrates other 110
Suggested reading 405
Sulfuric acid 261
Summit 350
Summit Aquatics 34
Summit Aquatics 149
Summit Aquatics 199, 236
Sump of trickle filter 158
Surface skimming 30, 40, 46
Switches 59-64
Switches : pressure 214
Switches uses 59
Switching electrodes 249
Switching timers 39
Sylvannia 127
Symbiotic algae 100
Syphon overflow 40
Syphons 29, 30
Syphons starting 373
System 1 75

T

Tank acrylic 25
Tank drilled 29
Tank fittings 69
Tank glass 25
Tank height 28
Tank location 28
Tank min. configuration 280
Tank of the future 274
Tank questionnaire 411-420
Tank shape 28
Tank size 26
Tank stand 49
Tank temperature 113
Tank width 26
Tanks covered 46

Additional Addresses

Macalaster Bicknell
Catalogue of instruments
169 Henry Street
New Haven CT 06510

Cole Palmer Instrument Company
Catalogue of Instruments
Chicago Illinois

LaMotte Chemicals
Tests
PO Box 329
Chestertown, Md 21620

Marine Aquarium Society of Toronto
Atoll Newsletter
Scott Dyer, President
130 Westbourne Avenue
Scarsborough, Ontario Canada
M1L 2Y7

Sigma Chemicals
PO Box 14508
St Louis, Mo 63178

Pfalz and Bauer Chemicals
Waterbury , CT 06708

Advanced Reef Keeping I

Table of Contents

Book 1
Theory, Equipment, Instrumentation, Installation

Part Three : Water Chemistry and Analysis

Appendices

Setting, Editing, Reviewing, Pagination, and final review completed in January 1989

Notes and Questions :

Notes and Questions :

....

....

....

....

....

....

....

....

....

....

....

....

....

....

Notes and Questions :

....

....

....

....

....

....

....

....

....

....

....

....

....

....

....

....

Notes and Questions :

....

....

....

....

....

....

....

....

....

....

....

....

....

....

Notes and Questions :

....

....

....

....

....

....

....

....

....

....

....

....

....

....